The Stravinsky Legacy

It has become increasingly apparent in recent decades that Stravinsky's music has had a far-reaching influence on the development of music in our century. Stravinsky's modernist innovations – evident in such features as his music's discontinuity, its stasis, its ritualised anti-narrative, its novel rhythmic and formal structures, its articulation of new kinds of musical time and its reinterpretation of music and materials from the past – have helped shape much of the music of our time. This book represents a first substantial attempt at evaluating Stravinsky's technical and aesthetic legacy. In Part I ('The Stravinsky Legacy') Jonathan Cross explores the breadth of Stravinsky's impact on the music of composers as diverse as Adams, Andriessen, Birtwistle, Boulez, Carter, Messiaen, Reich, Stockhausen, Tippett, Varèse and Xenakis. In Part II ('Stravinsky Reheard') he returns to Stravinsky's neoclassical music to examine how recent developments in composition and musicology affect our understanding of and analytical approaches to Stravinsky. The final chapter is concerned with a reevaluation of Adorno's notorious critique of Stravinsky.

Jonathan Cross is a lecturer in music at the University of Bristol, and is Associate Editor of *Music Analysis*.

Music in the Twentieth Century

GENERAL EDITOR Arnold Whittall

This series offers a wide perspective on music and musical life in the twentieth century.

Books included will range from historical and biographical studies concentrating particularly on the context and circumstances in which composers were writing, to analytical and critical studies concerned with the nature of musical language and questions of compositional process. The importance given to context will also be reflected in studies dealing with, for example, the patronage, publishing and promotion of new music, and in accounts of the musical life of particular countries.

Published titles

Satie the composer
Robert Orledge
0 521 35037 9

The twelve-note music of Anton Webern
Kathryn Bailey
0 521 39088 5

Arnold Schoenberg: notes, sets, forms
Silvina Milstein
0 521 39049 4

Franz Schreker, 1878–1934: a cultural biography
Christopher Hailey
0 521 39255 1

The music of John Cage
James Pritchett
0 521 56544 8

The music of Conlon Nancarrow
Kyle Gann
0 521 46534 6

The music of Ruth Crawford Seeger
Joseph N. Straus
0 521 41646 9

The Stravinsky Legacy

Jonathan Cross

CAMBRIDGE
UNIVERSITY PRESS

PUBLISHED BY THE PRESS SYNDICATE OF THE UNIVERSITY OF CAMBRIDGE
The Pitt Building, Trumpington Street, Cambridge CB2 1RP, United Kingdom

CAMBRIDGE UNIVERSITY PRESS
The Edinburgh Building, Cambridge CB2 2RU, UK   http://www.cup.cam.ac.uk
40 West 20th Street, New York, NY 10011–4211, USA   http://www.cup.org
10 Stamford Road, Oakleigh, Melbourne 3166, Australia

First published 1998

Printed in the United Kingdom at the University Press, Cambridge

Typeset in Minion 10.5/13.5 pt   [SE]

A catalogue record for this book is available from the British Library

Library of Congress cataloguing information data

Cross, Jonathan, 1961–
The Stravinsky legacy / Jonathan Cross.
    p.   cm. – (Music in the twentieth century)
Includes bibliographic references (p. 266) and index.
1. Stravinsky, Igor, 1882–1971 – Criticism and interpretation.
2. Stravinsky, Igor, 1882–1971 – Influence.   I. Title.   II. Series.
ML410.S932C87   1998
780'.92–DC21
98–17405   CIP   MN

ISBN 0 521 56365 8 hardback

For Emma, Alice and Rebecca

Tracing influences can be dangerous

(Louis Andriessen and Elmer Schönberger, *The Apollonian Clockwork: On Stravinsky*, tr. Jeff Hamburg (Oxford University Press, 1989))

Contents

Acknowledgements

Many people have helped bring *The Stravinsky Legacy* into the world. Arnold Whittall has had a hand in the project from start to finish: without his expert guidance, criticism and encouragement, this book would never have appeared at all. Various people have commented on drafts at different stages, and I am especially grateful to Craig Ayrey, Emma Cross, Julian Johnson, Kathryn Puffett and Jim Samson for their invaluable views. I am also grateful to Kathryn Puffett for her skilful and patient setting of the music examples. The University of Bristol Faculty of Arts Research Support Fund generously assisted in the cost of preparing these examples. David Allenby (Boosey & Hawkes) and Miranda Jackson (Universal Edition, London) have shown much kindness in helping me acquire scores, and I would have been completely at sea without the constant advice and support of Penny Souster at Cambridge University Press. Last, but by no means least, I acknowledge the immeasurable debt I owe to my parents, Margaret and John Cross, and to my three muses, Emma, Alice and Rebecca, whose support in countless ways sustained me through the many ups and downs of the book's writing. To them it is dedicated with love and gratitude.

Picasso's *Standing Female Nude* (1910) (Plate 2.1 and cover) is reproduced by permission: The Metropolitan Museum of Art, Alfred Stieglitz Collection, 1949. (49.70.34). All rights reserved, The Metropolitan Museum of Art, New York

I am also grateful to all the publishers who have kindly allowed me to quote extracts from published scores as follows:

Adams: *Short Ride in a Fast Machine*, Boosey & Hawkes Music Publishers Ltd. Andriessen: *Hoketus; M is for Man, Music, Mozart: De Staat*, Boosey & Hawkes Music Publishers Ltd. Berio: *Sequenza V*, Universal Edition (London) Ltd. Birtwistle: *Carmen arcadiae mechanicae perpetuum; Earth Dances; Secret Theatre: Silbury Air*, Universal Edition (London) Ltd. Boulez: *Domaines; Rituel*, Universal Edition (London) Ltd. Carter: First String Quartet. Copyright © 1955 (Renewed) by Associated Music Publishers, Inc. (BMI). All Rights Reserved. Used by permission of G. Schirmer Ltd. 8/9 Frith Street, London W1V 5TZ. Debussy: 'Sirènes' from

Nocturnes, Editions Joubert, Paris/United Music Publishers Ltd. Debussy: 'Voiles' from *Préludes* (Book 1), United Music Publishers Ltd. Glass: *Music in Similar Motion*, Dunvagen Music. Ligeti: 'Désordre' from *Etudes*, Schott & Co. Ltd. Maxwell Davies: *Vesalii Icones*, Boosey & Hawkes Music Publishers Ltd. Messiaen: *Cantéyodjayâ*, Universal Edition (London) Ltd. Messiaen: *Couleurs de la Cité céleste; Et expecto resurrectionem mortuorum*, Editions Alphonse Leduc (Paris)/United Music Publishers Ltd. Messiaen: *Turangalîla-Symphony*, Editions Durand (Paris)/United Music Publishers Ltd. Reich: *City Life*, Boosey & Hawkes Music Publishers Ltd. Reich: *Music for Pieces of Wood*, Universal Edition (London) Ltd. Stravinsky: *Petrushka; The Rite of Spring; Symphonies of Wind Instruments*, Boosey & Hawkes Music Publishers Ltd. Stravinsky: *Symphony in C; Symphony in Three Movements*, Schott & Co. Ltd. Torke: *Adjustable Wrench*, Boosey & Hawkes Music Publishers Ltd. Varèse: *Amériques, Intégrales* © G. Ricordi & Co. (London) Ltd.

PART I

The Stravinsky Legacy

1 Introduction: Stravinsky's modernism

Most histories of early musical modernism have concerned themselves with the same canonical list of works, among the most significant of which usually number Debussy's *Prélude à l'après-midi d'un faune*, Schoenberg's Five Orchestral Pieces and *Erwartung*, Strauss's *Elektra* and Stravinsky's *The Rite of Spring*. Their shared modernism – be it 'symbolist', 'expressionist', 'primitivist' – can usefully be summed up in the following remarks by Malcolm Bradbury which head an important recent study of early modernism:

> What Modernism and Postmodernism share in common is a single adversary which is, to put it crudely, realism or naïve mimesis. Both are forms of post-Realism. They likewise share in common a practice based on avant-garde and movement tactics and a sense of modern culture as a field of anxious stylistic formation.[1]

Christopher Butler, the author of that study, elaborates on this by adding that early modern artists shared in 'a general atmosphere of scepticism, which prompted a basic examination of the languages of the arts'.[2] In music before the outbreak of World War 1, this reaction against the (Romantic) past manifested itself variously by such means as a weakening or abandonment of tonality, a challenge to the 'tyranny of the barline' and a break-up of old forms and linear structures – though in most cases aspects of that Romantic heritage managed to survive in one form or another. After the War, such negativity appeared to turn itself into a shared project of reconstruction or of formalisation of new discoveries, a quest after new kinds of order – in the logic of the twelve-note method, or the security of neoclassicism, or the return to (revised) forms of tonality. And histories of a third phase of musical modernism in the aftermath of World War 2 have similarly stressed the commonality of composers' aesthetic ambitions: for example, in his first version (1981) of an account of the post-1945 avant-garde, Paul Griffiths wrote of 'the comparatively unified effort of the late 1940s and early 1950s, when composers . . . appeared to share similar aims and to some degree similar methods . . .'[3]

Such an apparently unified view of the evolution of musical modernism was shared by many of the central participants who were keen to perpetuate an idea of *la grande ligne*, whether in Schoenberg's famous claim that, in the twelve-note method, he had discovered something that would assure 'the supremacy of German music for the next hundred years',[4] or in Boulez's 1951 comment that 'since the discoveries of the Viennese School, all non-serial composers are *useless*'.[5] And what was true for its history was true for the music too: the Viennese School was at pains to point out the continuities within the music itself:

> Unity is surely the indispensable thing if meaning is to exist. Unity, to be very general, is the establishment of the utmost relatedness between all compo-nent parts. (Webern)[6]

> In music there is no form without logic, there is no logic without unity. (Schoenberg)[7]

It was, in part, for this reason that Theodor Adorno ascribed an authentic-ity to the twelve-note method because it clearly enacted the principle of 'identity in non-identity'. Furthermore, in Schoenberg's music Adorno still found embodied the idea of progress.

But for Adorno the picture of early modernism was more complex than the unitary view sketched above. He did not see a single modernism – or, at least, that modernism was dialectically articulated. Between the music of Schoenberg (which represented, in his view, the progressive, authentic, developmental and free subject) and Stravinsky (which represented the regressive, inauthentic, non-developmental and unfree subject) there was an irresolvable dialectic. Stravinsky's modernism was categorically different from Schoenberg's. From an Adornian perspective, Alastair Williams writes: 'Awareness of the simultaneous existence of heterogene-ous social spaces rather blunts the modernist aesthetic of a single advanced historical material. Instead, we are confronted with a sense of multi-layered history; each layer pursuing its own course through time.'[8] And such a view accords with recent rethinking of the evolution of modernism – witness, for example, the plural form of the title of Peter Nicholls's important study *Modernisms*, which argues for a recognition of the diver-sity of modernism in reaction to the tendency of *post*modern thinking to 'caricature' modernism as a 'monolithic ideological formation'. A modern-ism characterised 'primarily by its commitment to reactionary "grand nar-ratives" of social and psychic order . . . could [now] be seen to constitute only one strand of a highly complex set of cultural developments at the beginning of the twentieth century'.[9] In this light, only three years from the end of the twentieth century, Arnold Whittall is perhaps right still to be asking the question: what is modernism?[10]

If we look at what has happened to music and the arts since 1960, it is inevitable that a reevaluation of modernism should be seen to be necessary. Leonard Meyer's controversial identification of a situation of 'cultural stasis . . . a steady-state in which an indefinite number of styles and idioms, techniques and movements . . . coexist'[11] coincides with a postmodern reading of our present culture: 'the general situation is one of temporal disjunction which makes sketching an overview difficult'.[12] Paul Griffiths's second version of his history of the avant-garde (the very word is dropped from the title of the new book) not only struggles to find any real order in music since 1960 ('We live now with many musical histories, and many musical presents'[13]) but also revises what in 1981 had seemed a fairly simple plot regarding the musical activities of the 1940s and 1950s. Other figures complement the Boulez–Cage axis; space is allocated to the so-called 'classic modernism' of Schoenberg and Carter, and to the historically unparalleled 'elder responses' of Stravinsky, Messiaen, Varèse, Wolpe and Shostakovich. In other words, *la grande ligne,* the 'grand narrative', can no longer hold sway. The most significant shift in Griffiths's new history is the far greater prominence given to Stravinsky, whom in 1981 he had dismissed alongside 'other 12-note composers in America'. In particular, Griffiths is able to bring to our attention the increasing influence Stravinsky has exerted on recent generations of composers, the increasing recognition that Cageian indeterminacy or tonal reaction were not the only alternatives to the Schoenberg–Webern legacy that had been exclusively promoted by such important ideology-shaping institutions of the 1950s as Darmstadt and *Die Reihe.*

Indeed, for many composers now, despite Adorno's critical claims, Stravinsky, not Schoenberg, seems to have suggested some of the most productive ways forward, a fact evident, for example, in Glenn Watkins's extraordinary study of 'music, culture and collage from Stravinsky to the postmodernists',[14] and confirmed in Fredric Jameson's observation that it has begun to seem that 'Adorno's prophetic diagnosis has been realized, albeit in a negative way: not Schönberg (the sterility of whose achieved system he already glimpsed) but Stravinsky is the true precursor of postmodern cultural production.'[15] In 1989, the Dutch composer Louis Andriessen wrote that the 'true influence of Stravinsky has only just begun',[16] and in 1995 he commented that, since the death of Stravinsky, the forward path of serialism (the 'music of the future') has come to seem more of a cul-de-sac ('the dead end of what I may call German Romanticism') while 'that combination of high-brow and low-brow material [in Stravinsky] . . . will point out more possibilities for the future'.[17] Andriessen's is not a lone voice; composers from many generations have acknowledged the importance, the centrality of Stravinsky, to their own and others' work:

[*The Rite of Spring*] has not ceased to engender, first, polemics, then, praise, and, finally, the necessary clarifications. In seventy years, its presence has been felt continuously. (Boulez)[18]

I am a disciple of Jung and a lover of Stravinsky. (Tippett)[19]

I recall the first time I heard the *Sacre* . . . played live at Carnegie Hall, conducted by Pierre Monteux in the mid-twenties and decided there and then to become a composer. (Carter)[20]

I think that the *Symphonies of Wind Instruments* is one of the great masterpieces of this century . . . and certainly one of the most original, in that it's to do with the juxtaposition of material without any sense of development. . . . If someone said to me, what's the biggest influence on your life as a composer, I would say this piece. (Birtwistle)[21]

But there was one work in particular, Stravinsky's *Canticum sacrum*, which was a musical revelation to me: I must have heard its first performance broadcast from Venice in 1956, when I was 12. I didn't know at the time why it made such an impression, but it's remained a key work of the twentieth century for me. (Tavener)[22]

I consider it [*The Rite of Spring*] as a revolutionary piece also for the twenty-first century. (Andriessen)[23]

Musicologists, too, have joined in this reevaluation of the received history of modernism. For example, exploring the issues surrounding the alleged conservatism of Stravinsky's neoclassicism, Richard Taruskin makes a timely argument for the *modernity* of Stravinsky's 'antimodernism':

The reinstatement of *plaisanterie* – something made *pour plaire* – within the legitimate domain of art was a serious business for the postwar generation of 'antimodernists', with Satie and now Stravinsky at their head – a generation whose stance now seems, with the advantage of six decades of hindsight, so much more modern than the 'modernism', directly descended from Romanticism, with which it then contended.[24]

In developing what he has coined 'modernist analysis', Arnold Whittall has also called for a reexamination of the competing tendencies of progressive 'modernism' and traditionalist 'antimodernism' in the work (indeed, within the individual works) of a broad range of 'modernist' composers, including Birtwistle, Carter, Maxwell Davies, Stravinsky, Tippett and Webern.[25] He is thus able to distinguish analytically between a number of different musical modernisms: in Maxwell Davies, for instance, he examines the balance between complementary 'floating' and 'focused' tendencies ('"integration and disintegration are entwined" in Davies's modernist language'), whereas he once wrote of Carter's contrasting wholehearted embrace of modernism ('It is Carter who most unambiguously represents the "modernist mainstream" today'), a view which has, however, been subsequently revised in the light of Carter's later works (Whittall now proposes 'a sequence of events which presents the similarity/difference dialogue from ever-changing angles, and with different emphases'.)[26] And, in one of a number of notable departures from the inclusive post-War American theoretical/analytical orthodoxy (I am thinking, in particular, of Allen Forte's work on 'atonal' music: 'The inclusion of Stravinsky's name in the list [of Second Viennese composers] . . . suggests that atonal music was not the exclusive province of Schoenberg and his circle, and that is indeed the case'[27]), Pieter van den Toorn sets up a clear dialectic on technical grounds between Schoenberg and Stravinsky: 'It is . . . in matters having to do with opposition and superimposition, matters affecting all aspects of context, that Stravinsky's music is most appropriately addressed, that it can be distinguished convincingly from, say, much of Schoenberg's, a repertory which, in its vertical or harmonic grouping, tends to invite integration to a far greater extent.'[28]

Stravinsky's modernism, then, is just one strand among many which constitute the conceptual map of modernity. It is a strand which is many-faceted, thus suggesting a plurality even within itself and making it hard to pin down. It is perhaps only through an examination of the work of later composers, through an attempt to define his legacy, that it becomes possible to identify in greater detail the nature of Stravinsky's own modernism. There is, *pace* Cone, no Stravinsky 'method'. Unlike Schoenberg, Stravinsky had no pupils, nor did he write any works of theory. According to Adorno, this was because the Stravinsky style, 'based on whim', could not be taught, only copied.[29] Stravinsky has certainly had his imitators, both in Europe and America (despite the claim of Copland – the 'Brooklyn Stravinsky' and leader of the American Stravinsky 'school' – that 'there remains in Stravinsky's music an irreducible core that defies imitation'[30]). Yet it is becoming increasingly apparent (as evidenced by the composers quoted above), that, both at the time – preeminently in the music of Varèse – and certainly since World War 2, there has been a growing fascination with Stravinsky's creative provenance. Following the lead of Messiaen, composers have begun to look beyond the attractive surface diatonicism and rhythmic irregularity of Stravinsky's music, and have examined more deeply the ways in which in all his work, Russian, neoclassical and serial, Stravinsky found original solutions to the problems presented by modernism. Stravinsky worked with the defining traits of modernism – *inter alia*, its fragmentation, its discontinuity, its primitivism, its eclecticism, its pluralism, its oppositions – finding novel ways of balancing these power-fully contradictory elements without their losing their essential identity, their sense of difference. This Carter has described as Stravinsky's ability to achieve a 'unified fragmentation'. He continues:

> The idiosyncrasies of Russian folksong and liturgy, of jazz and military band playing, of the parlor parodies of Satie, seemed to have played a role in this, which, once it was developed, furnished a pathway out of Russian folklore into an ever broadening musical world of technique and expression – always marked by what came to be recognized everywhere as the highly original and compelling voice of Stravinsky.[31]

Yeats's (post-World War 1) analysis of the modern crisis –

> Things fall apart; the centre cannot hold,
> Mere anarchy is loosed upon the world . . .[32]

seems to offer a different understanding of modernism from Stravinsky's. *The Rite of Spring*, in its violence and its exploration of unconscious emo-tions, may invite superficial comparison with the destructive character-istics of expressionism, but it maintains an objectivity in particular through the obvious structuring provided by its block organisation and repetitions, and thus distinguishes itself from the apparently free, sub-jective expressionism of *Erwartung*. When Cocteau described *The Rite* as 'an organized "Fauvist" work',[33] he touched on the fascinating formalism of *The Rite*, the way in which an overwhelming expression of collective energy is simultaneously released and contained (this 'act of violence against the subject' was, of course, at the heart of Adorno's dispute with Stravinsky: *The Rite* as an 'anti-humanist sacrifice to the collective'[34]). Things may fragment and the *centre* may no longer hold, but anarchy never ensues. Carter's verdict on *The Soldier's Tale* could stand for most of Stravinsky: 'all the brief, almost discrete fragments, however roughly they connect with each other, end up by producing a work that holds together in a very new and telling way.'[35]

In *Adorno's Aesthetics of Music*, Max Paddison has elegantly demon-strated that 'Adorno's philosophy of art is also an aesthetics of mod-ernism'[36] through its quest for an understanding of fragmentation in twentieth-century culture; elsewhere Paddison has defined the Adornian 'dilemma of modernism' as 'the predicament faced by the artist caught between, on the one hand, the traditional demands of the art work for unity and integration (the harmonious relationship between part and whole) and, on the other hand, the loss of faith in any overarching unity on both individual and social levels in the face of the evident fragmenta-tion of modern existence'.[37] The negation of traditional kinds of synthesis

while preserving aspects of connectedness is thus central to an understanding both of modernism and of Adorno's negative dialectics: 'To
change the direction of conceptuality, to give it a turn towards non-
identity, is the hinge of negative dialectics.'[38] And this, in turn, raises
difficult questions for the analysis of modern music, traditionally dependent on theories of unity (stemming, once again, from the dominance of
the Schoenbergian/twelve-note theoretical tradition) – a questioning
begun by Joseph Kerman and finding its fullest expression to date in Alan
Street's seminal article, 'Superior myths, dogmatic allegories'.[39] Coming to
an understanding of these issues is a necessary aspect of the contemporary
(re)interpretation of Stravinsky's music – especially in the neoclassical
works where 'connected' surfaces disguise a deeper fragmentation, a
deeper discontinuity. Yet these works, too, despite their titular and formal
allusions to the connected and developmental genres of the eighteenth and
nineteenth centuries, eschew traditional unities and instead hold together
in 'new and telling ways'. So we return to the modernity even of
Stravinsky's 'antimodernism' (Taruskin), and to the on-going need for
appropriate kinds of 'modernist analysis' (Whittall).

The purpose of the remainder of this introduction is to sketch out, in very
general terms, a frame for our enquiry into Stravinsky's modernism. What
were the contexts for his modernism? How does it both distinguish itself
from and intersect with other modernisms? What is it in Stravinsky's
modernism that has informed, influenced and provoked later generations
of composers?

   Underlying any understanding of Stravinsky's modernism must be an
acknowledgement of his Russianness. In his monumental work of
scholarship *Stravinsky and the Russian Traditions* Richard Taruskin has
demonstrated categorically that Stravinsky's Russian origins shaped the
nature of his (anti-Teutonic) modernism: 'Even as he cultivated the
façade of a sophisticated cosmopolitan . . . Stravinsky was profoundly un-
and even anti-Western in his musical thinking', and no matter how much
he may have professed other allegiances, 'Stravinsky achieved artistic
maturity *and his modernist technique* by deliberately playing the traditions of Russian folk music against those of the provincial denationalized
Russian art music in which he had been reared.'[40] That Stravinsky's
Russianness impinges directly on the nature of his modernism is reinforced, from a different perspective, by Paddison's highly perceptive critique of Adorno (to which we shall return in Chapter 7) which indicates
how key facets of Stravinsky's modernism – for example, its 'orientalism'
and 'primitivism', its objectivity, its static and ritualistic characteristics, its

attitude to repetition – are a consequence of his being 'outside' the Austro-German tradition:

> What were for Schoenberg almost sacred elements of European art music – the need for organic unity achieved from within the material itself, for example – could not, considering his different heritage, have the same significance for Stravinsky. In what Adorno criticizes as a lack of a sense of the historical dimension of the material, can be seen from another perspective in fact as exactly what distinguishes Stravinsky in this century.[41]

One significant aspect of this anti-Teutonic, anti-organic stance is what Taruskin dubs *drobnost'*, defined as '"splinteredness"; the quality of being formally disunified, a sum-of-parts'.[42] The most far-reaching consequence of this attitude was the very antithesis of symphonic argument, namely, an exploration of 'block' construction, which first seriously manifested itself in *Petrushka* and found its most radical expression in the *Symphonies of Wind Instruments* (the subject of Chapter 2). Not that such thinking was without parallel: Debussy's *Jeux*, premiered in 1913 just two weeks before *The Rite of Spring*, also employed a kind of mosaic structure, though its dependence on its programme, and the mobility within its 'blocks' clearly distinguished it from Stravinsky's more radical, or at least more severe (and ultimately more influential), experiments.[43] There are clear associations with film too: when, for example, Watkins writes of 'the montage techniques of Eisenstein which juxtaposed and fused objects and actions to produce a new and separate meaning',[44] it resonates strongly with Stravinsky's *drobnost'*; Debussy was openly intrigued by the possibilities of applying to music the techniques of cinematography.[45]

A further outcome of these non-developmental structures is a music which has often been described as 'static'. Each block, once defined, remains unchanged; there is no sense of a directed (linear) motion through it. And even when the surface of the music seems to suggest conventional tonal voice leading, as in so many of the neoclassical works, the underlying structure appears to be equally non-directed. Taruskin's term for this is *nepodvizhnost'*: 'immobility, stasis; as applied to form, the quality of being nonteleological, nondevelopmental'.[46] Such a sense of stasis is generally brought about by means of repetition – at its most extreme, through 'immobile' ostinatos (aspects of *The Rite*, *Les Noces*, *Three Pieces for String Quartet*). Rhythm is thus brought into the foreground and takes on a structural role equal in significance to, if not greater than, pitch. Melodies, too, are 'static' in that they are built from limited motifs or cells which are then repeated/varied in various guises rather than developing thematically – what Adorno (critically) identified as 'only fluctuations of something always constant and totally static'.[47]

Such a reevaluation of musical time is another prominent aspect of the Stravinsky legacy. It is, in particular, in his positive attitude towards repetition (just as Nietzsche before him had joyfully embraced the notion of eternal recurrence: 'time itself is a circle'[48]) that Stravinsky defines his particular modernist strand and clearly differentiates himself from others. Repetition was central to Schoenberg's twelve-note method, too, but in a completely contrary sense: though at a deeper level the method was concerned with the constant varied repetition of a unifying, single twelve-note row, in its foreground working-out, repetition (of pitch class, of octave by doublings) was to be avoided at all cost (and hence, for Adorno, the method's embodiment of the 'identity in non-identity' dialectic). Stravinsky's music represents a complete inversion of this: foreground continuities through repetition; deeper (middleground) level discontinuities through fragmentation, opposition, disruption – *drobnost'*. And we can here again identify modernist concerns which overlap with Debussy's where repetition also has a non-developmental function and results, as Arthur Wenk has explored, in a static, circular music,[49] or as Derrick Puffett has argued for works such as the second book of piano *Images* (1907) where 'static, non-developmental textures – ostinato . . . [can] be regarded as an anti-developmental device substituting mechanical (!) repetition for German motivic development'.[50] Aspects of the anti-Teutonic characteristics of *both* composers' music certainly have their roots in Russia, especially in the shared models offered by Musorgsky – this is clearly a significant issue in any understanding of the pre-history of the parallel modernisms of Debussy and Stravinsky.

Another feature of this interest in stasis is what, from different angles, both Adorno and Taruskin have described as 'hypostatisation', that is, the focus on the moment as an independent event – something which both writers have discussed in relation to *The Rite of Spring*. Adorno views this negatively: he calls it the 'fetishism of the means' where effect is valued over 'musical meaning', a tendency whose origins he identifies in Wagner, and a view no doubt influenced by his identification of similar fetishism in popular music. Others have put a positive gloss on this uniquely twentieth-century phenomenon. Boulez, for instance, finds such thinking already evident in Debussy: *Jeux* moves from 'orchestration-as-clothing' (*orchestration-vêtement*) to 'orchestration-as-invention' (*orchestration-invention*).[51] There should be little doubt that, because it vitiates narrative argument, such thinking has proved to be an influential aspect of this modernist strand, revealed, for instance, in Messiaen's non-functional colour harmonies, in Stockhausen's moment form, and in the absolute focus on the present of much minimal music.

One other characteristic of *nepodvizhnost'* which is often related back to Stravinsky's 'motor' ostinatos in *The Rite*, *Les Noces* and elsewhere is that of the so-called 'machine' aesthetic. Fascination with the machine as symbol of the 'progress' of the modern age was a feature of many modern movements – most prominently Russian and Italian Futurism, Vorticism, Constructivism, De Stijl and at the Bauhaus – and also had its impact on composers as diverse as Honegger and Milhaud, Antheil and Varèse. Stravinsky's own fascination with the mechanical pianola from the late teens and into the 1920s was a catalyst to many contemporaries, and indeed to important successors such as Nancarrow. But it is to the 'mechanistic' aspect of his repetitions that most composers working with Stravinsky's modernist legacy have been drawn. Indeed, the 'proto-Futurism' of *The Rite*'s ostinatos is something which did not escape even contemporary attention.[52]

Ritual is another key feature of Stravinsky's modernism. It is emblazoned in the very title as well as the musical detail of that modernist paradigm, *The Rite of Spring*, but is to be found everywhere: in the stylised representation of Russian ritual in *Les Noces*, in the anti-narrative theatre of *Oedipus rex*, in the religious rituals of the *Symphony of Psalms* and the *Requiem Canticles*, in the formalism of *Agon*, as well as in instrumental works such as the *Symphonies of Wind Instruments* (itself, according to Taruskin, a veiled religious ritual) and the *Three Pieces for String Quartet*. As will be explored in greater detail in Chapter 4, Stravinsky's ritual structures chime with other modernist strands (Brecht, Cocteau, Meyerhold, etc.), which opposed the Romantic legacy of narrative, representational, cathartic theatre focused on the individual subject with stylised, formalised, collective kinds of theatre which often took their models from pre-Renaissance, pre-humanist societies, from folk art and from non-European cultures. Both Stravinsky's sources and his interest in non-narrative rituals bring into focus central aspects of his modernism – its so-called primitivism and orientalism, its representation of the collective, its 'neo-medievalism' (characteristically in the rhythmic domain) – which, while intersecting with other modernisms, is clearly distinguished from the Expressionist modernism of Schoenberg, demonstrating its continuity with Romantic traditions, its emphasis on individual experience and subjectivity, its developmental narrativity, and so on. Even where Stravinsky's and Schoenberg's modernist paths move closest, in the stylisation, the masks of *Pierrot lunaire*, Schoenberg's musical argument maintains its motivic continuities in a manner almost totally at odds with Stravinsky's methods.

It is his relationship to the past – whether to his 'Russian tradition', to the gamut of Western musical history, or to serialism – which has proved one of the most controversial and, arguably, one of the most influential aspects of Stravinsky's modernism. Andriessen puts it in a slightly different way: 'Stravinsky's influence can be seen . . . in a specific *attitude* towards already existent material.'[53] His neoclassicism, for instance, was not the retrogressive step that many, Adorno foremost among them, accused him of:

> It is by no means the least of Stravinsky's paradoxes that his unique New Objectivist, functionalistic procedure involves elements which had their purpose in precise functions of musical continuity which he now separates from these functions, making them independent and allowing them to ossify.[54]

The point is surely this: not that Stravinsky removes past music (or even contemporary popular music) from its context – that much is self-evident; rather, by placing familiar objects in new contexts he enables us to see them in new ways. A kind of alienation technique, one might say – an almost Brechtian desire to *prevent* the ossification of over-familiar conventions. Take *The Rake's Progress*, Stravinsky's ultimate neoclassical achievement. It was (and still is) misunderstood as mere pastiche, Mozart with wrong notes. Even as distinguished a figure as Deryck Cooke berated Stravinsky's Mozartian gestures because they did not behave in an authentic eighteenth-century manner – to which Brian Trowell has wryly retorted: 'as if Stravinsky were composing for the ear of the Emperor Joseph II'!'[55] For a start, *The Rake* is more than 'just Mozart'; it is an 'opera about opera', a 'collective generalisation of known operas into a "source opera"'.[56] Stephen Walsh puts it succinctly: 'By combining all these different traditions in one opera, Auden and Stravinsky were not so much re-creating classical opera in a modern image as using a variety of historically connected ideas as co-ordinates for plotting an essentially modern line of thought.'[57] It is Stravinsky's modernist *attitude* towards already existent material that is original, that is challenging (and, indeed, 'proto-postmodern'). And Stravinsky's appropriation of existent material extended as far as jazz (in whose rhythmic and harmonic language he recognised many common traits) and fashioned a fascinating accommodation between 'high' and 'low' which has also proved highly influential. But this is not the incorporation of jazz as found in, say, Milhaud or Gershwin, or indeed the affective reconciliation between popular and high art as in Berg's use of Wedekind's cabaret song in *Lulu*. This is another instance of Stravinsky's achieving a 'non-synthesising balance' (Elliott Carter's phrase) between opposed musical materials.

Which finally leads us to perhaps the overriding feature of Stravinsky's modernism, a feature on which we have already touched, and which brings together many facets: Stravinsky's objectivity. For Adorno, this represents a part of the regressive tendencies of Stravinsky's music: its depersonalisation, the alienation of music from the subject, the rejection of expression (cf. the infamous statement in *Chronicles of My Life* that music is powerless to express anything at all – though attributed to Stravinsky, a text actually 'ghostwritten' by Walter Nouvel), 'music about music'. But evidently many subsequent composers have read Stravinsky's objectivity differently: its playfulness, its sense of irony and critical distance from the musical materials, its eclecticism, its positive celebration of collective ritual, have all proved provocative and creatively fruitful. A distance from one's materials does not necessarily mean indifference to the subject matter, nor does it mean the abandonment of a free self. Stravinsky is reevaluating the relationship between subject and object and as such represents a return (a restoration, even) of earlier values, a move away from the dominance of subjectivity in nineteenth-century art. Adorno interprets this as anti-progressive. Others have found in Stravinsky's objectivity a very necessary counterbalance to the continuation of the Romantic tradition, even in the most radical music of Schoenberg and his followers. Schoenberg – to misappropriate Stravinsky's words on *Oedipus rex* – was interested in the fate of the person; Stravinsky, while not indifferent to it, was 'far more concerned with the person of the fate, and the delineation of it which can be achieved uniquely in music'.

> To the extent that terms like *stasis, discontinuity, block juxtaposition, moment* or *structural simplification* can be applied to modern music in general – a very great extent – and to the extent that Stravinsky is acknowledged as a source or an inspiration for the traits and traditions they signify – an even greater extent – the force of his example bequeathed a *russkiy slog* [Russian manner] to the whole world of twentieth-century concert music. To that world Stravinsky related not by any 'angle.' He was the very stem.[58]

These, then, are the key features of Stravinsky's modernism. They constitute Stravinsky's aesthetic legacy. But the Stravinsky legacy (appropriately) operates on many levels simultaneously: cultural, stylistic, technical. The impact of that cultural and stylistic legacy on the course of the development of twentieth-century music has been widely explored.[59] But Stravinsky's technical legacy has less often been addressed, and usually in passing or in relation to specific composers (often by those composers

themselves – as Messiaen and Carter have done). The possible reasons for
the lack of this kind of discussion are many. Partly, it has to do with the fact
that the wider influence of Stravinsky's music has, until recently, been
hidden by a historiography which has given preference to the twelve-note
legacy. Similarly, because Schoenberg's 'method' and the analytical techniques necessary to investigate it were clearly defined and widely theorised,
tracing and acknowledging influences was a relatively straightforward task.
By contrast, there is, as we have seen, no Stravinskian 'method', nor is there
any comparable agreement as to how to approach Stravinsky's music
analytically. As famously demonstrated by the unprecedentedly heated
exchange in the pages of *Music Analysis* over a passage from *The Rite of
Spring*,[60] the attitudes to Stravinsky analysis of Forte and Taruskin remain
at poles, with van den Toorn mediating between them, not to mention a
range of other competing voices (we shall return to these analytical contro-
versies in Part II). In the face of such profound disagreements, the task of
identifying Stravinskian procedures in later music, other than the most
superficial imitations, in a consistent and convincing manner would
appear to be something of an uphill struggle. Nonetheless, at century's end,
and given the frequency with which composers are now citing Stravinsky as
the *fons et origo* of their musical thinking, it is a task that must be undertaken. This book represents a first attempt.

The Czech novelist and essayist, Milan Kundera, has found a haunting
expression to sum up what he feels characterises that strand of modernism
I have appropriated for Stravinsky. His history of modernism is built
around a sense of the 'inimitable delight in being', and his list of participating artists is revealing:

> There are works in modern art that have discovered an inimitable delight in
> being, the delight that shows in a euphoric recklessness of imagination, in
> the pleasure of inventing, of surprising – even of shocking – by an invention.
> One might draw up a whole list of works of art that are suffused with this
> delight: along with Stravinsky (*Petrushka*, *Les Noces*, *Renard*, the *Capriccio*
> for Piano and Orchestra, the Violin Concerto, etc., etc.), everything by Miró;
> Klee's paintings; Dufy's; Dubuffet's; certain Apollinaire writings; late Janacek
> (*Nursery Rhymes*, Sextet for Wind Instruments, his opera *The Cunning Little
> Vixen*); some of Milhaud's works; and some of Poulenc's; *Les Mamelles de
> Tirésias* . . . In this listing of the great works of delight, I cannot overlook jazz
> music.[61]

To which we should add Kundera himself – perhaps the most 'Stravinskian'
of novelists.

Kundera's history of modernism, like mine, is selective. Furthermore,
the kind of modernism I have chosen to identify with Stravinsky is far

from exclusively his. In some cases, other musical modernisms anticipate and intersect in fascinating ways (Debussy's stasis, Bartók's rhythms, Ives's layering); in others, oppositions are more readily apparent (Schoenberg, Mahler, Berg), so that when similarities do emerge, they are all the more arresting (musical layering in *Pierrot lunaire*, Mahler's attitude to 'found' material, Berg's ostinatos). Certainly, the maintenance of an opposition between the non-developmental, non-narrative objectivity of Stravinsky and the subjective, Expressionist continuity with the Romantic tradition in Schoenberg is a convenience for my purposes here only insofar as such an opposition is still relevant to issues in modernism today – the on-going interplay between 'modernist' and 'traditionalist' tendencies. The integrity of Stravinsky's modernist thread depends on being able to demonstrate convincingly that there *is* something identifiably Stravinskian about the ideas and practices which have shaped much of the music of our time. By focusing on the notion of 'non-development', however it may manifest itself, and the hermeneutic difficulties it brings in its wake, what follows is an attempt to offer just such an interpretative framework.

2 Block forms

Picasso, Stravinsky and the *Symphonies of Wind Instruments*

Picasso's charcoal drawing of 1910 *Nude*[1] is one of the purest and most refined examples of what has become known as 'analytical Cubism' (Plate 2.1). Though at one level it is still a representation of a human figure, what is most striking is the dynamic balance it achieves between lines and curves to create a sense of shifting planes. There is a strong rhythm about the drawing which leads the eye with an uncanny inevitability from top to bottom. This view is supported, for example, by Georges Boudaille, who writes that the drawing suggests 'a being reduced to a graphic symphony' and 'a syncopated rhythm measuring out space'.[2] Such analogies with music were not uncommon even during the Cubist period itself, as documented by John Golding.[3] For instance, in discussing the painter Robert Delaunay's move around 1912 towards a more purely abstract kind of painting, Guillaume Apollinaire wrote that 'we are progressing towards an intensely new kind of art, which will be to painting what one had hitherto imagined music was to pure literature'.[4] Apollinaire labelled this purer, more lyrical phase of Cubism 'Orphism' (after his own *Bestiaire au cortège d'Orphée* of 1911): 'The works of Orphist artists should offer simultaneously a sensation of pure aesthetic enjoyment, a structure of which the senses are hardly aware and a profound content, in other words a subject. This is pure art.'[5] One of the principal concerns of this new phase of abstract painting – whose leading exponents were Delaunay, Fernand Léger and Francis Picabia – was that of simultaneity, 'a sense that the modern world was of such complexity that it could not be embodied in structures which show only finite objects in one moment in time'.[6] The concept is enshrined, for example, in Delaunay's *Sun, Moon. Simultaneous* series of paintings (started in 1913) in which (in language similar to that of Varèse's accounts of his own attitude to form, as discussed below) he became 'so involved in the "demands" made by the material that the structure seemed to be generating itself'.[7] Musical parallels were significant to these artists. For instance, 'Delaunay told Kandinsky that he had discovered relationships between colours which were "comparable to musical notes"', and that in many of his paintings of 1912, 'the use of the recurrent "motif" has a musical significance, as "variations on a theme"'.[8]

Plate 2.1   Picasso, *Standing female nude* (1910)

The first time I encountered Picasso's 1910 *Nude* it immediately struck me that it was in some ways the visual equivalent of Stravinsky's *Symphonies of Wind Instruments*. The musical/rhythmic aspects of Cubism in general and *Nude* in particular, and the obvious objective, almost constructivist aspects of the *Symphonies* immediately suggest a similar aesthetic (remembering, though, that the *Symphonies* was produced some ten years after the Picasso drawing. There is no evidence to suggest Stravinsky knew this actual picture). The basic elements of *Nude*, the means by which the space is articulated, could not be more simple: straight lines and arcs, with rougher 'shading' to break up a little the geometric sharpness of the drawing. These elements intersect in such a way as to produce a pattern of repeating shapes – repetitions, though, which are never identical (more like a sequence of variations) – as well as alluding to a veiled human figure. Stravinsky's *Symphonies of Wind Instruments* similarly articulates musical time by means of three basic (related) tempi which intersect (in the ratio 2:3:4) in such a way as to produce a pattern of repeating shapes, none of which is identical (variations?), as well as alluding to a veiled model (more obliquely than in the Picasso) – some sort of ritual (*in memoriam* Debussy), which Richard Taruskin has fascinatingly identified as the *panikhida* service, the Russian Orthodox office of the dead.[9] In the Picasso a variety of planes, individually characterised, are thus produced, the movement from one to the next forming the drawing's primary subject matter. In the Stravinsky a variety of musical blocks, individually characterised, are similarly produced, the movement from one to the next forming the work's primary subject matter. In both works, there is no obvious transition from one plane/block to the next: in other words, they 'proceed' at an immediate level by means of opposition, discontinuity (or 'stratification', to use the terminology coined by Edward T. Cone in his seminal analysis of the *Symphonies*[10]). Nonetheless, while not serving to undermine these fundamentally bold oppositions, there is, over a large scale, a degree of continuity which leads us through both works (Cone's term is 'interlock', where earlier blocks are regained and varied, compressed or extended): the interrupted vertical lines in the upper two thirds of Picasso's drawing or the arcs in the lower half, it seems to me, are instances of such 'interlock'.

Rhythm is an important articulatory feature of both Picasso's *Nude* and Stravinsky's *Symphonies*. Central to the definition of each of Stravinsky's blocks is the differentiation between the durational groupings of the blocks, and the organisation of repeating units within blocks. The rhythm of the Picasso is similarly achieved by repetition across the drawing and by the more local interplay of angles. The striking orchestration of

Stravinsky's blocks is perhaps matched by the different kinds of shading employed in Picasso's planes; certainly Stravinsky's choice of instruments and extreme changes in texture (from rich, full chords at fig. 1 to sparse three-flute writing at fig. 6^{11}) find parallels in both the extreme contrasts between light and shade and the changes in density of graphic activity in the Picasso.

The lower half of the drawing is quite different from the upper half, which alludes more directly to the human figure (head and face, a breast, shoulders, arms). It is as if the abstraction in the upper portion is only latent and is not explicitly realised until our eyes move to the lower portion. There is, nonetheless, a balance and continuity between the two halves which stand in contrast to, say, the conflict between Fauvist and Cubist representations of the women's heads in *Les Demoiselles d'Avignon* (clearly a transitional and 'incomplete' work). In a similar way, the chorale (composed first, on 20 June 1920) towards which Stravinsky's *Symphonies* is directed is not necessarily a consequence of the first half of the piece but comes more and more into view as the piece proceeds:

> The complete music was finished in abbreviated form by July 2, but a few days later I added two adumbrative bits of chorale to the body of the piece.[12]

Stravinsky's account not only betrays the 'cut and paste' approach he took to the *Symphonies* (a reading supported both by Cone's analysis and by Stephen Walsh's study of the work's genesis through the sketches[13]), thus drawing attention to the parallels with collage techniques used elsewhere in Cubist art, but also implies a certain rough or 'unfinished' quality. Certainly the way in which blocks of music are interrupted, shear off or fracture, gives a rough character to the work which is shared by Picasso's *Nude*. Such juxtapositions are not unique to the *Symphonies* (as discussed further below) but their roughness, their starkness, is foregrounded here and it is the audacity and originality of this approach to form-building which have made it such an influential work.

This roughness, too, is part of Stravinsky's legacy and can be heard in the work of many of his important successors: Varèse, Birtwistle, Andriessen, Xenakis. It is not just a roughness of orchestration where instruments (and instrumentalists) are pushed to extremes – though the high solo bassoon at the beginning of *The Rite* has, as fetish sound-object, almost come to symbolise early musical modernism. There are other roughnesses which are brought about, for instance, by the impact of folk music and jazz on Stravinsky – the coming together of 'high' and 'low', where sounds normally excluded within the context of 'art' music, such as exaggeration of squeaky upper partials in high clarinets, or the breath of a flautist, or the rasping of the reed in a saxophone, become a part of the music's colour – what, in a different context, Barthes referred to as the 'grain of the voice'.[14] There is a seeming 'hand-made' character to Stravinsky's invented forms (as demonstrated in his account of the making of the *Symphonies*), or in the neoclassical works in his transformation of received materials and forms (e.g. the 'roughing-up' of Pergolesi *et al.* in *Pulcinella*). There is even a certain roughness – by which I imply a degree of unpredictability or irregularity, something intuitively defined – in his handling of melodic and harmonic construction. Once again, this relates Stravinsky's work back to notions of primitivism, as does his involvement, from time to time, with what Peter Brook has described as a 'rough theatre'[15] – most notably in *Renard* and *The Soldier's Tale* (see Chapter 4). Along with this roughness goes a certain directness, a kind of plain speaking which maybe even consciously adopts a mode of naïveté, and which leads back to the boldness of the oppositions in the *Symphonies of Wind Instruments* and, indeed, to the essential simplicity of Picasso's *Nude*.

It might be instructive at this point to compare the analytical Cubism of Picasso (and Braque) with the near-contemporary work of the Dutch painter, Piet Mondrian, who was in Paris from the end of 1911 until 1914.[16] Even at its most 'analytical', Picasso's Cubism never became pure abstraction; most writers on Cubism at the time stressed its continuity with rather than opposition to realism. Of Picasso's work produced at Cadaqués in the summer of 1910 (the period of *Nude*), Golding has written:

> in Picasso's work and subsequently in Braque's, there was initiated a dialogue between the subject matter and the highly abstract way in which it was rendered. Looking at works of this second analytical phase of Cubism we are always aware of the presence of images, but sometimes they materialize only gradually from the complex of interacting transparent planes which surround and indeed constitute them, only to be reabsorbed into the painting's overall spatial flux.[17]

The same could also be written of the *Symphonies of Wind Instruments* whose 'images' are constituted by such ideas as familiar folk-like melodies, the chorale fragments, a fanfare, and so on, but these are glimpsed through their interaction, only to be reabsorbed into the music's overall spatial/temporal flux. Mondrian's work had moved beyond this stage into abstraction. Though, like Picasso, his paintings from 1913 onwards are made up of horizontal and vertical lines which enclose coloured planes, in no sense do they relate directly to observed phenomena (though this is not to say they do not have an important symbolic quality – as in, for example,

Mondrian's so-called 'oceanic' style). The rhythm of repeating lines, shapes and colours of his paintings is their *raison d'être*. Glenn Watkins draws parallels with the more obviously constructivist (Futurist? city-oriented?) music of Varèse and Antheil,[18] a view reinforced by Milner's reading of Mondrian as 'isolating the rhythms of the city and its dynamic restlessness'.[19] Certainly a sculpture such as *Interrelation of Masses* (1919) by the Belgian George Vantongerloo, a colleague of Mondrian's in the Dutch De Stijl movement, offers striking visual parallels with the music of Varèse. There are more recent parallels with Mondrian too, leaving aside his postmodern appropriation through the fetish for his lines and colours in popular 1960s design: in the graphic style of certain American experimental composers – the correspondence between, for example, Mondrian's *Composition in Blue, A* (1917) and Earle Brown's *December 1952* is unavoidable; and in the work of minimalist and post-minimalist composers. Louis Andriessen, for example, overtly aligns himself with Mondrian in *De Stijl* (1984–5), though his choice of the artist may have as much to do with Andriessen's own Dutch nationalist agenda as with Mondrian's proto-minimalist aesthetic. Mondrian's exploration of rhythm and process, vivid blocks of colour, restriction of means and non-expression suggest fruitful parallels with the classic American minimalism of the 1970s, most notably that of Steve Reich.

Glenn Watkins's account in *Pyramids at the Louvre* of Stravinsky's association with Cubist artists, and his accord with and participation in Cubism, is revealing. Stravinsky first met Picasso only in 1917 but, as Watkins argues, it is clear that 'Stravinsky was aware of and responded to the Cubist vision in the period around 1912–1914.'[20] He documents the composer's encounters with the ideas of the leading artists and art theorists of the time (Albert Gleizes, Jean Metzinger, Michail Larionov, Léon Bakst, Jean Cocteau, Jacques Copeau, Misia Sert, Blaise Cendrars, Delaunay, Picasso[21]), a number of whom even painted Stravinsky's portrait in decidedly Cubist terms; furthermore, his association during these years with both Cocteau and Diaghilev would have brought him into contact with these painters and their ideas.

Attempts to relate Stravinsky's music to its contemporary Cubist art date back to the time of the premières of the works themselves: 'He [Stravinsky] partakes of our aesthetic, of Cubism, of synchronism, of the simultaneity of some and the nervous, matter of fact onyrhythm of others.'[22] Watkins quotes Maurice Touchard's 1913 review of *The Rite of Spring* which describes the work's 'harmonic excesses . . . a kind of musical cubism'.[23] Subsequently parallels have been drawn, for example, by such commentators as the art historian Robert Rosenblum, who suggests an account of Stravinsky's structures as Cubist.[24] More common, however, than specifically Cubist accounts of, say, *The Rite of Spring*, are attempts to relate the work of Stravinsky and the Cubists by way of their shared 'primitivism', an exercise which clearly opens up further interesting parallels with the rawness and immediacy of Fauvism (an important prelude to Cubism), the aggressive rhythmic energy of Italian Futurism and the intuitive and often violent nature of Expressionism. As Stravinsky himself details in *Expositions and Developments*,[25] Debussy was among the first to recognise the primitivism of *The Rite* in his remark 'C'est une musique nègre'. Cocteau (quoted by Adorno[26]) wrote in 1926 that, 'When all is said and done, the "Sacre" is still a "Fauvist" work, an organized "Fauvist" work'. For Adorno such primitivism lies at the heart of his attack on Stravinsky, in which he relates the paganism of *The Rite* to the avant-garde attraction to African sculpture, before concluding that the 'aesthetic nerves tremble with the desire to regress to the Stone Age'.[27] It is a small step for Adorno from the human sacrifice of *The Rite*, the 'wild portrayal of the primitive', to the barbarism of the Third Reich. 'It is not only that the work actually resounds with the noise of the impending war, but it further reveals its undisguised joy at the vulgar splendor of it all.'[28]

Milan Kundera, for one, takes issue with what he calls Adorno's 'short-circuited method that, with a fearsome facility, links works of art to political (sociological) causes, consequences, or meanings; extremely nuanced ideas ... thereby lead to extremely impoverished conclusions'.[29] He objects to the fact that Adorno implicates Stravinsky in the destructive barbarism of our century. Stravinsky, according to Kundera, was the first 'to give barbaric rites a grand form ... Without its beauty, the barbaric would remain incomprehensible.'[30] To recognise the beauty in the barbaric is 'scandalous', but unless this scandal is understood, 'we cannot understand much about man'. *The Rite*, for Kundera, 'does not dodge the horror'.[31] And, in a strange way, Adorno too recognises this fact. 'Fascism, which literally sets out to liquidate liberal culture ... is for this very reason unable to bear up under the expression of barbarism. ... In the Third Reich – with its astronomical sacrifice of human beings – *Le Sacre du printemps* could never have been performed.'[32] Clearly, on one level, *The Rite* is a representation of destructiveness, and this parallels aspects of Cubist art: 'the *Demoiselles* is angular, harsh and grating ... the mood of the *Demoiselles* is quite clearly consciously disturbing, physical and erotic yet savage, simultaneously inviting and repellent'.[33] Adorno: 'With the elimination of the harmlessly grotesque, the work [*The Rite*] takes the side of the avant-garde – particularly of Cubism.'[34] But does such side-taking necessarily also imply an identification (Adorno's word) with the barbaric? 'If the liquidation of the young girl', Adorno asserts, 'is not simplistically enjoyed by the individual in the audience, he feels his way into the collective, thinking (as the potential victim of the collective) to participate thereby in collective power in a state of magic regression.'[35] I cannot accept that to listen to *The Rite* is to be complicit with the barbarism it represents; rather, like Kundera, I believe that such representation of destructiveness is necessary in order to be able to grasp its horror.

Herein lies the power of *The Rite*, and indeed the power of its influence. The analyses of Boulez, Forte, van den Toorn and others have clearly demonstrated that *The Rite* is a highly structured work; its forms, its processes, are ordered and consistent. If it were purely Dionysian it would truly be a terrible thing: we could only see in it, as Nietzsche famously argued, the 'horror or absurdity of existence'.[36] But, like Greek tragedy, the most fearful and primitive content (where 'everything subjective vanishes into complete self-forgetfulness'[37]), the Dionysian, is mediated through an 'Apollonian precision and lucidity'.[38] According to Adorno, in Stravinsky 'the structure is externally superimposed by the composer's will',[39] but, for *The Rite* at least, this simply does not accord with the subtle and complex ways in which Stravinsky organises his basic musical material. The unrelenting, unvaried and unsubtle repetitions of, say, Antheil's *Ballet mécanique* seem far closer to Adorno's description than does *The Rite*.

Is the structure of the *Symphonies of Wind Instruments* – a work which was so in keeping with contemporary developments in the arts generally, and which can be shown to have had a profound impact on subsequent composers – also merely 'externally superimposed by the composer's will'? What Adorno is asserting in this phrase is that, unlike Schoenberg, who 'hit upon objectively musical validities', Stravinsky's works were 'in no sense to be understood as the organ of an inner force'.[40] In other words, the form was imposed on the musical material rather than being a consequence of that material. Adorno's concepts of material and form are far more sophisticated and complex than this suggests, as Max Paddison has outlined in, for example, his chapter on 'a material theory of form': 'musical material is mediated not only because it is shaped, more or less consistently, within the form of the work itself, but precisely because it is already historically and culturally pre-formed before any individual act of composition even begins.'[41] And, as seen above in the discussion of the musical 'images' of the work ('historically and culturally pre-formed' material), this is certainly true of the *Symphonies of Wind Instruments*. But the 'shaping' of this material is certainly not achieved, in this work at the very least, by the imposition of some inappropriate formal 'given'. 'While his [Stravinsky's] musical structures juxtapose sound sections like Debussy, they rage against their flavour and rob them of their vitality,' wrote Adorno in his 1962 Stravinsky essay.[42] This does *not* accord with my experience of the work. Certainly, in its juxtapositions, as seen in relation to Cubism, there are aspects of the work that can legitimately be considered collagistic. But this is not its primary *modus operandus*, any more than it is Picasso's in his Cubist works. For one thing, as Cone's category of interlock makes explicit, as well as the analyses of Hasty and Jonathan Kramer,[43] the material is made to do some work. It is not just an assemblage of *objets trouvés* – Walsh's account of Stravinsky's 'empiricism' notwithstanding:

> the work – in its pragmatic, experimental being – seems to inhabit a world of variable possibilities, of observation and testing, a world in which right and wrong look like the mere arbitrary choice between one accident and another.[44]

In its pragmatism, its experimentation, the structure of the *Symphonies* perhaps begins to approach Adorno's concept of 'une musique informelle':

> a type of music which has discarded all forms which are external or abstract or which confront it in an inflexible way. At the same time, although such music should be completely free of anything irreducibly alien to itself or superimposed on it, it should nevertheless constitute itself in an objectively compelling way, in the musical substance itself, and not in terms of external laws.[45]

Though Stravinsky's work operates in quite different ways from the music for which Adorno's label was originally coined (e.g. Schoenberg Op. 11, No. 3, *Erwartung*, etc.), it nonetheless conforms (intriguingly so) to Paddison's description of a music composed from the 'bottom up', 'which freely chooses to go against the tendency of such forms towards integration and closure by denying the reconciliation of opposites and remaining deliberately open and fragmentary. This is seen as acting as an immanent critique of totality, of the universal, and of a wholeness which is seen as false.'[46]

The structure of the *Symphonies* is certainly not the kind of free form Adorno envisaged. But I believe that its originality and vitality (it is a work which has retained its freshness to this day) can be accounted for in terms of Adorno's category: the *Symphonies* resists 'integration' and the 'reconciliation of opposites' – the discontinuity of the variously-defined musical blocks, though mitigated in certain ways, remains unresolved to the end; it thus also remains, to a degree, fragmentary – it is built from fragments rather than musical wholes; and despite the 'morphology of closure' brought about by the concluding chorale, closure is nonetheless resisted: the musical fragments remain 'in play' beyond the end of the work. Immanent critique of totality? As we shall see in Chapter 6, even where Stravinsky adopts an apparent 'top down' approach to musical form by operating within (or, rather, against) a traditional formal given, an important element of critique is involved. In the *Symphonies* the critique of totality is much more explicit; its oppositions make little attempt at reconciliation. Herein lies the individuality (and influence) of the modernism of the *Symphonies of Wind Instruments*. As we saw in Chapter 1, the 'dilemma of modernism as Adorno understands it [is . . .] the predicament faced by the artist caught between, on the one hand, the traditional demands of the art work for unity and integration (the harmonious relationship between part and whole) and, on the other hand, the loss of faith in any overarching unity'.[47] And, it might be said, the analyst's predicament too.

Key analyses of the *Symphonies* – principally those of Cone, van den Toorn, Taruskin, Hasty and Jonathan Kramer – have all attempted to demonstrate how this work articulates the 'dilemma of modernism'. Cone's categories have already been discussed. The fragmentation of the form is achieved by 'stratification' while the most problematic feature is that of 'synthesis', which Cone defines as 'some sort of unification', 'the necessary goal towards which the entire composition points, for without it there is no cogency in the association of the component areas'.[48] This does rather imply too great a concern for the 'traditional demands' for 'unity and integration' involving, as Cone puts it, 'the assimilation by one [component] of all the others'.[49] There is perhaps not enough 'loss of faith' here, though '*some sort* of unification' at least allows for the possibility (as does Cone's graph) that not everything is resolved or assimilated.

Where, for Cone, the 'diverse elements are brought into closer and closer relation with one another, all *ideally* being accounted for in the final resolution'[50] (whose ideals? why is such a relation *necessary*?), for van den Toorn the 'final resolution' is more ambiguous. It has the morphology of a cadence, but does not function as such: 'the C-scale-on-C "resolution" has little to do with pitch organization generally . . . The "resolution" surfaces, rather, as a *terminating convenience*, an expedient, a "device"'.[51] Even the 'dominant-like articulation' of the earlier chorale fragments 'are in reality without dominant pretension',[52] though van den Toorn goes on to argue that 'only in the final measures – and only *retroactively*, strictly speaking – does the chorale's (G B D F/D A♭ F) articulation acquire the characteristic "feel" of a "dominant seventh" . . . "resolving" to its "tonic"'.[53] His hard-working inverted commas here draw attention to the terminological difficulties, but his analysis is admirable in its attempt to keep active both the continuous and the discontinuous elements of the work, resisting the urge to give priority to one over the other. This 'dilemma' he sums up as follows:

> Not until the first movement of the *Symphony of Psalms* (1930) . . . do we again confront a block juxtaposition as rigid, incisive, or abrupt as that in the *Symphonies*, or, as a seemingly inseparable coordinate, relations so unconditionally committed to a . . . symmetrically defined partitioning of the octatonic collection.[54]

Its octatonic pitch organisation serves to provide coherence, continuity, but this is nonetheless contradicted in various ways (usually – according to van den Toorn – in the rhythmic/metric domain). The stasis implied by octatonicism is imbued with a dynamism by rhythmic means; the implied dynamism/directedness of the allusions to 'dominants' and 'tonics' is contradicted by their static contexts. There is *simultaneously* opposition and synthesis, resolution and non-resolution.

Aside from Taruskin's brilliant revelation of the underlying liturgical structure of the *Symphonies* (a perspective he offers as a 'less abstract' and 'less radical' alternative in order to demonstrate the work's continuity with its Russian predecessors), he nonetheless presents it as the 'spectacular peak' of *drobnost'* in Stravinsky. The qualities of 'unending' and 'unbeginning' which go with this fragmentation make associations with *nepodvizhnost'*, 'a quality intrinsic to unisectional, ostinato-driven pieces [e.g. the first of the *Three Pieces for String Quartet*]. When such sections are multiplied [as in the *Symphonies*], one result is *drobnost'*'.[55] Where van den Toorn talks of abrupt block juxtaposition, Taruskin identifies 'splinteredness' in the work's refrains, interjections, alternations of opposed ideas and tempi, its 'halting' surface discontinuities, its non-directedness. Yet *drobnost'* also involves being a '*sum*-of-parts': this context is to be found in the harmonic organisation, where it is octatonic/diatonic interplay (mining the 'harmonic potential of the "Russian" tetrachords') that makes the work cohere. Taruskin's ultimate need to find 'organic' connectedness here stems from his desire to interpret the *Symphonies* as 'Stravinsky's "Russian" valedictory'.[56]

Jonathan Kramer's writings have focused on musical time in twentieth-century music, culminating in his important study, *The Time of Music*.[57] What is so refreshing about Kramer's approach to Stravinsky's music is the way in which he strongly resists the 'traditional demands for unity and integration' and instead places a primacy on discontinuity and 'nonlinearity'. Kramer certainly recognises the context and on-going significance of

Stravinsky's formal innovations which 'derive in part from those of Debussy, parallel those of Ives, Webern, and Varèse, and anticipate those of Messiaen and the Darmstadt school'.[58] Kramer deals with the balancing of discontinuous and continuous elements in a different way from Cone and van den Toorn: with regard to the *Symphonies of Wind Instruments* he argues for 'a subtle tension . . . , as this middleground stasis of form is contradicted by foreground details and background pitch connections that do progress through time'.[59] Like many analysts before him, Kramer specifies how blocks of material (what he calls 'moments' – so making explicit links with post-World War 2 developments) are defined and juxtaposed, but goes on to show how proportional (temporal) ratios offer the possibility of order, of consistency (Whittall's 'rules of containment'[60]), without undermining the primacy of the oppositions. He examines works from *The Rite of Spring* through to *Agon* but the 'real breakthrough piece' is identified as the *Symphonies*. There is a danger in his approach (not unique to Kramer by any means) of equating temporal and spatial proportions (they are *not* the same thing) and I am not convinced that a synthesising tendency is not lurking just below the surface. He often relies on an undefined notion of 'balance' to bring coherence to the music, and in *The Time of Music* he seems to backtrack on his earlier radical position by demonstrating a background, linear, stepwise progression. Coherence, in the way Kramer employs the term, is also a nebulous concept: 'Yet *Agon* magically coheres. The pervasiveness of one proportional ratio offers the single-mindedness absent from the work's surface.'[61] For single-mindedness read the 'unmistakable unity' to which Kramer had referred only two sentences earlier. And why 'magical'? – something beyond analysis, perhaps? Nonetheless, Kramer's analyses do offer further evidence towards an understanding of why Stravinsky's formal innovations have proved so influential. Stravinsky's modernism is clearly located in such discontinuities, and these analyses articulate Adorno's dilemma of modernism where artist and analyst are caught between the traditional demands for unity and integration and the loss of faith in unity in the face of fragmentation. Though not 'une musique informelle' as Adorno conceived it, this concept is nonetheless helpful in evaluating Stravinsky's achievement here. Furthermore, it is surely not without significance that, while Adorno condemns Stravinsky in general for a music 'stratified like blocks of marble'[62] and admits to the success of the Concertino for String Quartet and the Octet 'because they preserve the aggressive fragmentation of infantilism without deforming a model in any obvious way',[63] the *Symphonies of Wind Instruments* is conspicuous by its absence from Adorno's writings on Stravinsky.[64]

Petrushka

It has often been noted that the block juxtapositions of the *Symphonies of Wind Instruments* are not new in Stravinsky, merely more uncompromising than in the works that preceded it. Though van den Toorn identifies the beginnings of such block-like thinking in the repetitions of the Kastchei theme in the 'Danse infernale' from *The Firebird* (where the successive entrances of the theme are juxtaposed against a tutti A–E fifth, anticipating similar procedures in, for instance, *Les Noces* and the *Symphony of Psalms*[65]), the first clearly oppositional writing is to be found in the first tableau of *Petrushka* (1911, rev. 1947). The way in which 'static' blocks are broken off, only later to be repeated (in exact, varied or curtailed forms), is not only 'cinematic' in concept (cf. Stravinsky's comments on the origins of the *Symphony in Three Movements* in Chapter 6) – and thus relates directly to the programme of the ballet – but also, in enabling Stravinsky to quote explicitly from a number of Russian folk melodies and other popular tunes, it anticipates the eclectic juxtaposition of a wide range of distinct material (both 'newly-formed' and 'ready-made') in so many later works. Jann Pasler's fascinating account of the collaboration ('ballets as works of total theater', as she describes *Petrushka* and *The Rite*) between Stravinsky, Alexandre Benois (the score's dedicatee, co-author with Stravinsky of the story, and responsible for its original scenery and costume design) and Mikhail Fokine (choreographer) lends further support to a reading of the opening tableau of *Petrushka* in terms of block juxtaposition: 'By trying to follow the rapid succession of events in these tableaux, rather than any story, and to create a close coordination between his music and those events, Stravinsky was led to explore discontinuity in music.'[66] Fig. 2.1 details the discontinuous blocks of tableau 1, which are (variously) differentiated in terms of abrupt changes to such features as melodic material, orchestration, ostinato patterns, rhythm, tempo and metre. As one would expect of a music defined largely in terms of melodic repetition, pedal points and ostinatos, each block is, on the whole, static (with the possible exception of F, which retains the tonic–dominant alternations of the original popular song). Any sense of dynamism is generated within the blocks by means of rhythm, e.g. figs. 34–6 by the compression of the reiterated Gs in the melody, and by the increasing frequency of appearance of the triplet 'closing' group; by varying the rate of change between blocks, e.g. a greater frequency of change at figs. 42–51; and by the simultaneous layering of distinct musical ideas, e.g. F ('elle avait un' jambe au bois'), aspects of E ('barrel organ'), and A (opening 'crowd' music) all sounding together at figs. 24–6.

Fig. 2.1 Organisation of blocks in Stravinsky, *Petrushka*, first tableau (figs. 0–56) (1947 revised version)

Rehearsal figs.	Material
0–2	A (Shrovetide fair 'crowd' music)
2–2^{+3}	B
2^{+3}–3	A
3–7	B′
7–13	B″ (group of drunken dancers: Easter 'Song of the Volochobniki')
13–15	C (fair compère)
15–16	D
16–17	A
17–18	C
18–19	E (barrel organ player: 'popular Russian chanson'[67])
19–20	C
20–21	D
21–22	A
22–23	E
23–26	F ('elle avait un' jambe au bois')
25	A superimposed
26–28	E + G (cel/hp 'music box') simultaneously
28–30	G (cont.) + F
29^{+1}	A superimposed
30–33	C
33–34	A
34–36	B
36–42	B″ (drunken dancers)
42–44	C
44–45	D
45–46	A
46–47	C
47–48	D
48–51	C
51–53	D
53–55	A
55–56	A′

This detailed view of the individual blocks can usefully be compared with Taruskin's more general view of the overall shape of the first tableau, which he describes as a 'sort of rondo': ABACBABA, where A is the milling crowd and vendors' cries, B the barker or '*balagannïy ded*' amusing the crowd, and C the barrel organ and street dancer.[68]

Though discontinuity is clearly to the fore here ('What Benois calls the "illusion of life" projected by these tableaux comes not from any narrative, but from the sheer multiplicity of characters and events on stage'[69]), there are also clear continuities across the juxtaposed blocks (far more obviously than in the *Symphonies of Wind Instruments*). These are brought about, for instance, harmonically (in the blocks' shared diatonic D scale or diatonic–octatonic interaction[70]), motivically (in the fact that all melodic ideas but one – 'elle avait un' jambe au bois' – are characterised by a rising perfect fourth), rhythmically (by maintaining a constant pulse across changing metres – an early indication of the much more systematic 'tempo modulation' in the *Symphonies*), and by other means such as common pedal notes (e.g. the B♭ pedal across figs. 17–19). Once again, these various means of creating continuity give a degree of coherence to the music without unifying or directing ideas in any conventional sense – they offer 'rules of containment' which account for why these ideas belong here but do not specify fixed relationships between them ('It almost . . . does not matter in what order moments are heard, as long as we come to understand their proportional interrelationships.' '. . . the sense of rightness comes from the context of the whole piece'[71]). Even Adorno, who condemns *Petrushka* in *Philosophy of Modern Music* as infantile and 'grotesque',[72] nevertheless is prepared to admit that 'the montage of various fragments is based upon wittily organizational procedure'.[73]

The Rite of Spring

While Adorno still found some element of 'authenticity' in the montage-structure of *Petrushka*, this had completely disappeared in the out-and-out primitivism of *The Rite of Spring* where 'the atomization of the motif – so typical of Debussy – is transformed from uninterrupted passages of continually-merging color-splashes into a disintegration of the organic process'. '. . . he totally discards the concept of melody in favor of a truncated, primitivistic pattern.'[74] Van den Toorn asserts that:

> octatonic, diatonic, and octatonic–diatonic relations, being symmetrical and
> hence inherently static, non-progressive or inconclusive . . . are linked to –
> or may be said to prompt – a form constructed with relatively stable, self-
> contained blocks of material. These blocks are often abruptly cut off
> (without 'resolution' or cadential formulation) and subjected to (near)
> repeats in their respective contexts . . . [75]

Such a statement undoubtedly rings true – as demonstrated by van den Toorn's thorough examination of the pitch structure of *The Rite*[76] and confirmed by Taruskin – though the way in which the blocks are juxta-posed (and, therefore, the form-building processes) in this work is rather different from either *Petrushka* before it or the later *Symphonies of Wind Instruments*, in that blocks are defined either over longer spans or exhibit a greater degree of connectedness from one to the next (without at all contradicting the internally 'static, non-progressive' character of each block, large or small). Furthermore, there is generally a greater activity within blocks than in either *Petrushka* or the *Symphonies*, often achieved by the vertical (simultaneous) stratification of material – surely the most strikingly significant category of juxtaposition in *The Rite*, and clearly sig-nalled by the multiple layers of the 'Introduction' (see Chapter 3). Take, as an example, 'Les augures printaniers' (figs. 13–37). Van den Toorn's accounts[77] define the (harmonic) limits of this section principally in terms of alternating octatonic collections (his Collections I and III) with the occasional interpenetration of a diatonic scale; 'local (block) partitioning' is brought about by the different ways in which the same octatonic subsets are articulated. Put another way, an invariant B♭–D♭–E♭ subset (an osti-nato, first heard at fig. 12^{+3}, derived from the famous repeated '*Rite* chord' at fig. 13, which it might be understood to represent – a kind of musical metonymy or synecdoche) is present throughout the section as far as fig. 31 and provides, along with its insistent quaver pulse, a degree of linear continuity. Various 'non-progressive' musical ideas are layered on top of this or its repeated mother chord (or both), and it is the sequence of these ideas which articulates a sense of form made of blocks:

fig. 15	a: descending chromatic triplet idea
fig. 16	b: diatonic melody C–B♭–A–G (0235)
fig. 19	b': diatonic melody (bsns) B♭–A♭–G–F (0235)
fig. 25	b'': diatonic melody (hns) C–B♭–A–G–F (02357)
fig. 26	a
fig. 27	b'' (fl, transposed)
fig. 28^{+4}	+ b''': 'harmonised' diatonic melody (tpts) E♭–D♭–C–B♭ (0235)
figs. 30–37	many fragments and ostinati derived from foregoing material, layered and repeated in progressively greater density. Broken off by the entry of the 'Jeu du rapt' at fig. 37

However, as should be immediately apparent from this table, the similar-ities between ideas (especially between figs. 13 and 30) are, on the whole, more striking than the differences (though equally this is not meant to imply a unity of ideas with fixed relationships, as in a tonal work). Instances of quick, abrupt juxtapositions of blocks of material can be found throughout *The Rite* (exaggerated, in the orchestral version, by a parallel block-like approach to orchestration), but the above account of

'Les augures printaniers' would seem to suggest that, unlike *Petrushka* and the *Symphonies*, this is not the principal means of form-building. This is not to say that employing a terminology of 'blocks' is inappropriate, as large sections of the music are non-progressive and non-developmental, being built from fragmentary material; but the blocks are of a different order, and the motion within them is differently achieved. If the form of the *Symphonies of Wind Instruments* might be understood to be built from small, hand-coloured ceramic tiles, then *The Rite* is constructed from large, rough-cut blocks of granite or marble – though clearly neither is as static as such an analogy implies. The structural influence of *The Rite of Spring* would appear to lie more in the way in which simultaneous strata are organised than in the montage character typical of *Petrushka*'s first tableau or the *Symphonies*. For Stravinsky, the immediate consequences of *The Rite of Spring* are probably to be found in *Les Noces*, which might be understood as a kind of abstraction of the essence of *The Rite* in terms of its vast, ritualised, repetitive, non-progressive but rhythmically highly-charged blocks. For Taruskin, it is his finest achievement: 'Svadebka [*Les Noces*] is without a doubt the most convincing Turanian synthesis Stravinsky ever achieved. It unites all the strands that made up his multi-faceted Russian heritage within a single, strictly integrated perspective.'[78] In terms of Stravinsky's legacy, it is interesting that Christopher Butler selects *Les Noces* to illustrate the way in which innovations in Stravinsky's Russian works point to much more recent developments: 'Its central technical advance lies perhaps in the way in which the music is rendered statuesque by repetition, engendered by little shifts of "position" (which anticipate the minimalist procedures of Glass and others).'[79]

Edgard Varèse

As Jonathan Bernard has elegantly demonstrated, the aesthetic stance of Edgard Varèse was inextricably linked to that of his contemporaries in the visual arts – particularly the Cubists, but also the Futurists and the Blaue Reiter group.[80] Key features he identifies in Varèse's thinking – an interest in spatial considerations, adoption of multiple viewpoints, use of colour as an agent of delineation, etc. – not only have much in common with Picasso's Cubism, but (in the light of the above discussion of the shared aesthetic of Stravinsky and Picasso) also bring Varèse's music into proximity with the most radical aspects of Stravinsky's music.

There is certainly no doubting the radical and uncompromisingly modernist stance of Varèse as revealed in his writings, in which he adopts (like the Futurists) a quasi-scientific rhetoric:

When new instruments will allow me to write music as I conceive it, the movement of sound-masses, of shifting planes, will be clearly perceived in my work, taking the place of linear counterpoint. When these sound-masses collide, the phenomena of penetration or repulsion will seem to occur. Certain transmutations taking place on certain planes will seem to be projected onto other planes, moving at different speeds and at different angles. There will no longer be the old conception of melody or interplay of melodies. The entire work will be a melodic totality. The entire work will flow as a river flows.[81] (1936)

This account of a music made of interpenetrating (read: stratified?) planes and masses, devoid of any conventional counterpoint, is clearly closely related to an understanding of Stravinsky's music as made of juxtaposed static blocks.[82] Varèse's term for these blocks is 'zones of intensities':

These zones would be differentiated by various timbres or colors and different loudnesses. . . . The role of color or timbre would be completely changed from being incidental, anecdotal, sensual or picturesque; it would become an agent of delineation, like the different colors on a map separating different areas, and an integral part of form. These zones would be felt as isolated, and the hitherto unobtainable non-blending (or at least the sensation of non-blending) would become possible.[83]

Stravinsky's blocks, especially in the *Symphonies of Wind Instruments*, are delineated not only in terms of harmony, rhythm and tempo, but also by their instrumental timbre. Varèse opts (in theory, at least) to maximise the role of colour within the process of stratification and also attempts to make clear the absolute nature of the opposition of the resulting zones or blocks (his vocabulary of 'non-blending' here also anticipating Stockhausen's notion of moments). In practice, as we shall see below, the oppositions are rarely as stark as Varèse makes out. Nonetheless, the model provided by Stravinsky would appear to be significant for Varèse, who was producing a small but important body of works during the 1920s. Indeed, van den Toorn describes Varèse as a 'true descendant', particularly with regard to form: 'Stravinsky's "method" of abrupt block juxtaposition, particularly the kind of within-block registral and instrumental "fixity" this "method" poses with respect to reiterating fragments or simultaneities . . . does appear to have had a marked and lasting effect on Edgard Varèse.'[84]

Varèse's own concept of musical form seems to bear out van den Toorn's reading: he saw it as what he called a 'resultant', the 'result of a process', and so, like Stravinsky's *Symphonies*, the outcome of the way in which blocks of materials were juxtaposed, explicitly independent of received forms ('traditional music boxes'). Varèse's chosen analogy was with the phenomenon of crystallisation, which offered an appropriately scientific vocabulary for discussing the formation of a musical work:

> There is an idea, the basis of an internal structure, expanded and split into different shapes or groups of sound constantly changing in shape, direction, and speed, attracted and repulsed by various forces. The form of the work is the consequence of this interaction.[85] (1959)

A related ambition of Varèse was for what he called spatial music – paralleled a little earlier in the United States by the music of Charles Ives. Retrospectively Varèse identified a certain spatial freedom in his earlier works through, for example, the use of the siren in *Amériques* and *Ionisation*, and the Theremin (later revised to Ondes Martenot) in *Ecuatorial*; and he quotes the views in the 1920s of Zanotti Bianco who wrote of 'sound masses molded as though in space'.[86] However, his ambition for a genuinely spatial music remained only latent until the advent of the electronic tape, which then made possible both *Déserts* (1949–54) and the *Poème électronique* (completed in 1958 at the Philips Laboratories, Eindhoven, and played that year in the Philips Pavilion – designed by Le Corbusier and the architect-composer Iannis Xenakis – at the Brussels Exposition). Varèse paved the way for many post-World War 2 composers who have explored the spatial and dramatic possibilities of electronic music, or of the interaction of electronic and acoustic sounds (Berio, Nono, Stockhausen) and more recently the use of computers to transform sounds and throw them round the performing space (Boulez, Harvey, Stockhausen). His most obvious successor is Xenakis, whose scientific education, interest in the possibilities offered by electronics and computers, and concerns for the sonic and spatial aspects of music as well as its multi-media potential show obvious parallels with Varèse – despite the fact that Xenakis has repeatedly (and perhaps somewhat disingenuously) denied any influence.[87]

All this may seem a long way from Stravinsky – a composer who, though he lived well into the era of electronic music, never experimented with tape and electronics. Nonetheless, he knew and expressed an interest in electronic music, and, besides speaking of his admiration for Varèse's *Ionisation, Octandre, Density 21.5* and *Intégrales*, considered Varèse's 'tape recording the sound of New York City [the tape part for *Déserts*] – of the highest value and not merely as documentation, but as material of art'.[88]

Maybe such a view should not surprise us because, as Stravinsky himself pointed out, as early as *Les Noces* he had explored the 'problem of bringing together the live and the mechanical . . . an idea I abandoned only because I did not know how to co-ordinate and control both elements [pianolas and 'ordinary' orchestral instruments]'.[89] Stravinsky was fascinated by the pianola from his first encounter at the Aeolian Hall in London in 1914 until about 1930,[90] and his experiments with the instrument in *Les Noces* evidently influenced Antheil's original version of the *Ballet mécanique* for no fewer than seventeen pianolas (plus other items including an aeroplane propeller). Stravinsky's 'personal involvement with the machine aesthetic was anything but casual'[91] and, as we have already seen, situates him alongside contemporary artists such as the Italian Futurists, who were obsessed with machines and the speed of urban life ('we will sing of the vibrant nightly fervour of arsenals and shipyards blazing with violent electric moons . . .'[92]), the Bauhaus, the Constructivists, and film-makers such as Fritz Lang in his ground-breaking *Metropolis* of 1926.

Adorno had already condemned even *Petrushka* for its mechanical, 'lifeless' aspects because, he argued, it resulted in dehumanisation: 'The images of mechanical music produce the shock of a modernity which is already past and degraded to a childish level. . . . [It is] an act of violence against the subject with the enthronement of a mechanical factor as authority.'[93] As late as 1960, in his essay 'Music and new music', Adorno reiterated this view in relation to the latest developments in electronic music: he raises once again 'the evils of mechanization, the destruction of personality and dehumanization' provoked by electronic music; he argues that the 'pleasure taken in machines that work' derives from the 'how' rather than the 'what', i.e. it involves the fetishisation of the technological object; and he suggests that electronics are external to 'the immanent laws of music'[94] – though he does acknowledge the role of electronics in being able to work in new ways with timbre (precisely Varèse's project), and singles out Stockhausen's *Gesang der Jünglinge* (1955–6) for praise.[95] It is interesting to compare this with Walter Benjamin's influential discussion of the impact of technology, particularly the possibilities it offers for mass reproduction: while (like Adorno) he acknowledges the loss of the 'aura' of the original, unique artwork, there are compensatory advantages to mass access to art [96] – a view subsequently condemned by Adorno in his attack on the standardisation and depersonalisation of 'commodity music'. 'The liquidation of the individual is the real signature of the new musical situation,'[97] Adorno asserts, thus aligning his critique of popular music with his condemnation of Stravinsky.

Stravinsky's bringing together of the live and the mechanical is not restricted to his experiments with pianolas; it also extends outwards to the subject matter of *Petrushka* and *Pulcinella*, as well as to the opposition between the live (chromatic) and mechanical (diatonic) birds in *The Nightingale*. Indeed, Daniel Albright has gone so far as to suggest that *The Nightingale* lies symbolically at the heart of Stravinsky's aesthetic:

> This, I think, is what Stravinsky's music is 'about': the deep equivalence of
> the natural and the artificial. At the center of his dramatic imagination is the
> desire to juxtapose in a single work two competing systems – one which
> seems natural, tasteful, approved alike by man and God, the other of which
> seems artificial, abhorrent, devilish – and to subvert these distinctions as best
> he can.[98]

This throws interesting light on other significant oppositions in
Stravinsky's neoclassical music, principally that between the tonal (natural
– as Schenker argued – approved alike by man and God) and the non-tonal
(artificial, abhorrent, devilish) – an issue to be pursued further in Chapter
6. It also points forward to the incorporation of the natural and the
mechanical in the work of Stravinsky's major successors, such as
Messiaen's use of 'natural' birdsong within the context of highly repetitive,
'artificial' block structures (*Chronochromie* (1959–60), *Couleurs de la Cité
céleste* (1963) etc.), or Birtwistle's notion of the 'mechanical pastoral' – the
subtitle of his opera *Yan, Tan, Tethera* (1984) – which manifests itself in
many different guises, one example of which, the ensemble piece *Carmen
arcadiae mechanicae perpetuum* (1977) (discussed below) is also based on
the imaginary song of a mechanical bird (the subject of Paul Klee's 1922
painting, *The Twittering Machine*). Thus an understanding of the way in
which opposites are balanced in Stravinsky is going to provide a useful
model for understanding similar kinds of oppositions (though in very
different contexts) in more recent music.

   Closer examination suggests that Varèse's idea of a spatial music was
not so far removed from what Stravinsky was doing in many of his works –
though it should be noted that this was, at an earlier stage, a more explicit
feature of Ives's music, such as the specific physical placing of the three
groups (strings, flutes, trumpet) in *The Unanswered Question* (1908). It is
perhaps unsurprising that Stravinsky should demonstrate an awareness of
musical space in his dramatic works. In *Les Noces*, *Renard* and *The
Soldier's Tale* both performers and instrumentalists are a physical presence
on the platform/stage. In *Renard* stage characters are associated with particular instruments. In *Oedipus rex* the physical placing of the Chorus
becomes an issue; furthermore, as Judith Weir has perceptively remarked,
even the way the instruments are used shows an awareness of the space
their sound occupies: 'the way that Stravinsky keeps little groups of
instruments in very narrow wavebands. . . . Each instrument group operates at a different height in the score . . . and the voices are in between.'[99]
However, even in some of the purely instrumental works there appears to
be an implicit concern for the placement of musical instruments. Take, for
example, the much-discussed first of the *Three Pieces for String Quartet*.

Each voice is individually characterised, which, as in *Petrushka*, suggests separate physical locations for distinct yet simultaneous musical ideas: violin 1 has a (comparatively) long melody made from the pitches C–B–A–G; violin 2 punctuates with a descending four-note figure F♯–E–D♯–C♯; the viola provides an intermittent pizzicato 'drone' on the note D which coincides with a seven-crotchet-beat ostinato E♭–D♭/C–D♭ in the cello. Though it is possible to show (as Jonathan Kramer has done) that the movement as a whole is governed by an intricate proportional organisation,[100] or (as Pieter van den Toorn has done) that it can be interpreted 'as a piece in which octatonic relations . . . interpenetrate with the diatonic',[101] these remain merely the rules which (barely) contain the oppositions of these elements. The movement's novelty (indeed its modernity) lies in the way each component maintains its distinctiveness, implying a spatial as well as a musical distinction. It is for this reason that I am particularly drawn to Glenn Watkins's reading, which is worth quoting at length:

> in light of the fact that the first of the *Three Pieces for String Quartet* was conceived precisely at the time of Cocteau's discussions for the ballet *David*, Stravinsky's music may be plausibly seen as a direct response to Cocteau's call for a music that mirrors: the frontal (exterior) action of a clown/acrobat (violin 1); the backstage (interior) action of David's battle with Goliath, symbolized by means of preparatory gestures culminating in the seemingly unpredictable but highly controlled unleashing of his sling ('the magic bullet'), allied with David's difficulty in removing the head of his enemy (violin 2); and the simultaneous dance of victory (the cello/viola ostinato).[102]

As we have seen, the oppositions in the *Symphonies of Wind Instruments* operate horizontally (successively) rather than vertically (simultaneously) but otherwise the means by which musical ideas are differentiated are not so dissimilar. And though spatial concerns are not explicit in the work (there is a ritualistic quality to it which no doubt initially prompted Taruskin's investigation into its parallels with the *panikhida* service), it does not take a huge leap of the imagination to associate distinct musical blocks with different physical locations – something implicit in Varèse's choice of the word 'zone'. Varèse's own 'zonal' structures clearly owe a lot to Stravinsky, though he followed the electronic route in order to realise the spatial implication of such structures. Other composers, Xenakis included, have explored the theatrical implications of such bold designs in works of 'instrumental theatre' (discussed in Chapter 4).

The influence of Stravinsky on Varèse has often been remarked on. Paul Griffiths, for instance, pairs Varèse and Messiaen as opposite sides of the same (French) coin, though their similarities outweigh their differences: 'Both took from Stravinsky the principle of construction in disjunct blocks.'[103] Equally, their common interest in 'ancient cultures', and the fact of their 'best work' being written for ensembles of wind and percussion betray, as Griffiths put it, origins in the music of Stravinsky. (The same could be argued for Birtwistle and Xenakis.) Stravinsky himself, though admitting to never having heard *Amériques* and *Arcana*, claimed 'they *look* as though the shadow of *Le Sacre* had fallen over them'.[104] Xenakis comments on the 'immobility' of Varèse's music and suggests 'traces of Stravinsky in Varèse: tiny melodic patterns in *Amériques* and *Octandre*. That's probably why he decided on the immobility of pitch. What does change with him is rhythm, timbre, intensity and a specific mixture of these.'[105]

Amériques

The 'shadow of *Le Sacre*' is immediately evident in *Amériques*. It was completed in 1921 in New York, where Varèse had arrived from France at the end of 1915. No composer with a radical agenda writing in the years around the First World War could possibly have ignored *The Rite of Spring*: its influence was enormous. But *Amériques* is not just another *Ballet mécanique* which takes one aspect of *The Rite* (and its most obvious one at that) and pushes it to extremes (though there are momentary glimpses of 'machine music', e.g. fig. 20, which are reminiscent of works such as Mosolov's *Iron Foundry* as well as, more subtly, the 'Cortège du sage'). Nor is it just another of 'those little *Sacres* composed between 1920 and 1940 in the Soviet Union, Poland, Hungary, up to and including the Netherlands: umpa-pa, strings thumping away, never enough time-signature changes'.[106] Certainly there are motifs that appear to be almost direct quotations from *The Rite*, and its 'primitivism' is clearly in a direct line of descent from Stravinsky: a reliance on ostinatos, repeating rhythms, a vast battery of percussion, a revelling in the sheer power and volume that a symphony orchestra can produce – what Taruskin might call its '*stikhiya*'. Stravinsky's 'Pictures from Pagan Russia' here become, to coin a title, Varèse's 'Pictures of a New Found Land'. As Olivia Mattis has commented, 'America represented two concepts for the composer: industrial sophistication ("the future") and the undiscovered primitive West ("the source")',[107] so it should hardly surprise us if Varèse's first attempt at writing an 'American' music should work with that prime example of primitive music he had brought with him across the Atlantic (it should be remembered that the American premiere of *The Rite of Spring* did not happen until 1924). As one might expect of a work representing the Americas in all their diversity, it is much more eclectic than *The Rite* in the materials it employs. Like *The Rite*, there are allusions to 'native' folk music (real or imaginary) such as the 'Hispanic' melody in the strings at figs. 13–14 (reworked for high woodwinds at figs. 33–8) or the open fourths and fifths of the 'Puritan hymns' heard in the many versions of the opening alto flute melody. Sometimes, the contrast between the extremes of chromatic and diatonic material in *Amériques* can appear too severe, the 'collage' too disconnected, the materials themselves too raw (for example, the unadulterated playing of chromatic scales at figs. 17–18; or the incongruity of the laughing trombone at fig. 27 – and even, at times, of the siren). But such eclecticism is also the work's strength, resulting in a radical structure and suggesting striking parallels with the music of Ives, a 'native' American who had attempted to create a genuinely American music in not entirely dissimilar ways ('Eclecticism is part of [a composer's] duty'[108]).

There are many direct allusions to *The Rite of Spring* that sit, only partly digested, on the surface of *Amériques*. The opening bars begin with a solo alto flute melody (such woodwind solos are a familiar Varèse gambit), which inevitably calls to mind the Introduction to *The Rite*, to which is added a regular Bb–Db harp ostinato and a punctuating rising chromatic figure in the bassoon. The latter, shortened by one note, is otherwise virtually identical (same pitches, double reed timbre, triplet rhythms, *lento* tempo marking) to the cor anglais figure from the 'Action rituelle des ancêtres' (beginning fig. 129) (Ex. 2.1 – cf. Ex. 2.2). At fig. 130 in the Stravinsky, the cor anglais is joined by the alto flute playing a complementary repeating figure made up, initially, of four notes (B–D–G♯–C), very close to the first four pitch classes of Varèse's alto flute melody (B–C–G–D–A–E). Stravinsky's accompanying ostinato even starts with Bb–D. When Varèse's opening block returns, curtailed, after one bar's interruption at fig. 1^{+1}, an additional stratum of untuned percussion is added, followed (*più vivo*) by a new brass block which features a descending, repeated diatonic fragment on trumpet 1 and which, in a different guise, also characterises the next new layer added to the 'Action rituelle' (trumpets, fig. 132). It is possible to hear further allusions to this section of *The Rite* later on in *Amériques*: compare, for instance, the *ff* repeated horn motif at fig. 25 in the context of a number of ostinatos moving at different rates, with the *ff* horn entry at fig. 134 in *The Rite*.

An exhaustive directory of further correspondences between *Amériques* and *The Rite of Spring* is unnecessary here, but listed below are just some of the more obvious references:

Ex. 2.1 Stravinsky, *The Rite of Spring*, 'Action rituelle des ancêtres' (fig. 129)

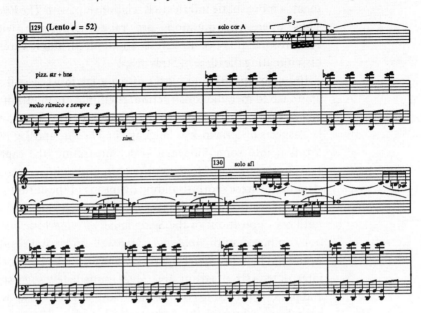

Varèse	Stravinsky
fig. 1^{+8} (hns)	fig. 99 (hns)
fig. 4^{+5} (picc, E♭ cl, tpts),	fig. 155^{+1} (picc, E♭ cl, tpt – same scoring)
fig. 5^{+11} (piccs, fls, tpts, xyl),	
fig. 6^{+27} (w/wind, brass)	
fig. 18^{+11} (piccs, fls, cls, tpts)	
fig. 5	fig. 13
fig. 18	fig. 48
fig. 26^{+1} (esp. melody in tpts)	fig. 64 (esp. melody in vn1 – same pitches)

The final section of *Amériques* (from fig. 44), an energetic coming together of much of the work's materials, shares the cataclysmic qualities of the closing stages of *The Rite*. And there are allusions beyond Stravinsky too: many half-references to Debussy; even suggestions of Expressionist Schoenberg (e.g. compare figs. 6 and 19 of *Amériques* with the opening of Schoenberg Op. 16, No. 4).

By themselves, the above examples do little more than confirm Stravinsky's hunch about 'the shadow of *Le Sacre*'. In Bloomian terms, one could probably argue of, say, the opening pages of the work that they represent instances of the revisionary ratios of *kenosis* (the fragmentation and reordering of the precursor) and *askesis* (separation from the precursor by interruption).[109] Nonetheless, *Amériques* is more than a collage of Stravinskian *objets trouvés*: these references are surface indications of

Varèse's familiarity with Stravinsky's music, and point to a deeper engage-ment, a more subtle intertextual relationship, with *The Rite* and *Les Noces*. Thus interesting questions are raised about the wider nature of Stravinsky's influence on Varèse, and, indeed, about Varèse's own role in disseminating the ideas of Stravinsky.

In its juxtaposition of blocks of material, in its overall structure, in its approach to melodic construction, rhythmic organisation and repetition, and in the assured way it deploys large orchestral forces, *Amériques* takes key aspects of Stravinsky's language in *The Rite* and *Les Noces* and trans-forms it into something new – demonstrating 'the capacity for meta-morphosis of a powerful language born under different auspices'.[110] Most striking is Varèse's form-building by means of the abrupt juxtaposition of blocks, a feature which did not manifest itself this boldly in Stravinsky until the oppositions of the *Symphonies of Wind Instruments* (which was not composed until *Amériques* was well under way, and which Varèse would not have heard in New York). The way in which blocks of music are interrupted (stratified) in *Amériques* immediately suggests a kind of 'cut and paste' approach to composition familiar from the above discussion of both Stravinsky and the Cubists, and it also corresponds to his own rhetoric of colliding sound-masses and shifting planes. Most striking is the way in which cross-block progressions take place (interlock), clearly antic-ipating Stravinsky's experiments in the *Symphonies*. As suggested above, a certain temporary 'synthesis' might be understood to be achieved in the final section of the work, but on the whole it eschews even the modest continuity and connectedness of the *Symphonies*. A structural model would undoubtedly have been provided by Debussy's *Jeux*, which Varèse knew well, though again *Amériques* lacks the integrative characteristics of that work.[111] The achievements of Debussy and Stravinsky are ultimately the more impressive for the very reason that they seem to handle the balance between continuous and discontinuous elements, between inte-grative and disintegrative elements, in a more assured way, without denying the primacy of opposition. Varèse's work is the more radical (and – arguably – the less successful) because of the absolute, and therefore less coherent, nature of its oppositions.

Fig. 2.2 shows the block organisation of the opening of *Amériques*. Each block is distinctly articulated in terms of timbre/orchestration, tempo and rhythm, and (perhaps only secondarily) harmony. Virtually every block here makes a feature of some sort of immediate repetition, usually in the guise of one or more ostinatos – indeed, the work as a whole would appear to be structured by means of the movement from one ostinato to the next. As a consequence of this, each block is static in that, once its material has

Fig. 2.2 Organisation of blocks in Varèse, *Amériques* (figs. 0–7) (Chou Wen-Chung edition, 1973)

Rehearsal figs	Tempo (crotchets/min.)	Material	
0–1	60	A	
1	112	B	
1^{+1}–1^{+3}	60	A	+ untuned perc
1^{+3}–1^{+4}	76	C	
1^{+4}–2	76	D	hn1 picks up sustained B from end of block A
2–2^{+2}	60	A	– perc and bsn
2^{+3}–2^{+7}	88	E	
2^{+7}–2^{+8}	60	A	+ timp motif from D
2^{+8}–4	60	F	though a distinct block, the vns/cel chromatic motif relates to the bsn in block A; sustained chord in lower strings cf. symmetrical chord (hn/tbns) from block D (fig. 1^{+5})
4–4^{+6}	72	G	1st entry of siren + 'Danse sacrale' motif
4^{+7}–5	60	A	solo afl final B sustained. + new layer
5–5^{+5}	60	H	E♭ cl takes over sustained B
5^{+6}–5^{+13}	60/92	I	cf. G (perc) + 'Danse sacrale' motif
5^{+13}–5^{+16}	92	A′	afl melody now on solo tpt, augmented
5^{+16}	120	trans.	'quasi cadenza' cf. new layer in A at fig. 4^{+8}
5^{+17}–6	*più moderato*	B	
6^{+1}–6^{+2}	*tempo/accel*	trans.	continuation of B?
6^{+3}–7	192	K	E♭ cl motif at 6^{+13} derivative of afl (A) 'Danse sacrale' motif at fig. 6^{+27}
7	64 (= 192/3)	L	vla cf. E♭ cl motif (K)

been established, it remains unchanged until the next block replaces it: there is no sense at all of 'development' within blocks. It is the simultaneous (vertical) juxtaposition of ideas within successive blocks that is one of the principal means by which any sense of motion is generated, a feature of 'accumulation' the work clearly shares with *The Rite*. This is at its most striking in the final long section of *Amériques*, which is made up of series of simultaneous ostinatos. As already suggested, there is also a certain degree of continuity/progression across repetitions of the same block (interlock).

Take, for example, the varied ways block A is treated at the start (Ex. 2.2). Its initial statement involves seven near-exact repetitions of the alto flute melodic fragment, where only the length of its first and last notes,

Ex. 2.2 Varèse, *Amériques* (opening)

including rests, is altered to give a pattern of durations in crotchet beats of 6.5, 5, 4.5, 6.5, 3, 3, 3.5, i.e. a general but inexact acceleration of events as the block proceeds (compare this with the subtle and sophisticated rhythmic alterations made to the opening bassoon melody of *The Rite*). As we have seen, two ostinatos – one continuous (harps), one periodic (bassoon) – accompany the alto flute. All subsequent appearances of block A involve just one statement of the melodic fragment with the initial B being regained at the end and sustained. The second appearance of A is varied by the addition of a new stratum of ostinatos for untuned percussion, but this has disappeared, as has the bassoon motif, at the third statement. The fourth appearance is severely curtailed, but with the timpani motif from block D added, while the fifth appearance of A allows the solo alto flute to be heard before a new layer is superimposed on the final sustained B (gesturally related to the 'quasi cadenza' which occurs just before fig. 6). The final appearance here is of the melodic fragment alone, now played by a solo trumpet, rhythmically augmented and transposed down a tone. Having been such a prominent feature of the score up to this point, the defining melodic fragment of block A is never heard again (though melodic fragments with a similar gestural/intervallic character can be heard at various moments throughout the work), with the exception of two brief statements of the augmented version: at fig. 18^{+13} (trumpet 1) and at fig. 21^{+7} (also trumpets). It is interesting to note that the first block of Stravinsky's *Symphonies of Wind Instruments* (the 'bell motif', or, in Taruskin's reading, the psalm intonation) does not survive in its original form beyond the first half of the piece (this, too, corresponds with Taruskin's division of the work according to the two main items from the Orthodox service: the *Tropar'* and the *Kanon*). However, what these descriptions of *Amériques* seem to reveal is that the interlocks across blocks do not make lines which continue to exert their influence 'even when silent', as Cone's analysis of Stravinsky's *Symphonies* proposed. Apart from anything else, there are many more blocks in Varèse than in Stravinsky, even in the first 100 bars, as Fig. 2.2 makes clear. Far from an effect of 'successive time-segments . . . counterpointed one against the other',[112] what we have here is much more the effect of a collage, the 'movement of sound-masses . . . taking the place of linear counterpoint'. The 'phenomena of penetration or repulsion' which, according to Varèse, occur when the sound-masses collide, coincide with the two kinds of juxtaposition employed in the work, that is simultaneous (penetration) and successive (repulsion).

Nonetheless, there are certain Varèsian harmonic fingerprints that mitigate, to some degree, the starkness of the collagistic oppositions in *Amériques*, most notably the predilection for forms of interval class 1. Furthermore, there is a far greater fluidity of material between blocks (a different kind of penetration, perhaps) than is found in Stravinsky, and this serves to reduce the absolute nature of the oppositions – Fig. 2.2 indicates how ideas initially associated with one block find their way into new ones. In order to maintain a significant difference between blocks, an increased emphasis is thus placed on changes in timbre/orchestration, as well as rhythm/tempo. With the exception of the explicit 3:1 relationship between successive tempi at fig. 7 (192:64), there is no obvious proportional relationship between blocks in the first part of the work; this further underlines their opposition.

The energy of *Amériques* is thus generated by the strength of the juxtaposition of its constituent blocks. The resulting structure is made up from both the local repetition of fixed musical ideas (the 'fixity' and 'immobility' of which van den Toorn and Xenakis respectively spoke) which are continually being recombined to form new blocks, and the larger-scale repetition/variation of blocks across the entire work. It is fascinating in its unpredictability, a genuine 'resultant' in line with Varèse's own accounts of fluid musical forms and 'crystallisation'. The influence of Stravinsky is apparent at every turn – not merely in the many superficial references to *The Rite of Spring*, or in the obsessive attitude to rhythmic procedures and repetition, but principally, as we have seen, in the music's block organisation (though this is much less tightly controlled than in Stravinsky, and eschews Stravinsky's contained continuities). *Amériques* is a radical work which, while building on the formal innovations of *Petrushka* and *The Rite of Spring*, nevertheless anticipates in a unique way the new, distinctive and influential structures Stravinsky was to begin to explore in the *Symphonies of Wind Instruments*. In retrospect, in the light of Varèse's formal experiments in *Amériques*, it is clear that his later experiments with tape were inevitable.

Olivier Messiaen

As Boulez reminds us, Messiaen's music 'has its roots in the music performed in Paris during the twenties and early thirties'. Messiaen was intimately familiar, as revealed through his teaching, with the work of the leading composers of the first part of the twentieth century – Bartók, Berg, Schoenberg, Webern – while the influence of Debussy, and to a lesser extent Ravel, is self-evident. However, it is Stravinsky who, according to Boulez, 'occupies a leading place'.[113] This is borne out by Messiaen's own writings, such as his famous analysis of Stravinsky's rhythmic language in his 1939 *Revue musicale* essay, and general comments in relation to his own music in *Technique de mon langage musical*.[114] And in his music, too, though such ideas and techniques may in general be identified as characterising early-modern music, the specific influence of Stravinsky is irrefutable. This manifests itself primarily in a challenge to our understanding of time through a new attitude to rhythm and metre, the consequences of which range from local additive and symmetrical rhythms to large-scale repetitions, simultaneities and innovative block and verse-refrain structures. Stemming from this are shared concerns for ritual and a fascination with so-called primitive, archaic and exotic cultures, as well as similar approaches to instrumentation and a predilection for the octatonic scale ('mode 2').

In fact, it was probably only Stravinsky's *early* works up to the *Symphonies of Wind Instruments* that influenced Messiaen most directly; his contempt for Stravinsky's turn to neoclassicism was as strong as his admiration for *The Rite of Spring*. And it seems to me that it is primarily in Messiaen's large-scale works of the 1960s that we finally see him consolidating and making his own the innovations he so valued in early Stravinsky. In terms of their formal novelty, it is to one of Stravinsky's works above all others that they owe their allegiance: the *Symphonies of Wind Instruments*. However, these works in their turn stem from experiments Messiaen himself undertook in a series of piano pieces written in 1949 and 1950 – *Cantéyodjayâ* and the *Quatre études de rythme* ('Ile de feu I', 'Mode de valeurs et d'intensités', 'Neumes rythmiques', 'Ile de feu II') – and which in turn had an immediate and profound impact on the young avant-garde of the day. *Cantéyodjayâ* is in many respects the key work, representing a transition from the vast, bold public statement of *Turangalîla* to the more 'chaste' birdsong works of the 1950s. Paul Griffiths, too, offers the likelihood of Stravinsky's *Symphonies* as primary model for *Cantéyodjayâ*, though equally he hazards the possibility that Messiaen's interest in the early *musique concrète* experiments of that time, and in film, could have suggested its radical collage structure.[115]

Cantéyodjayâ has an unusual structure made up of both fixed and free repetitions (see Fig. 2.3). The most fixed element is the *cantéyodjayâ* block itself (A), which punctuates the course of the work (Ex. 2.3); the most free elements are the couplets, which are themselves made up of many smaller units strung together (and to which Messiaen gives wonderful and faintly comical invented names combining French and Sanskrit, such as 'boucléadjayakî' and 'glRobouladjhamapâ'). The overall structure, while determined by cyclic verse-refrain repetitions, seems amorphous and inconclusive, though it does bear some vague resemblance to the overall shape derived from Greek tragedy that Messiaen was to adopt in *Chronochromie*. The *cantéyodjayâ* returns, extended, at the end, followed by somewhat incongruous contrary motion 'diminished sevenths', to call an artificial halt to proceedings. Perhaps after the tightly-controlled movements of *Turangalîla* Messiaen felt it necessary to try something more open-ended (we have already seen that the 'unending' nature of Stravinsky's *Symphonies* is an issue, and open-endedness of a rather

Fig. 2.3 Organisation of blocks in Messiaen, *Cantéyodjayâ*

A	B									
A	B									
A		C								
A			D							
A				E						
A			D		ref1	ref2	ref3	cplt1		
				E	ref1				cplt2	
				E		ref2				cplt3
					ref1					
		C								cplt3
A			D							

A = cantéyodjayâ
B = djayâ
C = râgarhanakî
D = alba
E = mode de durées, de hauteurs et d'intensités
ref = refrain
cplt = couplet

different sort was shortly to become a key issue in music on both sides of the Atlantic). What is perhaps most striking about *Cantéyodjayâ* and the *Quatre études* is the new kind of non-narrative time they articulate. It should hardly surprise us that Boulez was so fascinated by these works:

> these 'pieces' do not have an end, in the rhetorical sense; they simply *stop*. Their strict organization means that they are like fragments of some larger whole that is tacitly understood ... What we hear are fragments of an overall movement of which the composer gives us a glimpse virtually prolonging the mechanisms that he has momentarily set in motion for our benefit.[116]

Couleurs de la Cité céleste and Et expecto resurrectionem mortuorum

Two of Messiaen's major works of the mid-1960s might legitimately be labelled his own 'symphonies of wind instruments'. Both *Couleurs de la Cité céleste* and *Et expecto resurrectionem mortuorum* (1964) are scored for a large ensemble of woodwind, brass and percussion (including piano in the case of *Couleurs*). Both Stravinsky's *Symphonies* and Messiaen's two works are kinds of abstract ritualistic and religious dramas – explicitly so in Messiaen's case through both the specification of the physical layout of players on the concert platform and the prefacing of the scores with

Ex. 2.3 Messiaen, *Cantéyodjayâ* (block A)

Biblical quotations. In particular, in these works Messiaen exploits
Stravinsky's means of construction in distinct musical blocks – that is, a
structure built from opposed musical entities defined in pitch, rhythmic,
temporal and timbral terms. Timbre, or more specifically colour, is of
particular significance – indeed, Messiaen begins his preface to the score
of *Couleurs de la Cité céleste* by announcing that 'The form of this work
depends entirely on colours. The melodic or rhythmic themes, the com-
plexes of sounds and timbres, develop in the manner of colours.' In the
preface to *Et expecto* the composer describes its first performance in the
Sainte-Chapelle, Paris, 'where the blues, reds, golds, violets in each
window reverberate with the music'. *Couleurs* and *Et expecto* also share
something of Stravinsky's 'primitivism' – not just in Messiaen's naïve
simplicity and boldness, his foregrounding of rhythm and exotic percussion and his seemingly intuitive approach to harmony, but also in his
source materials: the sounds of nature (birdsong), pre-Renaissance
music and processes (Ancient Greek metres, plainchant, organum, a
'successive' approach to composition) and non-Western elements
(Indian deçî-tâlas).

The block construction of both these works helps articulate a new kind
of time (*drobnost'*, one might say, resulting in *nepodvizhnost'*), as symbol-
ised in Messiaen's description of the celestial city: 'Beyond all time, beyond
all place, in a light without light, in a night without night'. In part, this
manifests itself as another 'incomplete' structure, a work which starts and
stops rather than beginning and ending. Messiaen admits this explicitly in
the preface to *Couleurs de la Cité céleste*: 'the work does not end – having

Fig. 2.4a Definition of blocks in Messiaen, *Couleurs de la Cité céleste* (beginning to fig. 33)

A	quaver=126	*oiseau-tui*
B	quaver=126	*benteveo*
C	quaver=160	*troglodyte barré* (piano solo)
D	quaver=126	*mohoua à tête jaune*
E	quaver=108/120	Alleluia (8th Sunday after Pentecost) plus (on first appearance) the '7 angels with 7 trumpets'
F	quaver=126	*oiseau-cloche*
G	quaver=50/semiquaver=80	colour sequence (*topaze, jaune*, etc.)
H	quaver=160/80/116/96	'*l'étoile qui a la clef de l'abîme*'
I	quaver=176/30/58	'*comme un éclair qui sillonne le ciel!*'
J	quaver=104/160/126	*stournelle* (piano solo)
K	quaver=50	Alleluia (Holy Sacrament)

Fig. 2.4b Stratification of blocks in Messiaen, *Couleurs de la Cité céleste* (beginning to fig. 33)

```
A    B    C
     B         D
A                   E    F    G
              E         G
                   F
              E         G
              E    F    G
              E         G    H    I    J    K
```

never really begun: it turns on itself, interlacing its temporal blocks, like the flaming and invisible colours of a cathedral's rose window . . .'.

Fig. 2.4 shows the organisation of blocks (defined in terms of tempo, birdsong and colour, all of which are indicated in the score) in the first part of *Couleurs de la Cité céleste*. Though it is a work in a single span, the appearance of the 'Holy Sacrament' Alleluia, treated like a chorale, is an important punctuating point (after which a new sequence of bird songs is introduced, beginning with a group of Brazilian birds)(Ex. 2.4). This Alleluia occurs on only one other occasion (at the very end of the work), preceded by blocks H, I and J (varied) as on the first occasion. Such larger-scale repetitions suggest a grand cyclic plan, though the detail of the form is much harder to specify – a description of this work as an intuitively-constructed *kaleidoscope* (literally) of carefully-coloured blocks of varying length (the 'interlacing' of

Ex. 2.4 Messiaen, *Couleurs de la Cité céleste*, 'Holy Sacrament' Alleluia (figs. 32–3)

temporal blocks) would seem more appropriate. Fig. 2.4 does not represent the full picture. In some cases, there are very obvious connections between distinct blocks: for example, blocks A and F are virtually indistinguishable – same scoring, tempo and figurations, both imitated birds being natives of New Zealand. In other cases, individual blocks are themselves made up of smaller blocks: for example, block J alternates fragments marked *modéré* (a) and *vif* (b), plus one extra fragment marked *un peu vif* (c), in the order ababacb. Certain of these early blocks are a frequent presence throughout the work; others are hardly ever heard again. Take block D, the 'mohoua à tête jaune'. Its only identified appearance is at fig. 5, and so might be considered just an extension of the preceding birdsongs ('oiseau-tui' and 'ben-teveo') with which it shares its scoring and tempo. However, its closing gesture – a rapidly repeated demi-semiquaver chord (G–A♭–D♭) on wooden tuned percussion – does reappear later in the work: at figs. 53–5 (chord transposed to B♭–B–E) and at figs. 69–72 (G–A♭–C♯/D), on both occasions functioning as a local closing device. This 'personnage rythmique' (to mis-appropriate Messiaen's term derived from his analysis of rhythmic charac-ters in Stravinsky's 'Danse sacrale') is related to another called *vijaya*, which occurs as part of a texture of many such superimposed Indian and ornitho-logical 'characters' at figs. 43 ff and 63 ff (the three-note chord on these occa-sions forms a chromatic subset).

Perhaps because there are so many blocks and fragments in *Couleurs* as a whole, the processes of interlock are less obvious than in Stravinsky, or even in other of Messiaen's works such as *Et expecto*. As we saw in Varèse's *Amériques*, blocks do not seem so explicitly to exert their influence 'even when silent', a fact borne out both by the introduction of so much new material from fig. 33 (after the 'Holy Sacrament' Alleluia) and by the increasing fragmentation and multiple superimposition of ideas in the later stages of the work. When more local interlock does occur, there is no

Ex. 2.5 Messiaen, *Couleurs de la Cité céleste*, 'colour sequence' (fig. 11)

development of material as such but, rather, straightforward procedures of variation are involved. One of the most interesting of these is the colour sequences (block G) that occur between figs. 11 and 27. These consist entirely of twelve-note chords, each of which Messiaen associates with a different and specific colour. (It is fascinating to note the correspondence Messiaen appears to make between these 'celestial' passages and their opposite, a later block marked 'the abyss' (fig. 40 etc.) with which they share scoring and tempo; the eight twelve-note chords – 'the cry from the Abyss' – at the end of the first movement of *Et expecto* are similarly presented.) At fig. 11, the three chords represent three precious stones, the first two of which are among the foundation stones of the celestial city listed in one of the quotations from the Apocalypse which preface the score: yellow topaz, clear green chrysoprasus and crystal. They are differentiated only by their internal intervallic construction, spacing and emphasis[117] (Ex. 2.5). The next sequence, G^2 (fig. 13), begins with a twofold statement of the three chords, followed by two new gemstone chords (green emerald and violet amethyst), three new colour chords (red, orange and gold), and finally topaz and chrysoprasus again – all of them twelve-note verticalities in rhythmic unison. G^3 (fig. 18) is an exact repetition of G^1, while G^4 (fig. 24) takes one step back to G^2 (emerald and amethyst) before adding further twelve-note gemstones; similarly G^5 (fig. 26) starts from G^4 (red sardonyx) before adding pink, mauve and grey chords. Thus there is a kind of progression across the interlocking versions of block G, as one colour blends into the next, yet each block nevertheless remains static as one twelve-note chord is in essence the same as the next ('it turns on itself . . . like the flaming and invisible colours of a cathedral's rose window . . .'). Block G only ever makes one more appearance towards the end of the work (figs. 73–6), now marked 'infinitely slowly, ecstatic' and with the '8th Sunday after Pentecost' Alleluia superimposed on bells and gongs, eventually (fig. 76) itself being transformed into a 'violet' version of that Alleluia. Once again, Stravinsky's *Symphonies of Wind Instruments* offers a useful paradigm, where the 'bell motif' does not survive in its original form beyond the first half of the piece. Furthermore, though Messiaen can have known nothing of the possible Orthodox origins of the *Symphonies*, there is a wonderful coincidence of thinking in the punctuating roles of the 'Allilúiya' refrain Taruskin identifies in Stravinsky, and Messiaen's plainchant-derived 'Alleluias'. As in Varèse's *Amériques*, and two virtually contemporary works, the Second Piano Sonata of Tippett (1962; see below) and Birtwistle's *Verses for Ensembles* of 1969 (whose cyclic, block structure and wind and percussion scoring clearly owe much to *Couleurs*), Messiaen here invents a mosaic form which (in conjunction with a more atonal 'language') has far more the effect of collage than was the case in Stravinsky, but which nonetheless manages to achieve something of a synthesis of its many, opposed constituent parts by containing them within a controlled rhetorical scheme of larger-scale cyclic repetitions and of increasing density of superimposed ideas towards the work's conclusion. Like so many of Messiaen's works, it achieves the miracle of suggesting infinity through finite musical means.

Though *Et expecto resurrectionem mortuorum* shares with *Couleurs de la Cité céleste* its instrumentation, its concern for colour, its Biblical symbolism, its use of plainchant, birdsong and Indian rhythms, and a block approach to its structure, in other respects it is very different. For one thing, it is far less fragmented than *Couleurs*. It is not concerned with the kaleidoscopic opposition of multiple short blocks over a long single span; rather, it is a monumental and sustained expression of a non-specific religious ceremony in five movements.[118] Messiaen suggests that it is a work for vast spaces: 'churches, cathedrals, and even the open air and high mountains'. He also requests that one minute's silence be observed between each movement. In every respect, its ritual dimensions are exaggerated: the instrumentalists are the celebrants and the audience the participants. Though the origins of such thinking go back to medieval drama, if not to Greek theatre, more immediate musical precedents for such rituals can of course be found in Stravinsky. Once again, block forms are used to symbolise a new kind of non-linear time. Each of the outer movements consists, in essence, of a single, slow, sustained melody. The central three movements have block structures, but the number of blocks is much reduced compared with *Couleurs* (three in each case) and, though still non-developmental, each block has a much extended duration.

The fourth movement of *Et expecto* is the longest movement of the work to use block construction. It is prefaced with an amalgam of Biblical references: 'They shall be raised in glory, with a new name – amid the joyous concert of the morning stars and the shouts of the sons of heaven' (1 Corinthians 15:43; Revelation 2:17; Job 38:7); its music is similarly an amalgam of liturgical and natural references, plus quotations from all of the preceding movements. There are, in essence, three blocks, each of which is distinguished by a different tempo and (initially) by distinct material:

A *lent*   three long descending tam-tam strokes
B *bien modéré* (quaver=84)   Easter Introit 'transposed' into mode 3
                                           (percussion)
                                           Easter Alleluia 'transposed' into mode 7
                                           (trumpets)
C *un peu vif* (semiquaver=200)   song of the calandra lark

The overall shape of the movement, an arch form, can be represented as ABACABACABAA´. Stratification is achieved by abrupt interruption of blocks, and there is a degree of interlock across them (suggesting a limited linearity) achieved by such means as contraction and superimposition. The appearances of block A get progressively louder, a progression which is presented in microcosm on the gongs, bells and tam-tams in the last eight bars of the movement (from **pp** to **fff**), doubled by all the winds in a concluding 'chorale' (itself anticipating the massive chorale that constitutes the fifth and final movement). The very last chord is a nine-note 'acoustic' chord or 'chord of resonance' on D♭ (first heard in the third movement), that is, a chord with bell-like properties which locally resonates with the bells and gongs, and more generally sets up associations with Stravinsky's 'bell chords' such as at (explicitly) the end of *Les Noces*

Ex. 2.6 Comparison of final chords of Messiaen, *Et expecto resurrectionem mortuorum*, fourth movement, and Stravinsky, *Symphonies of Wind Instruments*

Messiaen   Stravinsky

and (implicitly) the end of the *Symphonies of Wind Instruments* (Ex. 2.6 shows the *Et expecto* and *Symphonies* chords). Stravinsky's favourite device of the chorale ending is also a feature of Messiaen's music of this time: in both *Et expecto* and *Couleurs de la Cité céleste*, at key moments in *La Transfiguration de Notre Seigneur Jésus-Christ* (1965–9), and even, arguably, at the end of *Chronochromie*. For Messiaen, as for Stravinsky, it is both a rhetorical and a ritual device, implying a kind of synthesis. Progression across block B is brought about, first, by compressing the distance between the entries of the Introit and the Alleluia and, second, by the addition of extra simultaneous strata: in B^2 the gongs superimpose the rhythm of the Indian deçî-tâla *simhavikrama* from the second movement, and in B^3 a fourth layer, the entire theme from the first movement, is added and 'harmonised' in the brass. The second statement of block C is also a varied reprise of the first.

Though, as we have already observed, individual blocks are much longer than those in Stravinsky's *Symphonies* and in *Couleurs de la Cité céleste*, there is no real development within them. Yet, equally, it would not be true to say that this is absolutely 'static' music. There is a sort of progression by means of accumulation, a process which has its origins in Stravinsky. Messiaen sets up a non-linear, non-narrative music which articulates a new kind of time, to which the notion of ritual (usually involving repetition) is closely allied. His use of simple and direct block structures is thus ideally suited both to the essentially non-developmental nature of the material he is working with (pre-tonal, non-Western, non-pitch-based) and to the larger metaphysical objectives of the work. Messiaen's achievement here, as elsewhere, is to take many of his ideas from Stravinsky (rhythmic and formal, ritualistic and dramatic) and to mould them into something new and distinct. If anything, Messiaen simplifies the ideas and materials he inherits from Stravinsky (Boulez: 'Messiaen does not compose – he juxtaposes'[119]), but instead of their resulting in mere Stravinsky pastiche as in the hands of so many inter-war imitators, Messiaen is able to invent a music of epic proportions and effect which is undeniably his own.

Karlheinz Stockhausen

If for no other reason, Stockhausen would have developed a deep acquaintance with Stravinsky's music as a member of Messiaen's analysis classes at the Paris Conservatoire in 1952–3. Karl Wörner tells us that, by the early 1950s, Stockhausen was 'familiar with almost every work of Schoenberg, Stravinsky and Bartók'[120] – though, as Robin Maconie adds, it may well be that not very much of that music was easily available in 1950.[121] More fascinating, perhaps, is Stravinsky's evident high regard for the younger composer. Stravinsky was familiar, at the very least, with *Zeitmasse*, *Zyklus* and *Carré* (partly, no doubt, through Robert Craft's involvement with performances of Boulez and Stockhausen) and spoke with evident enthusiasm of the group-structure of *Gruppen*.[122] Though Paul Griffiths has explored Stravinsky's 'elder response' to Stockhausen and the young, post-World War 2 avant-garde,[123] there is little immediate evidence to suggest any direct influence in the opposite direction. In the 1950s it may well have seemed that Webern was the key figure in Stockhausen's development, but his immense respect for the music of both Varèse and Messiaen was equally significant and suggests a strong sympathy with the Stravinsky legacy. Whittall has gone so far as to propose Stockhausen as the 'true heir of Varèse': it is Stockhausen's 'concern to mediate between diversities rather than to synthesize them into a higher unity which is his most "avant-garde", his most forward-looking attribute'.[124] It is this mediation between diversities, this Stravinskian balancing of discontinuities, which would appear to be Stockhausen's most decidedly Stravinsky-like attribute as well, one which was perhaps to manifest itself most clearly in *Momente* (first version 1961–4) but, equally, was apparent in different ways from the early 1950s.

'Stockhausen's most important contribution to the progress of music has lain in his search for new forms.'[125] The principal thrust of this chapter has been to argue a similar claim for Stravinsky, particularly through his radical block structures; in this regard, Stockhausen's attempt to build new forms independent of models from the past, devoid of the old kinds of narrativity and connectedness, parallels Stravinsky's efforts in *The Rite of Spring*, *Les Noces* and the *Symphonies of Wind Instruments*. Wörner writes:

> With Varèse and Stravinsky the ... conception was still a matter of collages ... In Stockhausen's work one can no longer speak of collages; one must speak rather of intermodulation. This means that apparently incompatible phenomena can be reciprocally modulated with each other in a way far transcending mere coexistence with and against each other; this procedure heralds the unity of a world which will maintain differences intact and at the same time will enable a total effect of 'higher unity' to be produced.[126]

At first sight this might seem to contradict Whittall's reading. But the 'higher unity' to which both writers refer is clearly the language of Stockhausen himself, the rhetoric of Stockhausen's own more recent musical 'cosmology',[127] and a way of thinking which was evident as early as 1956 when he spoke of a 'hidden power of cohesion, a relatedness among the proportions: a structure. Not similar shapes in a changing light. Rather this: different shapes in a constant, all-permeating light.'[128] Yet this musical unity is far more elusive than Stockhausen's confident assertions would suggest. What is interesting in both Wörner's and Stockhausen's statements is the way in which they argue for the persistence of difference, and that 'synthesis' (the 'higher unity') is only brought about, if at all, by mediating between differences. To categorise Stravinsky as a mere collagist, as Wörner does, is to miss the point: the music of both Stravinsky and Stockhausen – their shared modernism – appears to be concerned with suggesting continuities while simultaneously maintaining discontinuities.

The idea of 'straight' collage is certainly apparent in Stockhausen's work: in works for conventional instruments, such as the 'random' reading of nineteen musical groups scattered across the page of *Klavierstück XI* (1956); and in the *musique concrète*-like working of found objects in works with electronics such as *Gesang der Jünglinge, Telemusik* (1966), *Hymnen* (1966–9) and *Kurzwellen* (1968–9). It was Stockhausen's move in 1952 from composing with 'points' (for example, the withdrawn *Punkte* of 1952) to composing with 'groups' – a process articulated in *Kontra-Punkte* (1952–3) – which was the significant shift. In *Kontra-Punkte* each group of arpeggiated notes is clearly and distinctly defined/opposed in both harmonic and instrumental terms. One by one, instruments drop out during the course of the movement to leave just the piano at the end (maybe a suggestion of instrumental drama, of Stravinskian role-play): the original six timbres, formed by fixed groupings of the ten instruments, 'merge into a single timbre'. Thus is achieved, according to the composer, 'the idea of resolving the antithesis of a many-faceted musical world of individual notes and temporal relationships to the point where a situation is reached in which only the homogeneous and the immutable is audible'.[129] There is thus a vague but not inconsequential correspondence with the *Symphonies of Wind Instruments*, in that the final piano music of *Kontra-Punkte* has a similar 'synthesising' role to that of the chorale in the *Symphonies*. The opposition of groups in the Stockhausen does not generate a block form along the lines of Stravinsky – its structure, as suggested by Maconie, is the result of a complex scheme of proportional, pitch and tempo relations which owe far more to Webern and Boulez. Nonetheless, even Maconie alludes to a different Stravinskian parallelism: 'One may contrast

Stockhausen's progression from static accentual polyphony to dynamic rhythmic counterpoint, with precisely the opposite development in Stravinsky's *Rite of Spring*, from the static metrical complexity of the piece's early "dawn chorus" . . . to the dynamic accentual continuum of "The Sacrifice".[130] There was clearly something deeply 'Stravinskian' about Stockhausen's thinking in *Kontra-Punkte* to which the septuagenarian Stravinsky responded strongly in his own serial *Movements* (1958–9) for piano and orchestra. And Stravinsky's later comments on *Gruppen* confirm his regard for the way in which Stockhausen defined and worked with blocks of materials: 'each group is admirably composed according to its plan of volume, instrumentation, rhythmic pattern, tessitura, dynamic, various kinds of highs and lows'.[131]

Moment Form: *Klavierstück IX*

In the context of the post-War European avant-garde, the opening of Stockhausen's *Klavierstück IX* (begun 1954, completed and revised 1961) is audacious: nothing but one four-note chord repeated 142 plus 87 times. This was a clear signal of a new intention.

The single movement ten-minute work is essentially in two unequal parts: the first (the longer) involves a high degree of repetition and alternates ideas and tempi; the second is in a third tempo but is notated as free grace notes, a kind of fantasia of arpeggiated groups. Proportions are significant. Maconie's analysis[132] identifies thirty-three distinct sections in the work (indicated in the score by a heavy bar-line), organised in the proportion 24:9, i.e. 8:3, a Fibonacci ratio, and the same ratio as the alternating tempi in the first part (160:60).[133] What Maconie does not mention is that this relational schema is distorted in the music's temporal realisation by the widely divergent durations of sections, ranging from his section 7 (104 quaver beats at quaver = 60) to sections five, nine, eleven, fifteen and seventeen (each 4 quaver beats at quaver = 160). Herbert Henck's account of the piece[134] considers in more detail the proportions of sections, especially the use of Fibonacci numbers, and draws on Stockhausen's own annotated sketch of the piece, according to which there are only six 'structures' (see Fig. 2.5a). Henck then plots the overall shape of the piece to produce a familiar pattern of repetitions (Fig. 2.5b, Henck's Ex. 1). Once again, these Fibonacci proportions offer a 'rule of containment', governing the music's durations without undermining its structural oppositions.

In part one, the principal opposition is between the regular quaver repetitions (quaver = 160) of Henck's A sections, and the sections at quaver = 60, which are more varied rhythmically and are concerned, in

Fig. 2.5a Definition of blocks in Stockhausen, *Klavierstück IX*

	bar first appears	Maconie's section no.	character
A	1	1	chord of four notes, repeated regularly
B	3	2	ascending chromatic melodic line
C	17	4	polyphonic sequence
D	94	22	staccato chords with reduced resonance (half pedal)
E	112	24	isolated chords and notes of weak intensity
F	117	25	rapid figurations weakening in intensity towards the top of the piano, with accents. Isolated low notes as fundamentals.

Fig. 2.5b Stratification of blocks in Stockhausen, *Klavierstück IX*

	A	B	C	D	E	F	
1	A¹						b.1
2	A²						b.2
3		B					b.3
4	A³						bb.4–16
5			C¹				bb.17–45
6	A⁴						bb.47–57
7	A⁵ +		C				bb.58–63
8			C²				bb.64–89
9	A⁶ +	B					bb.90–93
10				D			bb.94–108
11	A⁷ +			D			bb.109–11
12					E		bb.112–15
13	A⁸						b.116
14	A⁹						b.116
15						F	bb.117–53

Maconie's words, with 'the sustaining and ornamentation of a chord'. There is a degree of connectedness evident across some of the sections (an incipient sort of interlock), especially, as Henck indicates, the decreasing (Fibonacci series 2) number of chords in subsequent sections A: 142–87–53–35[32]–16[19]–11–6–3–1 quavers. However, equally striking is the gradual overlapping of the concerns of distinct sections. These differentiated sections and their relationships are defined by Stockhausen himself as '[r]igid, "monotonous" events [which] are transformed into flexible, "polytonous" ones; sometimes the two are abruptly juxtaposed, sometimes they intermingle in constantly fresh conjunctions'.[135] Part two might in some ways be understood to be a consequence of the quaver = 60 sections of part one – partly in the obvious doubling of the tempo to quaver = 120, partly in elevating the ornamental figurations to the status of exclusive subject matter. But it is also meant to be something quite different. Evidently a new kind of form is being explored here.

Is it too fanciful to interpret this much shorter second part as a kind of equivalent of the concluding chorale from the *Symphonies of Wind Instruments*? It certainly seems to relate to the main body of the work in a manner not dissimilar to the relationship between the chorale and the rest of the *Symphonies*. It can be shown (as Cone demonstrates for the chorale) to synthesise certain aspects of the earlier music. It is more consistent than the first part, with its persistent oppositions, and gives the impression of continuity even though the music itself is not continuous (the chorale is the longest and most sustained block of the *Symphonies* – in terms of duration, the ratio of the main body of the work to the chorale is approximately 3:1). It is the most lyrical moment of the work. Maconie's phrase about the second part of *Klavierstück IX* might equally well apply to Stravinsky's chorale: 'a triumph of lyricism over structure'.

Thus the novelty of Stockhausen's form, if not actually dependent on new forms suggested by Stravinsky, at least parallels them in intriguing ways. As far as Stockhausen himself was concerned, the most important aspect of his piano piece was its attitude to time, its bringing together of what he called different forms of musical time. Both parts of the piece are fascinating in that each suggests, in a different way, what Stockhausen was later to describe as 'an immanent concentration on the present'[136] – achieved in the opening minutes of the first part by extreme repetition of a simple entity (a practice and aesthetic being paralleled in the early 1960s on the other side of the Atlantic by the likes of La Monte Young and Terry Riley), and in the second part by the increasing isolation of events. *Klavierstück IX* was completed in the year Stockhausen began work on *Momente*, his fullest expression of the new moment form. The kind of group form first witnessed in *Kontra-Punkte* reached its culmination in *Gruppen* where '[g]roups of sounds, of noises and of combined sound and noise, are wholly autonomous units. Each group moves in its own temporal space, and above all with its own tempo',[137] though elsewhere they can come closer or even 'coalesce' – evidently a reinterpretation of Stravinskian block structure. Moment form would appear to be the logical continuation of this. 'His invention of moment form was symbolic at a time when the unified thrust of the 1950s seemed to have gone from music.'[138] Stockhausen's reevaluation of block structures was a response to the challenge of finding new forms in a post-serial context. In this, as we have seen, he was not alone.

Momente

Like Messiaen's *Turangalîla*, which is a massive exploration of time and love (human and divine, erotic and spiritual), Stockhausen's *Momente* for solo soprano, four choirs and thirteen players, is about love and time. Both *Turangalîla* and *Momente* are 'abstract dramas', both have a ritualistic character. Furthermore, *Momente*, in its use of the chorus, in its specification of the disposition of singers and instrumentalists on the platform, in its eschewal of a single, linear narrative, suggests Stravinsky's *Oedipus rex* as an antecedent. The new approach to form in *Momente* reflects new attitudes towards time and duration which in turn relate to new kinds of (non-)narrative rituals. It is striking that in Stravinsky's most ritualistic works – *The Rite of Spring*, *Les Noces*, *Symphony of Psalms*, *Mass*, *Threni* – he invents block structures which place a primacy on opposition, discontinuity, non-development. Similarly Messiaen's most ritualistic works of the 1960s – principally *Et expecto resurrectionem mortuorum*, *Couleurs de la Cité céleste* and *La Transfiguration de Notre Seigneur Jésus-Christ* – are among his most uncompromising in their block structures, such forms being appropriate to a non-linear, non-directed music which expresses new kinds of 'timeless' time. Though they achieve it in different ways and for different purposes, it is interesting that both Messiaen and Stockhausen are concerned with the 'end of time', with a music where time 'flows forgotten. The lovers are outside time.'[139]

   Momente, according to the composer, is a 'polyvalent composition containing independent events. Unity and continuity are less the outcome of obvious similarities than of an immanent concentration on the present, as uninterrupted as possible.'[140] Its polyvalence (literally 'many links'), or at least the possibility of it, is offered by the openness of the form: in principle, if not in practice, the ordering of the 'independent events' is mobile. Such procedures were not, in themselves, new: Cage had, of course, been experimenting with variable forms for some time (and though Stockhausen knew Cage's work well, he claims his own developments were achieved independently of Cage), Boulez had produced his new open form works in the late 1950s and early 1960s (Third Piano Sonata, *Pli selon pli*, etc.), and Stockhausen himself had written the mobile *Klavierstück XI*. What is new about *Momente* is the way in which each musical moment (or block) is apparently independently defined, aiming to achieve an absolute focus on the present, avoiding continuity with the past and the future.

There are three 'pure' moments which Stockhausen labels M ('Melodie': melody/monody-heterophony), K ('Klang': timbre/homophony) and D ('Dauer': duration/polyphony). There are also I-moments (informal, indeterminate) which 'neutralise' the three groups of moments. However, there are also other moments between the 'pure', 'self-reflecting' moments that 'reflect both themselves and one or both of the others', which Stockhausen explains as follows:

> When, in one of these double reflections, the reflection of the other compo-
> nent is weak, the latter is indicated in lower case; if it is almost as strong, then
> two capitals are used together. M(m) is a moment with 'feed-back' self-
> reflection; so is D(d-m), but this time having a transition of the self-
> reflection into a reflection of M; at DK(d) and DK(k) the feed-back
> reinforces one component of the double reflection.[141]

The mobility of the form is thus necessary on two principal counts: firstly, to ensure the independence of individual moments (if continuities were fixed, then the independence of moments would be compromised), and, secondly, in order to allow for a web of possible relationships, only some of which can be realised in any one performance. However, the 'absolute' ideal of moment form, i.e. the independence of the moment, is brought into question in a number of ways. The interpenetration of moments of course means that one moment becomes dependent on another (so suggesting a past or a future for any given moment), something Griffiths, for one, is prepared to permit on dramatic grounds: 'characteristically, ideology is not immune to the claims of drama'.[142] Furthermore, as the work evolved over many years, versions of its form became fixed – the 1965 'Donaueschingen version' was recorded by Wergo/Nonesuch, and the 1972 'Bonn version' (Stockhausen's formal scheme for which is given in Fig. 2.6) remains its 'final' form.

A random collage of totally disconnected *objets trouvés* was never the intention of *Momente*. Indeed, as has already been discussed and as Stockhausen's own statements reveal, 'unity and continuity' may well be achieved in the work, not by an expression of the utmost connectedness of phenomena, but, in Whittall's phrase, by mediating between diversities. This means the work can never be closed; rather, it transcends closure: 'In all these considerations about unending [*Unendlich*] form one notices a peculiar tendency to overcome the time that "ends" – death.'[143] Connections remain relative, not absolute: as Boulez wrote in relation to his Third Sonata, 'definitive, once-and-for-all developments seem no longer appropriate to musical thought as it is today, . . . which is increasingly concerned with the investigation of a relative world'.[144] Above, I

Fig. 2.6 Stockhausen, *Momente* (from Maconie, *The Works of Stockhausen*)

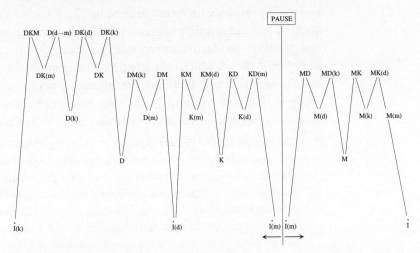

suggested the possibility that the block form of Stravinsky's *Symphonies of Wind Instruments* resists closure, that despite evidence of connection and continuity in the work, the structure remains open and unresolved – one of the first instances of an 'unending form'. In this sense, it clearly provides a model for Stockhausen's moment form;[145] both works offer an 'immanent critique of totality'. *Momente* is thus the logical successor of the *Symphonies*.

Michael Tippett

Ian Kemp has described the music of Michael Tippett in the period framed by his second opera, *King Priam* (1958–61), and his fourth, *The Ice Break* (1973–6), as 'heterogeneously homogeneous'.[146] What prompts this evaluation is Tippett's sudden apparent change in stylistic direction following the completion of his first opera, *The Midsummer Marriage* (1946–52), a move which can be generalised as one from an essentially tonal, lyrical and continuous music to a more decidedly atonal, fragmented and discontinuous one. 'I found this style change immensely stimulating and exciting.'[147] Kemp's historical gloss accounts for the change in terms of what he calls the 'feel of the time' – indeed, he goes so far as to suggest this is the 'decisive compositional determinant'.[148] A new conception of musical time evolved – one where, as we have already seen was the case for Stravinsky, directedness, even for a composer such as Tippett who had to work with rather than against tonality, became less of an issue, where circularity and 'non-ending' grew as important aesthetic considerations. A fascination with simultaneous progress and stasis emerged (preeminently, Kemp argues, in *The Vision of Saint Augustine*). Such an account certainly suggests parallels with neoclassical Stravinsky, and provokes productive interpretational strategies for Tippett's works since *The Ice Break*, which have attempted some sort of accommodation of their 'progressive' and 'traditional' attributes. But as far as the works of the *Priam* period were concerned, the immediate emphasis was more on the heterogeneous than on the homogeneous elements. As Kemp writes:

> The organization of Tippett's gestural language [in *King Priam*] postulates juxtapositions and superpositions, as opposed to the developments and gradual transformations appropriate to material that invites rather than resists change. . . . Tippett proceeds by sudden contrasts and by the rearrangement of the components of such contrasts. His music is 'non-developmental', in the sense that it contains no transitions, or at least seems to have none. Nevertheless it still contains the stuff of dynamic movement for its components generate their own interior tensions which then find release in switches to other components.[149]

Tippett had always looked to Stravinsky's music, if not for technical guidance at least for an aesthetic justification of his thinking, especially in the period leading up to *The Midsummer Marriage*, which had coincided with Stravinsky's neoclassical years. It is interesting that the 'style change' for both composers, the search for new kinds of structures, took place at around the same time, but where Stravinsky turned to the greater 'homogeneity' offered by the serial method, Tippett sought models in the structural 'heterogeneity' of earlier Stravinsky, in works such as the *Symphonies of Wind Instruments* and, most obviously, the *Symphony in Three Movements* in his Symphony No. 2 (1956–7).

King Priam and Piano Sonata No. 2

The first performance of *The Midsummer Marriage* in 1955 had received a hostile reception in the London press, the principal objects of criticism being the libretto and the plot. The manifest change in direction in *King Priam* was understood, even at the time of its premiere, as a reaction to that criticism: a 'constructive response', as Kemp describes it. The narrative of *King Priam* is clear and straightforward. But this suggests a contradiction at the heart of the work: in order to project what is undoubtedly his most direct, linear plot, Tippett opts for a musical structure predicated on fragmentation, juxtaposition and discontinuity. When Stravinsky chose to work with classical subject matter in *Oedipus rex*, he abandoned any pretence of a single narrative by separating the spoken narrations (which are in the vernacular) from the main body of the work (which is in Latin), this non-linear structure being supported by the work's fragmentation – explicitly a '*Merzbild*, put together from whatever came to hand'.[150] Even a dramatic work with as blatantly linear a plot as *The Rake's Progress* (a linearity enshrined in the opera's very title) is stylised through its adoption and adaptation of a 'classical' number opera structure, as well as through its broad-ranging allusions to operatic discourse from Monteverdi to Verdi and beyond.[151] In other words, in his last overtly neoclassical work Stravinsky was still undertaking what he suggested was his aim in his first overtly neoclassical work, *Pulcinella* – namely an act of criticism, making plain the distance between his various historical models and the new work, and thus disrupting any simple narrative expectations.

At heart *King Priam* is a simple narrative. In order to tell this story as directly as possible, Tippett, like Stravinsky, adopts familiar musical conventions but, unlike Stravinsky, he does not keep his critical distance. (For me, this is the central difficulty with much of Tippett's music – the lack of critique of the materials he chooses to work with, the absence of Stravinsky's 'objectivity'. The eclecticism of speech in *The Ice Break*, or of musical languages in *New Year*, or of philosophies and source material in *The Mask of Time*, is in many respects so personal, so rooted in the composer's own autobiography, that I at least am never quite sure what to do with it – it strikes me as being ingenuous, albeit sincerely so, and for that reason almost beyond interpretation.) Take the Prelude and opening scene of the opera, which presents a mosaic of generally static musical blocks, in the majority of which various well-worn clichés are adopted: courtly heralds playing dotted fanfare figures on trumpets and drums to announce the start of the work, while a wordless offstage chorus moan in a portentous but non-specific manner; solo oboe playing a cradle song for a restless child (fig. 10); the entry of Priam in *marche militaire* style and alluding to the conventional triumphalist key of D (fig. 17); slow, low bassoons and bass clarinet representing the Old Man (fig. 26); a dissonant, loud off-beat stroke on the word 'death' (as ill-judged a gesture as the chorus's shout of 'slain!' at the narration of the death of Belshazzar in Walton's *Belshazzar's Feast* – a work whose rhythmic vitality, if nothing else, owes much to Stravinsky), followed by clock-like tintinnabulation of percussion and high woodwind ostinatos representing 'time standing still' (fig. 34). Tippett treads a fine line between the establishment of memorable 'motifs' in the opening blocks, which are unequivocally linked with the characters they accompany, and a naïveté unintentionally bordering on the comical. For Tippett, this memorability is absolutely necessary in order to sustain a workable block structure over the large span of an opera – that is, the blocks do have to be sharply and boldly defined so that they retain their identity even after transformation. Kemp accounts for the importance of such gestures as 'a consequence of Tippett's decision to present the natures, thoughts and behaviour of the characters in his opera as a series of unequivocal facts – of statements so categorical that they would naturally arouse the critical comment and "examination" of the opera's inter-ludes'.[152] Thus the developmental possibilities of such music are severely restricted. Instead, a large number of ideas is presented and juxtaposed/ superimposed, and it is the nature of these oppositions, their ordering and repetition in accordance with the requirements of the drama, which sus-tains the opera.

King Priam is a bold, brave and, in many respects unique, musico-dramatic project. In operatic terms, it appears to be without precedent. The recurrence of musical ideas identified with particular characters or situations is as old as opera itself, but here it is elevated to a primary princi-ple. It is not Wagnerian because the material does not develop (Tippett's approach is more like Debussy's parody of Wagner's leitmotif technique: musical 'calling cards') – hence, perhaps, the necessity for the wider associations of motifs beyond the work itself. Berg's alliance of characters and instruments in *Lulu* (vibraphone for Lulu, piano for the Athlete etc. – and, interestingly, low instruments, including a prominent bassoon, for the old man Schigolch) is closer to what Tippett is trying to achieve. Tippett's scoring was influenced directly by Stravinsky, as he acknowl-edges:

> From Stravinsky's instrumentation [of *Agon*] I derived some clues as to how to deploy an operatic orchestra in an entirely new way – treating solo instru-ments as equals both within the ensemble and against the voices on stage, writing for heterogeneous mixtures of instruments.[153]

And, at much the same time as Tippett was writing *King Priam*, other opera composers were trying out similar means of characterisation: Benjamin Britten, for instance, in *The Turn of the Screw* (1954) associated his ghostly characters exclusively with the gamelan-like sounds of tuned percussion, and Hans Werner Henze's *Elegy for Young Lovers* (1959–61, to a libretto by *The Rake's Progress* team of W. H. Auden and Chester Kallman) identifies characters with specific instruments throughout. But Tippett was the first to follow Stravinsky's *dramatic* models – the latent drama of the block structure of the *Symphonies of Wind Instruments*, the abstract drama of *Oedipus rex* and *Agon* – and apply them to an entire opera. The 1960s were to see a renewed interest in Stravinsky's theatre (discussed in Chapter 4), ranging from the dramatic rituals of Messiaen, through the instrumental theatre of Birtwistle, to the overt music theatre of Peter Maxwell Davies (where *The Soldier's Tale* was, at least in part, a model). But these were radical kinds of theatre, alternatives to the operatic genre with its inappropriate narrative structures and inflexible institutions. *King Priam* is a compromise between a reactionary narrative genre and a radical non-narrative structure.

I sense at times Tippett's lyrical instincts are barely held back – maybe even frustrated – by the constraints of his non-developmental structure. This is most apparent at conventional operatic nodes such as the aria, of which there are a number in *King Priam*. Kemp's conclusion is that the music 'does not take wing often enough'[154] (one moment where it does is Helen's Act 3 scene 1 aria, 'Let her rave'), but the point is that, more often than not, the structure precludes such fully-fledged lyrical flights. Priam's aria[155] in Act 1 scene 2 ('So I'd hoped it might be') is a case in point. It is the emotional climax of the scene and its text is structured as a classic soliloquy showing Priam's examination of himself and of the past, and his movement towards self-reconciliation and decision ('Let it mean my death'). Priam's vocal line articulates this directed emotional progress by moving freely and fluently between lyrical aria ('I have a deepening anguish'), arioso ('Do I now with my own hands . . .') and recitative ('because he chooses with the certainty of youth . . .'), and achieving the highest note, E, at its very end (on '*my* death'). It is well shaped and controlled. To some extent, the more fragmentary accompaniment supports these rhetorical switches, but contrariwise, because it re-presents only slightly varied versions of musical blocks familiar from scene 1 (Priam's entry march, the Old Man's stuttering bassoon/bass clarinet utterances, the nurse's music, the opening fanfares etc.), it also serves to subvert that movement.

We shall see in Chapter 6 how it is possible to come to an understanding of Stravinsky's music in terms of a balancing of the continuous and the discontinuous, the linear and the circular. Tippett, too, preoccupied (as was Stravinsky) by different notions of time, expressed a fascination with simultaneous progress and stasis:

> There is a sense of Time as unique, from Genesis to World's End. And there is a sense of Time as repetitive, or circular – the myth of the Eternal Return. I am uncertain how objective is my feeling that the movement of these two ideas, one against the other, is another aspect of the new world picture.[156]

Kemp argues that Tippett's finest achievement of 'the movement of these two ideas, one against the other' is in *The Vision of Saint Augustine* (1963–5). But in *King Priam* there is less a sense of 'synthesis' of its contradictory elements – the tension between progress and stasis is not an entirely productive one. The fragmentary musical structure is driven by the drama which, as exemplified by Priam's aria, pulls in different directions. And when the music does fully 'take wing', as for example in Paris's Act 1 aria ('Carried on the wind of love') with a consistent accompaniment supporting the music's drive towards his call to Zeus, it seems strangely anachronistic – despite its atonality – in the larger context of oppositions, as if it should somehow be in inverted commas. But it is not. Once again we see Tippett adopting a nineteenth-century mode of discourse but without the critical distance adopted by Stravinsky in, say, Jocasta's aria from *Oedipus rex*. Throughout the opera, Tippett employs various devices for interrupting narrative continuity, such as the sung interludes; what is odd about Paris's aria (among others) is that it suspends the narrative thread – as conventionally one would expect of an aria – but with a music which emphasises continuity, in opposition to the musical discontinuity characteristic of the dramatically dynamic parts of the opera. Smaller-scale continuity is opposed to larger-scale discontinuity.

Yet, despite the fact that block structures seem to work much better for abstract or ritualistic dramas than for linear narratives, and despite the contradictions and structural weaknesses of *King Priam*, it is nonetheless effective in the theatre. When in operation, the process of stratification lends a stylised character to the work in keeping with what one might expect of a Greek drama, or indeed a Baroque opera. The passionate, lyrical and more continuous moments, when they come, do not alienate in a Brechtian (or a Stravinskian) way but, taken on their own terms, speak simply and directly – we recognise the traditional operatic rhetoric for what it is, spoken in Tippett's accent. And the legacy of Stravinsky is everywhere, even if not fully absorbed: in the presentation and organisation (successively and simultaneously) of musical blocks; in its rhythmic dynamism; in so many aspects of scoring and harmonic language; even in specific allusions – to give just one example, the figure and scoring of the idea associated with the Old Man bears a striking similarity to the music for the old men of *The Rite of Spring* (bass clarinet figures from fig. 140 of the 'Action rituelle des ancêtres').

One of the immediate consequences of Tippett's structural experiment in *King Priam* was his Piano Sonata No. 2 (1962–3) which, like the Concerto for Orchestra (1963), signals its allegiance to the opera by incorporating musical material directly from it (tempi 2 and 7 employ ideas from Act 2) . It is one of Tippett's most uncompromising works and, perhaps because it is freed from external dramatic and formal constraints or expectations, is his most successful use of a block structure (that it was explicitly concerned with such structural issues is indicated by its original

Fig. 2.7 Ordering of tempo blocks in Tippett's Piano Sonata No. 2

1	2	3	4	5	6	7	8
1	2	3	4	5			
			4	5			
			4				
	2				6		
		3	4				
		3	4	5		7	
			4				
	2	3					8
	2	3	4		6	7	
					6	7	
					6		
			4			7	
					6	7	
					6		
		3					8
						7	
		3					
1							

discarded title, 'Mosaics'). Stravinsky's *Symphonies of Wind Instruments* is selfevidently the primary precursor. Each of the eight principal blocks is clearly defined and distinguished in terms of harmony, rhythm and piano texture (though equally there are subtle links between the blocks). Tippett also follows Stravinsky's lead in identifying each block with a different tempo, though here each tempo is unique and in no significant proportional relationship with the others (in this sense there is a distant likeness to Stockhausen's *Klavierstück XI*). The disposition of tempi is given in Fig. 2.7.

What this chart does not indicate, however, is the relative proportions of these blocks. Some are quite extended and contain a number of sub-elements, such as the first appearance of tempo 6 (crotchet = c.58), which is 66 bars long, i.e. more than a fifth of the entire work. Other statements, especially towards the end of the work (bb. 265 ff), become highly fragmented and interrupt one another in rapid succession (in a programme note, Tippett suggests that if this work were for more than one player, many of these closing fragments might occur simultaneously – a 'jam session'[157]). This diversity, and particularly the periodic introduction of new material (tempi 6, 7 and 8), has led Kemp,[158] among others, to suggest that a more conventional four-movement sonata design underlies the surface mosaics: a 'first movement' which moves 'from rhetoric to lyricism', the first appearance of tempo 6 represents a rondo 'slow movement', tempo 7 (crotchet = c.132) introduces a new 'scherzo' theme, and tempo 8 (crotchet = c.40) begins the 'slow finale' with a new chordal theme.

Such a reading, however, while possibly helping to account for the greater expansiveness of certain sections than one finds in Stravinsky, undermines the radical nature of Tippett's form by imposing an inappropriately unified view. In Stravinsky's neoclassical works (such as in the first movement of the Symphony in C as discussed in Chapter 6) there is a productive tension between the 'morphology' of a classical form and the discontinuity of the disposition of Stravinsky's material. This is not the case here, partly because one cannot be certain of the presence of the earlier sonata model. Discontinuity remains to the fore. The work's dynamism springs from the way in which widely divergent materials are pitted against each other in a balanced way, without offering the possibility of reconciliation (despite the recurrence of the opening idea at the end – which then just vaporises). In applying Cone's categories to this sonata, Robert Jones relates the notion of synthesis to what he calls its 'sense of an ending', which is achieved 'not through arrival at a stable sonority but by creating the effect of a precarious balance between two forces that are incapable of further reduction'.[159] Such is Stravinsky's achievement, and therein, according to Arnold Whittall, also lies the key to Tippett's modernism: 'the "balance of similarities and contrasts" as a means of achieving an adequate degree of formal coherence, through juxtaposition rather than superimposition'.[160] Stravinsky's music offered Tippett a model of 'heterogeneous homogeneity' which is creatively exploited in his Second Piano Sonata.

Harrison Birtwistle

> I think that the *Symphonies of Wind Instruments* is one of the great masterpieces of this century . . . and certainly one of the most original, in that it's to do with the juxtaposition of material without any sense of development.[161]

The influence of Stravinsky on the music of Birtwistle is profound, and one that the composer regularly acknowledges. It will be evident on a number of occasions throughout this book that an understanding of Stravinsky's modernism has a deep bearing on how we might develop appropriate analytical lines of enquiry for Birtwistle's music. Though Birtwistle was perhaps at his most stridently 'Stravinskian' in works of the 1960s that were explicitly concerned with exploring violently juxtaposed musical blocks in ritualised musico-dramatic contexts, everywhere can be felt the influence of Stravinsky's attitude to repetition and variation, his 'unified fragmentation' in the layering of conceptually opposed musics (linear and circular), and an understanding of the power of ritualised forms and structures. Occasionally, very specific Stravinskian paradigms can be identified. One such case is *Earth Dances* (investigated in Chapter 3), one of the most original orchestral works of the latter part of the twentieth century, which can be seen as a direct creative response to *The Rite of Spring*. Another, *Carmen arcadiae mechanicae perpetuum*, is, in quite a different way from Tippett's Second Sonata, a later twentieth-century reconsideration of the *Symphonies of Wind Instruments*.

Carmen arcadiae mechanicae perpetuum

Composed in 1977 for the London Sinfonietta, *Carmen arcadiae mechanicae perpetuum* (literally, the Perpetual Song of Mechanical Arcady) is a homage to the painter Paul Klee. Its title, Birtwistle states, 'is a title he [Klee] could have invented',[162] and the model is explicitly Klee's *The Twittering Machine* (1922), a painting which represents four mechanical birds in a strangely coloured ('natural') landscape.[163] It is not, I think, too fanciful to suggest that the sounds with which Birtwistle's work opens represent the chirrupings of a rather peculiar mechanical menagerie (Ex. 2.7).

The oxymoron of Birtwistle's title, the notion of the 'mechanical pastoral', is also apparent in Klee's work. The machine and the naturally-occurring phenomena co-exist in Klee's drawings and paintings; through-out his *Pedagogical Sketchbook* – Birtwistle's 'musical bible'[164] – Klee discusses the simultaneous operation of the regular/geometric and the irregular/natural.[165] Once again, this calls to mind the 'deep equivalence of the natural and the artificial' of which Albright spoke in reference to Stravinsky's music, while Klee's fascination with Cubism and his later association with the 'constructivism' of the Bauhaus make interesting parallels with Stravinsky as well as Varèse. Furthermore, Klee was an accomplished musician and considered music and painting analogous because they were comparable 'temporal' arts.[166] His theoretical writings are full of musical references, particularly to the movement dynamics and rhythm of pictures, and this in turn suggests the proximity of his thinking to that of Varèse. It is interesting to note that Klee, Stravinsky and Varèse were all in Paris at some point during 1912, and all would have moved among the same artistic circles – for instance, Robert Delaunay was an acquaintance of all three. Varèse, too, has been an important formative influence on Birtwistle (Birtwistle's first published work, *Refrains and Choruses* of 1957, might almost be a homage to a work such as *Octandre*): at the very least, their shared interest in the visual arts as a stimulus for musical thought

Ex. 2.7 Birtwistle, *Carmen arcadiae mechanicae perpetuum* (opening)

reveals parallel compositional procedures. It is thus clear that the roots of a later-twentieth-century musical modernism can be identified explicitly in the circle of musicians and artists around Stravinsky whose shared concerns throw interesting light on definitions of Stravinsky's own modernism.

Birtwistle's customarily cursory programme note for *Carmen* suggests further parallels with Klee, Stravinsky and Varèse:

> It consists of six mechanisms which are juxtaposed many times without any form of transition. The dynamics of the piece have a time-scale independent of that of the mechanisms, creating an independent dynamic life of their own. This process is also applied to the registers of the piece.[167]

In other words, he is suggesting a fundamental opposition between the pitch and rhythmic organisation (a 'mechanical' process which, once set in motion, will work itself out 'automatically'), and the dynamics and registers (which are 'natural', 'intuitive', 'hand-crafted'). The most striking aspect of this score is its juxtapositions: the music is composed of discrete musical blocks (six 'musical mechanisms') separated, usually, by refrain-like sustained notes or chords. The aesthetic of its structural organisation clearly owes an immense debt to the *Symphonies of Wind Instruments*, as shown by Fig. 2.8. The principal 'identifier' of each block on its recurrence appears to be a rhythmic one because it is the rhythmic identity which remains more-or-less constant across the various transformations of the material. The role of tempo in defining the blocks is striking: with the exception of block A (discussed below), material returns on each occasion at its initial tempo. However, in order to maximise the oppositions between blocks, and to avoid any sense of transition or immediate continuity, there is no significant proportional relationship between the two tempi used (they stand in the ratio 23:21). In this regard, Birtwistle seems to share more of Varèse's structural concern for opposition than Stravinsky's, certainly as explored in the *Symphonies of Wind Instruments* with its precise tempo relations (Birtwistle had himself explored such 'metric/tempo modulation' in *Silbury Air*, written immediately prior to *Carmen* and discussed in Chapter 3).

A different proportional logic would appear to govern sectional relations, and in this sense, if we follow the lead established by Kramer's proportional analyses,[168] *Carmen*'s patrimony in the *Symphonies* is reasserted. What we see is what might be termed 'proportional modulation'. For example, each of the first six blocks (including two exact repetitions) is of the same relative length, i.e. 36 quaver beats, irrespective of the *actual* sounding length of the quaver unit as a result of the tempo differences. The

Fig. 2.8a Characteristics of blocks in Birtwistle, *Carmen arcadiae mechanicae perpetuum*

A   Regular pulsation involving triplet quavers. Rotation of three or four pitches in each voice contained, usually, within the range of a fourth and together forming a chromatic aggregate
B   Simultaneous strands made up of long–short rhythmic cells. The principal strand is usually shared between a pair of voices and is contained within the range of a fourth. High degree of cell repetition. Quaver=168
C   Three-note clusters in piano, usually occurring in pairs, contained within a small interval. Sometimes accompanied by regularly pulsed vertical sonority and always by an irregular horizontal idea. The block is never repeated exactly. Crotchet=92
D   Homorhythmic motion employing a variety of rhythmic patterns (durational values range from sextuplet semiquavers to triplet crotchets); each strand often covers a wide intervallic range. On two-thirds of its appearances it is accompanied by a descending idea in longer note values. The block is never repeated exactly. Quaver=168*
E   Pitch rotation and repetition as in A. Material more diverse and contains non-rotational chromatic elements. Voices not generally coordinated vertically and, although there is constant semiquaver movement, there is no regular rhythmic patterning. Quaver=168
F   Distinctive homorhythmic patterns made up of straight and triplet quavers and semiquavers. Each individual strand fills out chromatically the interval of, usually, a perfect or an augmented fourth, but without any regular rotation of pitches. Resulting parallel movement of voices (often within a consistent containing outer interval) gives impression of a kind of chromatic organum. Crotchet=92

* NB this is marked *crotchet=168* at fig. 3, the only time this mark occurs. Elgar Howarth and the London Sinfonietta, in the première recording of the work, read this consistently as *quaver=168*. KTC 1052 (Amsterdam: Etcetera, 1987)

Fig. 2.8b Stratification/interlock of blocks in Birtwistle, *Carmen arcadiae mechanicae perpetuum*

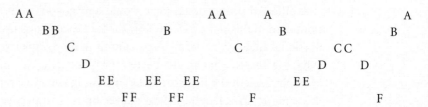

number 36 governs the length of many of the other blocks in the initial part of the work: the appearances of F at fig. 6; of E at fig 8; and of A at fig. 9, whose two statements together make up 36 quaver beats, the moment of repetition after 18 beats being almost precisely the half-way point of the work (beat 615 of 1227); nearly all other blocks are proportionally related, with a lowest common denominator of 4 quaver beats. However, the proportions of the second half of the piece, following the entry of a transformed version of A at fig. 11, take on a less regular, less predictable character; on the whole, blocks are longer. The final A block is by far the longest section of the work. This suggests the A material has a Stravinskian 'signalling' role. Its appearance at the beginning and the end of the work, albeit in quite different forms (reflecting their different functions?), suggests a framing role, while its appearance at fig. 11 signals a structural change. This sense of a new beginning, of a reviewing, is reinforced by the return of the sustained F♯ (trumpet, b. 8 of fig. 11) familiar, at the same pitch level, from the 'refrain' at the start of the work. As we have seen, the only other statement of A signals the exact half-way point.

It should be evident, then, that the organisation of blocks in *Carmen* – the process of stratification – is brought about by a comprehensive disruption of local continuity, confirming Birtwistle's express desire for the absence of transition. Nonetheless, a larger-scale connectedness – interlock – is apparent across appearances of the block or mechanism. For example, block A^2 (fig. 9) is a compressed version of A^1 where the processing mechanism and pulsation are the same but the material on which they operate is altered slightly, as well as incorporating piano trichords derived from C (this incursion or 'penetration' of material across blocks we saw as a characteristic of Varèse's forms). A^3 (fig. 11) continues this diversification by disrupting the even triplet pulsation to produce a new rhythmic grouping. The process is interrupted, however, and does not find its fulfilment until A^4 (fig. 19), which quickly settles into the routine of bar-length repetitions to which all the A sections seem to have been aspiring (a certain 'directedness', perhaps? See Ex. 2.8). This is the most stable and predictable music of the entire work, which might also account for its being the longest. Comparison with the chorale from Stravinsky's *Symphonies* might also be appropriate here, given the way both musical blocks appear initially in a fragmentary state and only achieve their fullest form as the culmination of their respective works.

However, such an account is perhaps guilty of overplaying the connections. The A blocks are, in fact, altered quite radically during the course of the piece – so that the similarities between A^1 and A^4 are not immediately easy to discern. A^1 divides the ensemble into four separate strands (woodwind,

Ex. 2.8 Birtwistle, *Carmen arcadiae mechanicae perpetuum* (figs. 20⁺⁶–20⁺⁹)

brass, string quartet, and marimba and double bass) distinguished by their rhythmic groupings. The motion of the whole is governed by a constant triplet semiquaver pulse at crotchet = 120. This tempo marking only occurs twice in the piece, the other occasion being its obvious reworking, A^2. A^4 organises the entire ensemble homorhythmically with a distinctive pattern of a pair of triplet quavers followed by three quavers, and at the slower tempo of quaver = 184. The only evident progenitor for this material is the passage I have labelled A^3, which, though it has more widely divergent pitch material, nonetheless possesses a similar rhythmic organisation, dividing the 5/8 bar into three triplet quavers and three quavers at a tempo of quaver = 168. The initial intention would thus appear to be that these musics should sound very *different*. Their similarities, as the composer's own account might lead one to expect, are a result of the mechanism that operates on their pitch materials, rather than that material in itself. Each individual voice concerns itself with the rotation of a set of three or four pitches contained, usually, within an interval of no more than a fourth. This high level of repetition, combined with the relative regularity of the rhythmic organisation, makes for a distinctive and 'static' music – in the sense that it is 'non-progressive' and the rotations stop only when each section has filled its allotted durational/proportional span. These are clearly variants of the same idea, a familiar Birtwistle preoccupation of 'viewing an object from many different perspectives' – the 'objects' in the case of *Carmen* being the processes, the 'mechanisms', themselves.

As far as other blocks are concerned, the processes of interlock vary greatly – it is certainly not as consistent as that demonstrated by Cone for Stravinsky's *Symphonies*. Block F, for instance, retains a strong identity on each of its appearances: it proceeds accumulatively and gets progressively longer. The transformations of D, by contrast, are more enigmatic, where one individual instance of the mechanism offers only a partial glimpse of the whole object, which is never fully revealed (like looking at a three-dimensional sculpture).

Given the diversity of materials and processes in *Carmen*, along with the wholehearted atonality of its musical language, it should hardly surprise us if Cone's category of synthesis ('some sort of unification') is not immediately apparent. Though, as we have seen, there are elements which seem to point towards the end of the piece – and, as the piece unfolds, connections across *different* blocks also seem to become more apparent – yet there is clearly no complete convergence or resolution of ideas. But, as with the *Symphonies*, this does not make for an incoherent whole. For one thing, we have seen how the proportional scheme imposes some sort of (admittedly artificial) order on the pattern of juxtapositions; further, the precise ordering of the blocks – the 'wave' shape revealed in Fig. 2.8b – suggests a 'rough symmetry' not uncommon in Birtwistle, and involves a reversal towards the end (compare this, for example, with the formal outlines of *Tragoedia* (1965), *Punch and Judy* (1966–7) and *Verses for Ensembles* (1968–9), all derived from Birtwistle's reading of the formal structure of Greek tragedy[169]). This is no synthesis, though a balancing is achieved which might well be considered the equivalent of the 'nonsymmetrical balance' Klee discusses in his *Pedagogical Sketchbook*: 'the balancing and proportioning power of eye and brain that regulates this expansion of the object toward equilibrium and harmony'.[170]

But there is one other element of *Carmen arcadiae mechanicae perpetuum* that engenders a sense of continuity across the entire work, and takes the form of a refrain-like music which recurs between every block. Cone's identification of bridge passages in Stravinsky's *Symphonies* is helpful here. A bridge, he writes, is a device for 'mitigating the starkness of the opposition between the strata[,] . . . an area with a life of its own . . . Although acting as a bridge in the immediate context, it reaches forward to its next appearance in the interlocking pattern.'[171] Examples can be found elsewhere in Stravinsky, such as the punctuating Prelude/Interludes from *Agon*, a work which, like *Carmen*, is 'highly discontinuous', which has 'puzzled commentators by its disparity of materials yet unmistakable unity',[172] and one of Stravinsky's works with which Birtwistle is allegedly most (analytically) familiar.[173] *Carmen*'s refrains would seem to coincide with Cone's bridging characteristics. They are not transitions between mechanisms, but they do mitigate the starkness of the oppositions, signalling the end of one block and the beginning of the next. They stand temporally and gesturally outside the main sequence of oppositions, although they do often overlap with the blocks they interrupt, thus implying certain connections. The refrains are characterised by a sustained note or chord and, sometimes, an acciaccatura figure. Successive appearances of the refrain interlock across the work to form a stratum which is seemingly far more connected than any other music in the work. Indeed, the refrain almost becomes a seventh 'mechanism' in its own right – witness the prolonged, climactic refrain just before fig. 8, or the sustained wind/strings chords in block F at fig. 10. Nevertheless, any continuity suggested by the refrain is contingent on its difference from all the other blocks, whose juxtaposition it ultimately serves to reinforce. Its lack of rhythmic focus stands in complete contrast to the highly-charged rhythmic energy of the six principal mechanisms.

In formal terms, *Carmen arcadiae mechanicae perpetuum* is Birtwistle's most overtly Stravinskian work. It is fascinating to see how, more than seventy-five years after its composition, the *Symphonies of Wind Instruments* continued to exert a strong and direct influence.

Conclusions

Though the anti-organicist stance of Stravinsky's *drobnost'* may seem utterly modern in that it stands in distinct opposition to the Western

Romantic tradition, its roots actually lie deep in nineteenth-century Russia. As Taruskin has revealed to us:

> The kuchist position [the Balakirev circle of Russian nationalists, the "Mighty Handful"] had always valued the piquancy and the separate integrity of the individual moment over the generalized impression, even the coherence of the whole. Such a standpoint is the essence of "realism" in all artistic media, and can be traced, for example, in countless dicta of Musorgsky.

He then quotes a letter from Musorgsky to Rimsky-Korsakov outlining the differences between Russian thought and that of reasoned, German symphonic development.[174] Nor, as we have seen, was Stravinsky's stance necessarily unique among early modernists: in many ways Debussy, similarly influenced by Russian thinking, anticipated so many of Stravinsky's 'innovations' – not least in the nascent block structure of *Jeux*.[175] There is thus a danger in focusing on one work as if it were the sole source of the twentieth century's reevaluation of structure. Like the 'legend' of the rhythmic innovations of *The Rite of Spring* (explored in the next chapter), the *Symphonies of Wind Instruments* has come to be seen as a watershed in the history of musical form. The construction of Stravinsky as the 'only begetter' has actually grown stronger as recent composers have come to recognise the radical significance of *all* Stravinsky for their own work (a radicalism which different accounts of the century's history had served partly to hide).

This having been said, as with all legends there is a core of truth. Taruskin's claim that Stravinsky 'bequeathed a *russkiy slog* [Russian manner] to the whole world of twentieth-century concert music' needs to be considered carefully.[176] And in the boldness of its oppositions, the conviction of its fragmentation, the radicalism of its various (and contradictory) continuities, the satisfying novelty of its overall structure, it is the *Symphonies of Wind Instruments*, like no other work before it, that has made possible the structural innovations that have followed. It would be difficult to claim, for example, that the mobile form of Henry Cowell's celebrated 'Mosaic' String Quartet (1935) owes much to Stravinsky; or that the 'non-narrative' distribution of the René Char poems across Boulez's *Le Marteau sans maître* (1955), and the interlock between their associated instrumental tropes, are primarily derived from Stravinsky's *Symphonies*; or that the 'static' internal construction and freedom of arrangement of the blocks of the first movement of Lutosławski's *Jeux vénitiens* (1960–1) are any more 'Stravinskian' than they are 'Bartókian'. Stravinsky and modernism are not synonymous. Equally, though, a climate was created by Stravinsky which may, to a greater or lesser extent, have influenced the structural thinking of these composers.

A more recent example comes from a composer who identifies his primary allegiance with *Schoenbergian* modernism: Brian Ferneyhough. The 'open' structure of Stravinsky's *Symphonies* relates to a feature Paul Griffiths has recognised as a general characteristic of many of Ferneyhough's works, where 'the arbitrary becomes absolute in being composed',[177] works which could easily have had different formal outcomes. And there are more specific Stravinskian resonances in, for instance, the episodic structure of *Bone Alphabet* (1991–2) for solo percussion.[178] An idea is established in one tempo, only to be interrupted by a new idea at a different tempo, and a third, and so on. The composer's account of the work would seem to support a comparison with the *Symphonies*: he describes a process whereby thirteen strands or 'compartmental areas' were separately composed, only then to be chopped up and 'kaleidoscopically redistributed'.[179] Such stratification inevitably results in 'sharp contrasts and unpredictable changes of direction', yet there is an overarching shape, an emotional coherence, a timely placing of events, where the principal climax (*fffff brutale*) occurs at the point of Golden Section, and a slowing and fragmentation takes place towards the end.

My point is this: Stravinsky's modernism (I prefer this term because it neutralises the potential problematics of Taruskin's Russo-centric interpretation) and in particular the radical structure of the *Symphonies of Wind Instruments* helped create a climate in which formal experiment, in which non-directed, non-developmental, unending structures, were seen not only as possible but legitimate. For these reasons alone, even though the direct technical influence of the *Symphonies* may often be difficult (and unnecessary) to substantiate, I would argue we are justified in regarding it as a structural paradigm for the twentieth century.

3 Structural rhythms

The topic of the influence of Stravinsky's rhythmic practices on the music of the twentieth century is vast. Though the rhythmic achievements of other key figures in the emergence of musical modernism, notably Debussy, Bartók and Ives, later Cage and Messiaen, are undoubtedly of significance, it is to Stravinsky that the most far-reaching innovations have consistently been credited. In works from *Petrushka* to the last serial pieces, it was Stravinsky's resolute challenge to received rhythmic and metric conventions, his bold embrace of rhythmic practices from folk, popular and non-Western musics, and his construction of new kinds of non-linear musical temporality that have had so profound an impact on those that came after. One work in particular, *The Rite of Spring*, has cast a long shadow over the century; there is scarcely a single composer who has not come under the influence of *The Rite* to some degree or other. As Taruskin puts it, 'Stravinsky's rhythmic innovations in *The Rite*, hardly less conspicuous than his harmonic ones, are, if anything, even more of a twentieth-century legend. . . . The force of rhythm is the elemental force, the "Scythian" force of *stikhiya* ['elemental dynamism'] that Stravinsky was not alone in attempting to unleash. Not alone in the attempt, but all alone in the realization: for the better part of a century now his ballet has been hypnotizing, inspiring, and compelling all who have come into contact with it.'[1] In this sense, a history of rhythmic practices in twentieth-century music *is* a history of the legacy of *The Rite*. If nothing else, *The Rite* indicated – in a way that had not been true since medieval times – that, in Boulez's words, rhythm could act as a 'principal structural agent'.[2] It certainly seems probable that, without Stravinsky's complete reinterpretation of the role of rhythm in music, the advances of much music since World War 2 would simply not have been possible. This chapter will explore just some of the imaginative structural outcomes of Stravinsky's extraordinary innovations.

Stravinsky's own limited discussion of rhythm in *Poetics of Music* is notoriously simplistic, a paltry echo of the sophistication of the music itself, though it is useful insofar as it initiates a discussion of definitions and distinctions. Music, he argues, being based on 'temporal succession' and requiring 'alertness of memory', is a 'chronologic' art in the sense that painting is a spatial art: 'Music presupposes before all else a certain organization in time.'[3] Rhythm, according to Stravinsky, requires metre in order to be understood: metre provides the regular framework against which rhythm is understood to operate. Metre is 'a purely material element, through which rhythm, a purely formal element, is realized.' More significant are Stravinsky's views on musical time (views, it is generally agreed, that were essentially those of his close friend, Pierre Souvtchinsky[4]), what he calls the '*chronos* of music'. Paralleling the distinction between metre and rhythm, he defines a distinction between two kinds of music: 'one which evolves parallel to the process of ontological time [real or clock time]', the other which 'runs ahead of, or counter to, this process', that is, 'psychological time'. 'All music, whether it submits to the normal flow of time, or whether it disassociates itself therefrom, establishes a particular relationship, a sort of counterpoint between the passing of time, the music's own duration, and the material and technical means through which the music is made manifest.' Stravinsky goes on to associate music based on ontological time with the principle of similarity, 'inducing in the listener a feeling of euphoria and, so to speak, of "dynamic calm"', while music which adheres to psychological time proceeds by contrast, being unstable and therefore 'particularly adaptable to the translation of the composer's emotive impulses'. Stravinsky, not surprisingly, aligns himself with the former.

The problems with these definitions should be clear enough. Apart from anything else, Stravinsky begs the question of what he actually means by time – indeed, he tries to have it both ways by arguing that time is an objective, external phenomenon which 'flows' and against which music is required to be evaluated, and also that time is something that is actually articulated by music. Souvtchinsky was certainly familiar with the writings of Henri Bergson, and it is Bergson's distinction between 'temps espace' and 'temps durée' which strongly informs this chapter of the *Poetics*, though the latter is seemingly devoid of the richness of the context of Bergson's argument.[5] 'La durée réelle' (real, subjective time) for Bergson is time as it is actually experienced; clock time is an abstract concept, a mathematical contingency (just as Kant understood time and space as necessary *a priori* concepts, as argued in the *Critique of Pure Reason*, modes necessary in order to perceive the world, not physical facts), and has little to do with temporal (musical) experience. For Stravinsky to claim that his 'musical time' is identical with 'clock time' is a nonsense because musical perception depends on memory; clock time is purely sequential and is therefore independent of memory. Moreover, for Stravinsky to argue thus was to play into the hands of some of his fiercest critics, Adorno chief among them:

Stravinsky and his school bring about the end of musical Bergsonianism. They play off *le temps espace* against *le temps durée*. The procedural method originally inspired by irrationalistic philosophy establishes itself as the advocate of rationalization in the sense of that which can be measured and counted without memory.[6]

For Adorno, the eradication of memory means in effect the liquidation of the subject. But is this really what Stravinsky achieves in *The Rite*? For Taruskin (see also below), though this is a music 'not of process but of state', it nonetheless derives momentum and coherence (and is therefore dependent on memory) from the very exploitation of 'this interplay of utter fixity and its opposite, utter mutability'.[7] Stravinsky creates a new kind of 'musical time', a 'virtual' time ('la durée réelle') which can never be confused with clock time. Only in those relatively rare passages where there seems to be little else occurring than regular repetition of an unchanging object, is the effect for the listener the suspension of memory because time appears to 'stand still'. The effect is of a non-directed 'timelessness' – that is, something quite the opposite of a sense of the mere measurement or division of an objectively perceived temporal flow. And it is important to remind ourselves that Stravinsky was not alone in attempting to articulate new kinds of time; indeed, it could well be argued that time ('durée') became *the* defining issue of early modernism, whether in the 'dream' time(lessness) of the Freudian id in *Pelléas et Mélisande*, *Erwartung* and *Salome*, or the 'ritual' time(lessness) of the Jungian collective unconscious in *The Rite* and *Les Noces*.

Such thinking about time and rhythm in music was not without precedent. In particular, the innovations of the early-fourteenth-century ars nova, as revealed in Philippe de Vitry's treatise of the same name, demonstrated that rhythm was a primary concern. The medieval historian, Richard Hoppin, summarises:

> the notational system established by Philippe de Vitry did indeed constitute a new art of rhythmic organization. Other elements also contributed in some degree to the novelty of fourteenth-century music, but the real break with the music of the ars antiqua came in the field of rhythm. Never before had composers had at their disposal a notation that gave them such freedom of rhythmic expression in a variety of different meters. . . . In large part we may say that concern for rhythmic organization is the chief characteristic of French music in the fourteenth century. That concern manifests itself both in the development of large-scale forms based on rhythmic repetitions and in the creation of rhythmic complexities unequalled in any period before the twentieth century.[8]

Ex. 3.1 Stravinsky, *Petrushka*, first tableau (figs. 30–2 and 34–6; piano duet version, rev. 1947)

(a)

(b)

Substitute 'Stravinsky' for 'de Vitry' and it reads almost as accurately. Such parallels between a medieval aesthetic and Stravinsky's modernist aesthetic not only reinforce aspects of Stravinsky's 'primitivism' but also more generally coincide with the views of certain cultural theorists who have observed a fascination with the Middle Ages in modern times. Umberto Eco, for one, has noted that 'a number of "medieval" preoccupations appear . . . to have a contemporary resonance, [such] that our [(post)modern] age may in a number of significant respects be described as "neomedieval"'.[9] Stravinsky's 'new art of rhythmic organisation', his 'freedom of rhythmic expression', is just one aspect of this aesthetic, one distinctive facet of his modernism.

Example 3.1 shows two key moments in early musical modernism and in the reassessment of rhythm in twentieth-century music. Taruskin describes *Petrushka*'s rhythmic originality as 'momentous':

> for it marks the first time that folklorism and modernism coincided in Stravinsky's music. The quality of the rhythmic periods here – static, additive, nondeveloping ostinati of variable length that continually break off and

start up again – is unprecedented in Russian art music. It is instantly recognizable as Stravinskian: it is, in fact, one of his trademarks, and one of his most influential innovations.[10]

These rhythmic innovations were developed and most clearly and uncompromisingly presented in *The Rite of Spring* and in principle changed little throughout Stravinsky's subsequent career. Despite the fact that these innovations have, as Taruskin commented, taken on a mythical status in the twentieth century ('the stamp of his originality', as van den Toorn puts it, 'his unique contribution, his little "niche" in Music History'[11]), Stravinsky's rhythmic language has not been widely discussed in any sustained way.[12] Nonetheless, in terms of what constitutes the influential surface features of his rhythmic practice, there is broad agreement, even if the way in which those features are interpreted differs widely – from the devoted admiration of Andriessen and Schönberger to the harsh critique of Adorno. It will be useful briefly to catalogue these features here if for no other reason than that of their ubiquity in the music of our century – they are one of the most obvious outward signs of Stravinsky's legacy. The reasons for the attractiveness of Stravinsky's techniques are as many as the individual pieces that employ them, but in general terms it is possible to say that, in the early modern period, they offered a challenge to the common-practice hegemony in the rhythmic domain in the same way that the abandonment of tonality had done for harmonic practices. More than this, by focusing on repetition/recurrence as a means of challenging the dominant aesthetic of wholeness, connectedness, unity, continuity and directedness, they offered the possibility of an alternative, modernist aesthetic of fragmentation, discontinuity and opposition in a non-narrative, non-developmental music which nonetheless remained consistent and coherent. 'Development' was replaced by 'recurrence'; 'becoming' was replaced by 'being'. Taruskin sums up:

> he made determined efforts . . . to scotch the symphonic, the developmental, the transitional, wherever they might chance to raise their heads. . . . Henceforth Stravinsky's music would no longer meet the normative criteria traditionally deemed essential to coherent musical discourse. There would be no harmonic *progression*, no thematic or motivic *development*, no smoothly executed *transitions*. His would be a music not of process but of state, deriving its coherence and its momentum from the calculated interplay of 'immobile' uniformities and abrupt discontinuities.[13]

Taruskin and van den Toorn agree on the two basic aspects of the rhythmic language of *The Rite*. The first is what Taruskin calls the 'immobile' ostinato and corresponds to van den Toorn's 'rhythmic Type II' which is characterised by foreground metric regularity. The most obvious example of a dominating, undifferentiated, 'hypnotic' beat is to be found in the 'Action rituelle des ancêtres', though such regularity can also be disguised by syncopation and other accents, as in the treatment of the famous *Rite* chords in the 'Danse des adolescentes'. One does not have to look far to find countless examples of the use (and abuse) of such repetition in music from the time of *The Rite* to the present day. Immobility also allows for the possibility of the 'superimposition of two or more motives that repeat according to periods, cycles, or spans that are not shared but vary independently of, or separately from, one another' (van den Toorn) – as in the 'Cortège du sage'. Such layering, or 'tiling', to use Boulez's term, suggests rich structural possibilities and is discussed at length below. The second basic aspect of the rhythmic language of *The Rite* is described by Taruskin as of an '"invincible and elemental" kind, and it was truly an innovation – for Western art music, that is. . . . This is the rhythm of irregularly spaced downbeats, requiring a correspondingly variable metric barring in the notation',[14] and resulting in variable metric stress. This corresponds to van den Toorn's 'rhythmic Type I', which is characterised by 'foreground metric irregularity; an irregular or shifting meter' and which he further associates with the definition of block structures. Once again, aside from substantive exploration of new metric structures, examples can be found everywhere of music that contents itself with the imitation of Stravinsky's irregular groupings and continually changing time signatures (from the alternating 4/4s and 3/8s of the 'Dance' from Orff's *Carmina burana* to countless Hollywood soundtracks).

For Taruskin, the coming together of these two rhythmic categories is one of the most fascinating features of the music of *The Rite*, and beyond. This results in further examples of layering, where one independent regular stratum can be pitted against another irregular one. Taruskin's example (from figs. 114–15 of the 'Glorification de l'élue') shows a regular four-quaver ostinato in lower strings and a pattern of groups of five and six crotchets in the violins where the ostinato 'shifts in and out of phase with the variable downbeats of the main tune'.[15] His choice of vocabulary is telling, given the use to which regular repetitions and shifting metres have been put in much process music since the late 1960s. Such a technique culminates in the 'Danse sacrale', which Taruskin not only regards as the apogee of 'hypostatisation' (confirming Adorno's reading but not his interpretation), that is where each moment seems to stand for itself only, but also the most radical example of the variable downbeat technique where 'the shifting meters are coordinated on the "subtactile" level – that is, by an equalized value that is less than the duration of a felt beat'.

Put another way, this is a music with a perceived pulse which provides rhythmic continuity but where the metre is in a constant state of flux. The violence of *The Rite* is in part the result of this severe and apparently incoherent disruption of regular periodicity (despite van den Toorn's attempt to show in the 'Danse sacrale' a 'concealed 2/8 periodicity' as well as higher level groupings in threes[16]).

Closer examination of the rhythmic detail shows how these two principles are brought into play, the techniques being familiar from so much later music. Rhythmic ostinatos, used singly and resulting in motoric patterns (the placing in the foreground of 'pure' pulse, formerly a background feature), or variously superimposed to produce something more complex, polyrhythmic/polymetric and continuously varied; regular repetitions varied by means of augmenting or diminishing aspects of the rhythmic motifs themselves, or the durational intervals between repetitions; use of accentuation and syncopation; and, as Boulez demonstrated in his analysis of *The Rite*, varied ways of opposing and balancing rational and irrational, symmetrical and asymmetrical, fixed and changeable patterns. Messiaen went further and identified less obviously foreground rhythmic features of *The Rite*, such as the so-called 'non-retrogradable' rhythms, additive rhythms and simultaneous process of augmentation, diminution and stasis in the 'personnages rythmiques', which were not only fully exploited in his own music but had a profound influence on his pupils, including Boulez. Taruskin shows us how, for Stravinsky, these practices originated in his Russian musical heritage. But it is interesting, too, how so many of these foreground features coincide with the rhythmic innovations of another new music of our century: American jazz. The impact that jazz (whose 'primitive' origins in many ways overlapped with the 'primitive' sources of Stravinsky's modernism) had on European music of the 1920s would not have been so strong were it not for the fact that so many of its radical aspects – syncopations, irregular patterns, the hypostatisation of particular harmonies and sounds – had already been explored by Stravinsky, as well as Bartók, and their contemporaries. Of course, such features became the *lingua franca* of much American music from Gershwin to Bernstein.[17] And, conversely, the decidedly Stravinskian character of much of the music of, say, Duke Ellington is particularly striking, a fact not lost on jazz critics of the time:

> It [Ellington's Jungle Band version of 'Dreamy Blues'] is a poignantly restrained and nostalgic piece with glorious melodic endowment and scoring that even Ravel and Stravinsky might envy. Indeed it actually recalls those hushed muted trumpets of the beginning of the second part of the 'Rite of Spring'.[18]

Thus, though Stravinsky was not the sole promoter of the revolution against the received understanding of rhythm in the early years of the twentieth century, and though in general there was a growing awareness of musics outside the Western tradition as important sources for the revitalisation of the rhythmic domain, Stravinsky's influence has nonetheless been profound, primarily because in *The Rite of Spring* he demonstrated definitively that rhythm could be the principal structural agent. He produced a music about which it is frequently true to say that the conventional, tonal dependence of rhythm on pitch had been completely reversed. The consequences of Stravinsky's 'discovery' were enormous. His innovative practices have become the rhythmic paradigm for the century, and *The Rite of Spring* their exemplar.

Layers

Chapter 2 examined in detail musical forms made from the juxtaposition of successive, sharply differentiated blocks of musical material – in Cone's terminology, the process of stratification. The novelty and consistency of this means of form-building in Stravinsky was explored, as was its significant impact on the formal thinking of his contemporaries and successors. Given that the character of any particular musical block conveys 'little internal sense of harmonic progress, such progress being possible only *between* blocks', Pieter van den Toorn argues that this is a fundamentally rhythmic concept, his 'rhythmic Type I'. But, as we have just seen, this is not the only kind of juxtaposition to be found in Stravinsky. The *simultaneous* juxtaposition of differentiated musical materials in musical layers or strata is also a highly characteristic device, corresponding with van den Toorn's contrasting 'rhythmic Type II'. His favoured instance of this technique – 'one of the lengthiest of its kind in Stravinsky' – is the 'Danse de la terre', which forms the climax of Part I of *The Rite*. Boulez's less prosaic term for this process is '"tiling" – the layering of developments one on top of another', and *his* favoured instance is the Introduction to Part 1 of *The Rite* 'with its remarkable aggregations of individual developments' resulting in a 'complex structure'.[19] The other significant writer to draw attention to such layering, from a somewhat different perspective, is Messiaen. His identification of 'personnages rythmiques' in Stravinsky (and in his own music) is necessary in a context where the individual constituents of layered sections need to be clearly differentiated. What unites the readings of, among others, van den Toorn, Boulez and Messiaen is their agreement that these structures are primarily rhythmic in concept.

Just as it is possible to look to pre-tonal and folk musics in order to discover forerunners or prototypes for aspects of Stravinsky's block structures (especially verse–refrain forms), and just as we saw that a concern for rhythmic organisation was preeminent in certain kinds of medieval music, so precedents for the simultaneous layering of ideas can be found in the successive compositional approach adopted in some of the first polyphonic works (from the earliest motets of Leonin and Perotin to the sophistication of Machaut's *Messe de Notre Dame*). We have already commented that this confirms an aspect of the 'primitivism' of Stravinsky's approach. But for early twentieth-century composers there were also other more immediate models for this renewal of structural interest in rhythm. In particular, the Paris Exposition of 1889 has frequently been cited as a seminal event in the emergence of modernism and, as is well known, Debussy's discovery there of the Javanese gamelan had a profound and lasting effect on his musical language, as well as wider consequences for the development of musical modernism. Though, as Glenn Watkins has colourfully demonstrated, such 'orientalism' (linked, in many senses, to an early modern concern with the 'primitive') was widespread in later nineteenth- and early twentieth-century Western European art, its particular significance for Debussy and Stravinsky was far reaching. In Debussy's case, aspects of the rhythmic layering of the gamelan in a static harmonic context (with the lowest gongs playing at the slowest tempo and the highest metallophones at the fastest) have clearly had an impact on his structures. Especially at moments of greatest tonal ambiguity and harmonic stasis he will construct rhythmically layered textures in order to maintain the music's momentum, creating a sense of motion within stasis. Combined with his imaginative orchestration, the result is a music which seems to shimmer in a manner equivalent to that of the gamelan. It should hardly surprise us that, in the face of the collapse of tonality with its guarantee of directedness, early twentieth-century composers should look to the rhythmic parameter in order to find new means of investing their apparently harmonically static and non-developmental music with a renewed dynamism.

Two brief examples from Debussy will provide useful comparisons with Stravinsky. The first, a page selected almost at random from 'Sirènes', one of the orchestral *Nocturnes* (1897–9), shows the shift from one static harmonic block to the next, marked by a change in orchestral texture (Ex. 3.2a). What is immediately clear is how each block is made up of a number of superimposed ostinatos, each with its own characterising durational unit, ranging from dotted crotchets to sextuplet semiquavers. This is just one example among many of what Derrick Puffett has dubbed 'Debussy's ostinato machine', which, he argues, left its technical 'imprint' on so many

Ex. 3.2a Debussy, 'Sirènes' from *Nocturnes* (figs. 2^{+10}–3^{+1})

Ex. 3.2b Debussy, 'Voiles', *Préludes*, Book 1 (opening)

subsequent composers, including Stravinsky, and also Ravel, Messiaen and Birtwistle.[20] The second example is from the first book of piano *Préludes*: an excerpt from 'Voiles', whose outer sections, built from one unchanging form of the whole-tone scale, is entirely static harmonically (Ex. 3.2b). Yet the music as a whole does express a certain dynamism by means of the layering, both rhythmically and intervallically, of the piano texture. Once again, the sound of the gamelan is never far away: the layers above a slow-moving, low pedal B♭ (gong) move progressively faster. In both these examples, there is a high degree of coherence to the music – even though there is a productive tension between its static and dynamic component parts – in part because the differences (other than durational ones) between the layers are not significantly marked. In other words, there is a loosening of the strict ties between 'contrapuntal' layers but not a complete dissociation; connectedness, on the whole, still outweighs disconnectedness.

This is probably not true of the most extreme examples of layering in the music of Charles Ives. The superimposition of preexistent and invented materials in such works as *Central Park in the Dark* (1906) results in extraordinarily polyrhythmic structures but ones in which, unlike in the situation in Debussy, it is virtually impossible to identify each separate component – what Cage described as 'the mud of Ives'.[21] Ives's collages are just that: disconnected collections of unrelated materials. What 'unites' these found materials is their common expressive or programmatic context, and rhythmic differentiation is only one aspect of the process of layering. Elsewhere, such as in the piano sonatas or the Fourth Symphony (1909–16), Ives experimented in a more sophisticated way with polyrhythms, which certainly had an important bearing on the thinking of later American composers, but in general his playful imagination far exceeded his technical musical achievements. Ives's ideas were both in tune with and significantly different from contemporary developments in Europe. It is often thought that this was because he worked in complete isolation from European developments, but Elliott Carter has argued that Ives 'was far from being the recluse that some have pictured'. As can be seen from *Essays Before a Sonata*, he clearly knew and had strong views on the music of Brahms, Wagner, Strauss and Debussy. And as Carter comments:

> In all of this, Ives, like every composer, is seeking his place and his own style in relationship to other music as he hears and experiences it, and this is as true of his discussions of old music as it is of his criticism of Stravinsky's *Firebird*, which he heard in 1919 or 1920 when he wrote, 'I thought it was morbid and monotonous; the idea of a phrase, usually a small one, was good enough, and interesting in itself, but he kept it going over and over and it got tiresome.'[22]

The reason that Ives exerted little influence, even in America, in comparison with Stravinsky, was in part because his music was little known and rarely performed until much later in the century. Any influence Ives's music had took place in the context of the sounds of Debussy and Stravinsky, which were already known. In 'The case of Mr. Ives' (1939), Carter writes:

> I came to know the [Concord] sonata in the years when Stravinsky first scandalized America in person . . . A keen time with lots of enthusiasm and lots of performances of new music to which I sometimes went with Ives himself . . . new music was new and very 'modern' and Ives was much

interested. Often he would poke fun, sit down at the piano to play from memory bits of a piece just heard, like *Daphnis and Chloé* or the *Sacre*, taking off the Ravel major seventh chords and obvious rhythms, or the primitive repeated dissonances of Stravinsky, and calling them too easy. 'Anybody can do that' he would exclaim . . .[23]

The Rite of Spring

But could they? Perhaps the clearest example of layering in Stravinsky is to be found in the first movement of the *Three Pieces for String Quartet*, which was discussed in Chapter 2. There we saw how each voice is individually characterised in terms of pitch, rhythm and 'dramatic function' and how, despite a number of possible 'unifying' schemes, each component maintains its distinctiveness and remains in opposition to the others throughout. (Mis)appropriation of Messiaen's designation of 'personnages rythmiques' would seem to be highly apt here because, though each idea is clearly defined in terms of pitch (no more than four contiguous pitch classes in each case), it is the rhythmic working of those pitches into distinctive ostinatos which moulds their individual identities. Furthermore, as van den Toorn has pointed out,[24] the subtle organisation of each 'personnage' into periods of differing lengths (violin 1, twenty-three beats; viola and cello, seven beats; irregular punctuations from violin 2) makes for a structure which seems to be built from immediately audible and regular repetitions and yet which, as a whole, never repeats itself exactly. In essence it is an extremely simple idea and it stands as a paradigm by which other layered structures might be evaluated; in practice, it has proved to be a highly sophisticated and influential means of musical structuring.

The 'tiling' evident in the Introduction to *The Rite of Spring* is discussed at some length by Boulez. His summary of the importance of this music is insightful:

> Over and above its extraordinary diversity of rhythmic variation; over and above its quite exceptional use of oppositions between rational and irrational values and its tight imbrication of long and very short values . . . over and above the perfection of the rhythmic structures by which it is organised . . . I believe that the Introduction of *The Rite* presents an architectural phenomenon of the greatest interest: a kind of development by progressive overlapping which is thus very difficult, not to say impossible, to analyse on a series of more or less contrasted planes as with all the other developments in *The Rite*.[25]

Clearly, given the length and scoring of this Introduction, and the fact that it acts as a prelude to a still larger structure, the simplicity of the

Ex. 3.3 Stravinsky, *The Rite of Spring*, 'Introduction' (fig. 6)

organisation of the *Three Pieces* would be inappropriate and incapable of sustaining itself. And the difference between, say, a layered movement by Ives and Stravinsky's Introduction lies not only in the way in which each individual element or motif is handled (indeed, 'developed' is the term Boulez employs) but the control of the manner in which they combine to create a seemingly dynamic overall structure.

Boulez distinguishes four principal phases: an introductory first phase (from the beginning to fig. 3^{+1}); a more involved second phase (fig. 3^{+2} to fig. 9), itself made up of a number of smaller distinct subdivisions; a third phase which introduces another new motif (oboe 1, fig. 9) followed by a climactic superimposition of principal motifs (figs. 10–12); and a simplified reprise of the opening phase, preparing the way for 'Les augures printaniers'. By far his most engaging idea about the overall structure of the Introduction is his account of how principal motifs generate secondary motifs which, 'once presented, can assume their own periodicity, detach themselves from the principal motif which gave them birth, and form the link between two subdivisions of a structure'.[26] What Boulez here seems to be suggesting is that a dynamic structure is built from seemingly static, repetitious motifs, that the overall structure, far from being (as in Ives) moulded independently of its musical materials, results directly from the way in which those materials are handled. He gives the example of the cor anglais principal motif (marked '*en dehors*' – a kind of *Hauptstimme*) – itself a variant of the principal cor anglais motif first heard at fig. 2 – and the alto flute counterpointing motif (*Nebenstimme*), which appear together at fig. 6 (the third subdivision of the second phase). The two motifs are clearly related: they share an (0,2,5) set (3-7) for the opening three main pitches, the third of which is decorated with a grace note, as if the faster (triplet quaver) secondary motif were troping the principal motif; they also demonstrate a kind of rhythmic voice exchange whereby the movement from a pair of quavers to triplet quavers in the principal voice is reversed by the secondary voice (see Ex. 3.3). At fig. 7^{+3} and fig. 7^{+5-6}, the two motifs again occur together but with the secondary motif

transposed down an octave. (Here is another instance of block organisation where these bars interrupt and alternate with the mechanical repetitions of motifs that began at fig. 7, showing once again that processes of
successive stratification and simultaneous layering often coexist. An interesting point here in relation to the larger-scale organisation of the work is
that the total harmonic content of the bars at fig. 7^{+3} and fig. 7^{+5-6} is set 9-7
(0,1,2,3,4,5,7,8,10), the complement of 3-7 which, as we have seen, is
shared by the two motifs' openings, and which will become the principal
three-note motif of 'Les augures printaniers'.) At fig. 8 (fifth subdivision of
the second phase) the secondary motif achieves independence from the
principal motif, assuming 'extreme importance by virtue of its abundant
rhythmic variation',[27] and in this form it is heard to accompany both the
'third principal motif' on the oboe at fig. 9 and a related new motif on the
piccolo clarinet at fig. 9^{+2}, signalling the start of the third phase. In other
words, the subsidiary motif has served to connect two principal motifs:
'Having accomplished its transitional role between the second and third
phases, the motif vanishes from the second subdivision of phase 3.' Boulez
sums up:

> beneath a structure articulated on specific planes by principal motifs, sec-
> ondary motifs are inserted so as to soften and shade off that structure by a
> constant process of renewal and by their diverse ways of combining with the
> principal motifs . . . [a] dual plane of development.[28]

One of the most extraordinary passages of the entire work is that which
occurs at the end of the third phase, figs. 10–12. It forms the tumultuous
climax to the Introduction by means of the gradual superimposition of
nearly all the main and subsidiary motifs heard up to this point. These
motifs (variously defined) are shown in Table 3.1, arranged into two
general groups – though the boundaries between these two boldly defined
groups are not strict, that is, certain motifs share characteristics of both.
Group A, what might loosely be termed the 'background' group, is
characterised by regular rhythmic ostinatos and static harmony. At the
heart of group A is motif i, a regular and unchanging pulsating pizzicato B
on a solo double bass, later joined by a solo cello. This provides the pulse
frame (to borrow from the title of a Birtwistle work[29]) for the entire
passage, though it is virtually swamped by the other voices clamouring to
be heard by the end of the passage (fig. 12). The other motifs from group A
are layered above it, proliferating out from it, so that motif ii, for instance,
later joined by motif iii, fleshes out the harmonic context of motif i, while
motif iv elaborates rhythmically on motif i and harmonically (the addition
of the G♮) on motif ii. Taken together they form a multi-layered expression

Table 3.1 Motifs in *The Rite of Spring*, 'Introduction' (figs. 10–12)

of a regular musical background. There is a slight sense of progression in that, particularly through the addition of extra instruments to these layers, these background processes are accumulatively reinforced as the passage proceeds (for example, bassoons and horns join motif iv at fig. 11, motif iii does not appear in viola and alto flute until fig. 11^{+1}).

I have notionally collected three other motifs together in group A because, though they might equally well belong in group B, characteristics of A are, arguably, dominant. Motif v consists of just two alternating pitch classes, G♯ and D♯, and for this reason, along with the fact that it shares a regular triplet subdivision of the metre, I have grouped it with the other harmonically limited elements; it has a subsidiary, 'background' character. Nonetheless, both gesturally and because of the less regular nature of its repetitions, it might be understood to belong as a subsidiary layer in group

B. Alternatively, we might choose to interpret the motif as forging a connection between the principal characteristics of both groups. Motif vi also seems to effect a link between the two groups: it begins with a pair of triplet E♮s which clearly belongs with motif iv but then continues with a demi-semiquaver gesture more typical of group B, even though harmonically it remains within the ambit of motif iv. Eventually this second segment becomes detached from the opening triplet, so aligning itself more closely with group B. Motif vii really belongs to neither group but forms a separate punctuating strand rather like violin 2 in the first of the *Three Pieces for String Quartet*. Its falling chromatic segment, 'harmonised' with Debussy-like parallel seventh chords (forming, in fact, a sequence of octatonic tetrachords), belongs with neither group, though gesturally it might once again be understood to belong more to group B than to group A. However, like motif vi, I have grouped it with A because, as the passage proceeds, it comes to be associated with the trilled G♯ (motif iii).

Group B, the 'foreground' group, contains most of the principal melodic motifs of the Introduction and is characterised by rhythmic flexibility as well as, in general, a different shared harmonic context from group A. It can be seen from Table 3.1 that all the motifs begin with an F–B♭ rising fourth, with the exception of motif xi which reverses this to produce a falling B♭–F dyad (though note that the motif's first appearance at fig. 9 *does* begin on F, falling a fourth to C); motif viii, which begins on F but continues chromatically; motif ix-a, which is in any case a continuation of an aspect of motif ix; and motif ix-a′, which consists entirely of string harmonics (it is really only a colouration of motif ix-a, with which it is always associated). Motif viii belongs in group B because it is undeniably foreground material (marked '*très en dehors*'), its falling chromatic character providing a continuity with the supporting motifs from the beginning of the work (something noticeably absent from the reprise of the opening bassoon solo at fig. 12). The remaining motifs are all closely related harmonically, articulating forms of the diatonic subsets 5-23 (0,2,3,5,7) and 4-23 (0,2,5,7); more specifically, there is a high level of pitch-class invariance between the motifs because they all draw on a single diatonic set (C,D,E♭,F,G,A♭,B♭). For these reasons alone it should be clear that each motif requires a distinct rhythmic (as well as timbral and registral) identity in order to differentiate itself within a dense texture. Put another way, each motif needs to become a distinctive 'personnage rythmique'. This is achieved variously and subtly by, for example, the lengthening of important notes within a motif through the addition of a dot or tie (motifs viii, ix and xi), or a shortening of note values as the motif proceeds, often involving irrational subdivisions of the quaver beat; by contrast, and characteristic of group A, other motifs maintain regular durations throughout (as, for instance, in the distinctive septuplet demi-semiquavers of motif vii). Boulez offers a detailed account of 'the extraordinary rhythmic diversity deployed by Stravinsky throughout this Introduction',[30] and in particular of how rhythmic development is achieved by means of the rational and irrational subdivisions of the basic durational unit, varied repetitions, symmetries and contrasts. Such complexity is unusual even in Stravinsky; as Boulez observes: 'this kind of experiment is exceptional . . . [S]uch refinement in periodic symmetry and asymmetry, and such constant variation of rhythm through the use of irrational values, are almost never found again in his work.'[31]

Each of the motifs identified in Table 3.1 is layered (or tiled) one on top of the other. The layers are gradually introduced from fig. 10, and from fig. 11 the frequency of repetition of the motifs from group B increases progressively to build to a savage climax at fig. 12. At the point where the texture could hardly get any more dense (and is therefore unable to sustain its intensity further), the music is violently broken off, each motif stopping abruptly at whatever point in its cycle of repetitions it finds itself. All that is left is the solo bassoon as at the beginning and in the original slower tempo (Ex. 3.4).

It should be clear from this account that the rhythmic organisation of this passage is its 'principal structural agent'. Though it is built essentially from repetitions in the context of group A's incessant ostinatos, both the variation in the rhythmic identities of the group B motifs and the change in the rate of their repetition ensure that a far from static structure is the result. It is this balancing of the essentially circular, non-directed repetitions of group A and the more 'developmental', directed nature of the motifs of group B that gives this music its extraordinary power (and we shall see how, in very different contexts, this balancing of the circular and the linear remained a fertile constructive principle for Stravinsky even in his neoclassical works – the essence of his modernity). The balancing is brought about in part because the music is *not* a collage of unrelated fragments. We have already seen how all motifs in group B are harmonically related: by retaining a background harmonic commonality while severing strong vertical foreground connections (through their rhythmic individuality), the superimposition of layers produces the effect of a shifting kaleidoscope of hues – the breakdown of elements of connectedness does not necessarily result in disconnectedness. Similarly, the wide variety of foreground durational subdivisions employed in the layers is contained by the background regularity of the double bass's 'pulse frame', without

Ex. 3.4 *The Rite of Spring* (figs. 11⁺²–12)

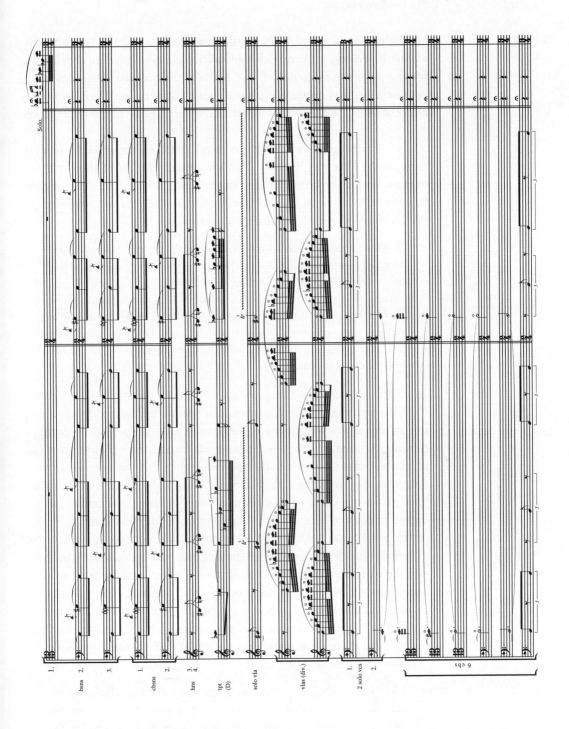

ever being subsumed by it. The music surrenders its singularity (unity) for a nonetheless coherent and rich multiplicity. Herein lies one of the reasons for the immense influence of *The Rite of Spring* on the development of twentieth-century music, and it is also what distinguishes *The Rite* from so many of its two-dimensional imitations. By no means 'anybody' could do it.

Even Adorno admitted that 'Stravinsky's imitators remained far behind their model'.[32] In the light of the above interpretation of the rhythmic organisation of the layering of the Introduction, it might be instructive at this point to look at Adorno's critique of *The Rite* as presented in *Philosophy of Modern Music*. Adorno states:

> In all cases, the differentiations derived from the motivic model [i.e. the most 'elementary principle of rhythmic variation' – the redistribution of accents on repetition] appear to be the result of a simple game of chance. In this perspective, the melodic cells seem to be under a spell: they are not con-densed, rather they are thwarted in their development. For this reason, even in those works of Stravinsky which are most radical from the standpoint of surface sound, there is a contradiction between the moderated horizontal and the insolent vertical.[33]

To answer the last point first, we have just seen that there is indeed an opposition in the Introduction between the horizontal and the vertical, but rather than viewing this as a problem (because it does not conform to Adorno's Schoenbergian twelve-note model, where the horizontal and the vertical collapse into one another), I have argued that this generates a pro-ductive tension which is replicated across various dimensions of the struc-ture. As for the 'game of chance', it is true that Stravinsky relinquishes a degree of control over vertical correspondences of motifs, but this does not mean that the contribution of each individual motif to the structure of the whole is not carefully planned. Boulez confirms the view explored here that the structure results from the 'development' of motifs rather than its being imposed from the outside on 'passive' material. The subject may become fragmented as a consequence, but it is certainly not destroyed as implied by Adorno (indeed, a multiple expression of subjectivity might in reality be far more appropriate than the unitary one pursued by Adorno).

Adorno further asserts:

> Rhythmic structure is . . . blatantly prominent, but this is achieved at the expense of all other aspects of rhythmic organization. Not only is any sub-jectively expressive flexibility of the beat absent – which is always rigidly carried out in Stravinsky from *Sacre* on – but furthermore all rhythmic rela-tions associated with the construction, and the internal compositional

organization – the 'rhythm of the whole' – are absent as well. Rhythm is underscored, but split off from musical content. This results not in more, but rather in less rhythm than in compositions in which there is no fetish made of rhythm; in other words, there are only fluctuations of something always constant and totally static – a stepping aside – in which the irregularity of recurrence replaces the new.[34]

There are, of course, many instances in which it is possible to confirm Adorno's reading; where there is, for instance, a regular 'inflexible' beat, it is for good reason (the absolutely necessary 'ritual' metric regularity, for example – with the exception of the passage between figs. 135–8 – of the 'Action rituelle des ancêtres', resulting once again in an extraordinarily richly layered music in which the role of rhythm is primary in differentiating these strata). Nonetheless, these features are as often absent as present. We saw above how the inflexibility of group A was complemented by the flexibility (Boulez's balancing of rational and irrational) of group B material. The music is not static, decorated by local fluctuations feigning dynamism; it derives a very real dynamism from, *inter alia*, the manipulation of its rhythmic cells. The careful layering of materials, itself a rhythmic consideration, shows a deep understanding of the consequences for the 'rhythm of the whole'. It is true that Stravinsky's motives do not in themselves develop into something new (that sense of 'becoming' characteristic of the developing variation) but nor do they remain entirely static – Boulez's argument about the way principal themes spawn subsidiary themes which themselves effect transitions to new themes is a compelling one and certainly flies in the face of an argument that says the music is simply going round in circles. Indeed, it is possible to argue that the alleged fetishisation of rhythm in *The Rite* was brought about not primarily by Stravinsky but by subsequent reinterpretations and misinterpretations of his work. Of course *The Rite*'s handling of rhythm is new and challenging, and is often placed in the foreground, but this is not to the exclusion of harmonic considerations, as Allen Forte has exhaustively shown.[35] If anything, the principal innovation of *The Rite of Spring* is the way in which rhythm and harmony work to structure the music as equal partners – something which could not, despite Adorno's best efforts, be said to be true of many of Schoenberg's twelve-note works.

Taruskin's account of the innovations of *The Rite* can be seen simply and directly to rebut Adorno. Whereas Adorno tried to evaluate Stravinsky in an Austro-German context, for Taruskin the enormity of Stravinsky's achievement and, indeed, the very root of his modernity are a result of his willingness (unlike Tchaikovsky, for example, who constantly battled with his aspiration to 'real mastery of German techniques') to be an out-and-out Russian composer:

> From now on [after *The Rite*] he would revel in the *drobnost'* ['the quality of being a sum-of-parts'] that, according to Musorgsky, came naturally to a Russian composer, and he would turn it into a high esthetic principle. Guided by this principle, he made determined efforts – efforts that may be traced in the *Rite* sketchbook in engrossing detail – to scotch the symphonic, the developmental, the transitional, wherever they might chance to raise their heads.[36]

Even the kinds of 'motivic developments' discussed above are not, in this light, to be read as vestiges of a Teutonic thinking but rather as elements of a new kind of continuity within the context of a discontinuous musical structure. They work alongside the basic formal procedures identified by Taruskin, gloriously exemplified by the *Rite*'s Introduction: 'extension through repetition, alternation, and – above all – sheer inertial accumulation.'[37]

After *The Rite*

I have often alluded, both here and in Chapter 2, to the many imitators of *The Rite* who took up often superficial aspects of its innovatory language, especially with regard to rhythm, and decontextualised them to produce music where it *is* true to say (with Adorno) that rhythm had been fetishised. Taruskin similarly writes of the impact of the 'more superficially arresting maximalisms on the likes of Prokofiev (the *Scythian Suite*) or the "Futurists" of the early Soviet period with their *Rails* (Deshevov), their *Dnepr Dams* (Meytus) or their *Foundries* (Mosolov)',[38] to which list we might further add the obvious examples of Prokofiev's *Pas d'acier* and, from outside Russia, Antheil's *Ballet mécanique*. We further saw in Chapter 2 how Varèse was among the first to understand more deeply the implications of Stravinsky's innovations and to engage with them through his own striking musical experiments. Layering of musical ideas, as in *Amériques*, was one of the means by which he constructed larger musical blocks, a fact reinforced by Varèse's own rhetoric of interacting strata or 'planes': 'Certain transmutations taking place on certain planes will seem to be projected onto other planes, moving at different speeds and at different angles.'[39] *Intégrales* (1924–5), described by Arnold Whittall as 'a rare example of a work composed in the mid-1920s which is both truly radical and convincingly coherent',[40] clearly demonstrates the imaginative and structural employment of layering – not least as a consequence of the necessity to distinguish rhythmically between the varied elements of a large collection of untuned percussion. The opening Andantino section (from the beginning to fig. 3), and continuing into the slower Moderato section which follows (up to the commencement of the Allegro at fig. 5^{+2}), shows the ways in which a layered texture grows out of the continually present, rhythmicised B♭ played by the E♭ clarinet. Other layers 'proliferate' outwards from it and are characterised not just timbrally but by the (Stravinsky-like) ways in which they reinterpret the rhythmic character of the initial idea – that is, 'other planes' result, 'moving at different speeds [rhythms] and angles [registers/timbres]'. This process culminates just before the final Presto section (what Whittall designates as the coda) in a polyrhythmic coming together of the initial planes, still in the presence of the initial high B♭ (this time played by the oboe), but now climactically superimposed (see Ex. 3.5). There is thus here an integration (as implied by the work's title) of the musical materials but in such a way as to maintain their opposition. It is surely not without significance that Varèse should choose to articulate a key musical climax by means of a kind of rhythmic layering reminiscent of the similarly articulated climaxes of *The Rite of Spring*.

It is appropriate to mention at this point two later American responses, not only to Stravinsky, but also to Ives. The music of Conlon Nancarrow is an extreme response to Stravinsky's rhythmic practices, and it has many eminent champions: Boulez, Carter and Ligeti among them. At the heart of Nancarrow's output is the series of more than fifty studies for player piano whose organisation is preeminently rhythmic. Their rhythmic structures, as Kyle Gann has recently exhaustively demonstrated, are meticulously calculated.[41] The layering of (often individually inaudible) rhythmic patterns and tempi results in a complex polymetric music whose aesthetic effect, if nothing else, closely parallels that of Ives. But it is in the careful organisation of each constituent layer from rhythmic motifs – by such means as regular repetition, proportionally calculated accelerandos and ritardandos, complex and unusual time-signatures, intricate rhythmic canons, and so on – that Nancarrow betrays his Stravinskian origins, pushed to extremes (arguably at the expense of other musical parameters, which are impoverished).

Analogous layers are also to be found in the music of Elliott Carter, though Carter's harmonic concerns are quite different and rhythm is never removed entirely from such contexts: 'stratification of musical elements by metrical and other means became very important for me in such works as my *First String Quartet*'; 'Here [Second String Quartet] the four instruments are stratified according to their repertoire of intervals, their repertoire of rhythms, and their repertoire of musical gestures.'[42] In one

Ex. 3.5 Varèse, *Intégrales* (bb. 195–7)

Ex. 3.6 Carter, First String Quartet (bb. 22–6)

interesting respect, the First Quartet (1951) is Carter's homage to Ives and Nancarrow: he quotes both the opening theme of Ives's First Violin Sonata (see, for example, the cello at bb. 27ff) and a rhythmic idea from Nancarrow's First Study at the start of the quartet's final variation section. Nonetheless it is to Stravinsky that Carter gives primary credit for his rhythmic innovations:

> Works such as the *Rite of Spring* and others of Stravinsky showed [a . . .] re-examination of various rhythmic and durational procedures. We were all aware almost intuitively at that time that these procedures were going on, but it was only later that the exact systematic significance of these developments became clear to us.[43]

Such 'systematisation' is evident, for example, in the 'metrical stratification' of the first section of the First Quartet, where each instrument presents a theme of strikingly different character. As early as b. 22, these ideas sound simultaneously: Ex. 3.6 shows how each voice maintains its own gestural and intervallic identity as well as an invariant durational unit such that the ratios between the voices (vn1:vn2:va:vc) is 40:15:8:12. The equivalent passage at the end of the first section (beginning b. 312) shows an even greater metrical diversity, the voices being in the ratio 6:10:20:75. Such layers are not preserved throughout the piece; the voices come together at various points and in a general sense the quartet's musical argument is about the ways in which degrees of reconciliation can be forged between widely divergent materials. In Carter's Second String Quartet (1959), using Ives's Second Quartet as a model, he takes these ideas one stage further in ascribing abstract dramatic roles to each of the instruments ('actors'). A different sort of metrical stratification can be found in, for instance, the Double Concerto for Piano and Harpsichord (1961), whose complex polyrhythmic organisation is carefully planned in terms of conflicting musical 'speeds'.[44] In the central section (bb. 314–466), speeding up, slowing down and regular pulsation are combined, and the opposition between harpsichord and piano (dramatised throughout by their positioning on opposite sides of the concert platform) comes to a head at b. 453, where the harpsichord and orchestra begin a controlled ritardando at the same time as the piano begins an accelerando. Stravinsky himself heard this work and dubbed it a 'masterpiece'.[45]

The layering of complementary musical ideas was also a feature of much music of the European avant-garde of the 1950s and 1960s (and of some famous and influential works at that), though whether this was necessarily a consequence of the continuing influence of Stravinsky, as was the case with Carter, or as much a result of, say, experiments with the newly-developed electronic tape, is a moot point. We saw in Chapter 2 how Stockhausen's thinking was in part influenced by Varèse and Messiaen; a work such as *Gruppen* is, in some senses, an obvious response to those composers in its reevaluation of musical time, and one in which, in keeping with integrally serial thought, there is an intimate relationship between durational and pitch structures – as explored in his essay, '. . . how time passes . . .'.[46] The structure of *Gruppen* is essentially rhythmic, that is, according to an intricate scheme of different tempi which interact simultaneously, resulting in a work for three orchestras each requiring its own conductor. At much the same time, Bernd Alois Zimmermann was exploring his notion of the 'sphericality of time', most notably in the opera *Die Soldaten*, where past, present and future interact, and at whose cataclysmic conclusion there is an extraordinarily plural layering of all manner of musical materials. (Zimmermann is one of the many composers listed by Andriessen and Schönberger as having been influenced by Stravinsky, without saying in what respects.[47]) The third movement of Berio's *Sinfonia* (1968–9) offers a further example of how a stratified musical structure – here, found fragments are layered on top of the scherzo from Mahler's Second Symphony – is employed in the context of the expression of a musical pluralism. For all these works, we should be prepared to acknowledge, as Carter was, that in *The Rite of Spring* Stravinsky pointed the way towards the systematic, structural operation of rhythmic and durational procedures, and of new understandings of musical time, though we should equally be aware that in many cases such thinking is as much characteristic of modernism in general as it is of Stravinsky.

György Ligeti, another prominent figure of the European avant-garde of the late 1950s and 1960s, often cites Stravinsky as one source of his musical thinking, alongside his fellow Hungarian, Bartók, whose influence at least on local rhythmic practices is everywhere felt. But, since he first encountered it in 1980, it is the music of Nancarrow, Reich and Riley, and certain African musics, that have had the most immediate impact on Ligeti's work. Not that polymetric structures were new to him: as Richard Steinitz has recently brought to our attention, an interest in layered polyrhythms is obvious even in some of his earliest works (the *Polyphonic Study* of 1943, for example, combines four independent repeating melodic phrases, each of different length[48]) as well as in such key pieces as the Second String Quartet (1968) with its overlaying of ticking clocks in the third movement ('come un meccanismo di precisione'), or the third movement ('movimento preciso e meccanico') of the Chamber Concerto (1969–70), or *Monument-Selbsportrait-Bewegung* (1976), whose rhythmic layers and canons uncannily parallel those of Nancarrow. The everexpanding set of piano *Études* (the first set of six was published in 1986; the most recent, No. 15, 'White on White', was premiered in January 1996), demonstrates, among other things, an on-going fascination with the layering of independent and competing processes (usually identified with the separation of the pianist's hands) in the context of an unchanging, often very quick pulse. The first *Étude*, 'Désordre', aptly illustrates this Nancarrow-like machine aesthetic (see Ex. 3.7). The two hands begin together, articulating groups of three and five quavers (cf. Bartók; there are also striking parallels with Debussy, e.g. compare the white note/black note opposition of 'Désordre' with, say, the opening of 'Brouillards' – *Préludes*, No. 1, Book 2); then, by the regular diminution of the right-hand patterns by one quaver, the two patterns quickly move out of synchronisation. The synchronisation of the hands is later reestablished, only for the left hand to be progressively augmented by one quaver. Though it is certainly possible to argue that such repetitions and additive processes have their origins in Stravinsky, they suggest more immediate associations with the 'classic' process music of Reich from the 1960s and 1970s, even if Ligeti could rarely be accused of having adopted Reich's minimalist aesthetic – a connection claimed by Ligeti himself in the middle movement of *Monument-Selbsportrait-Bewegung* which has the full title 'Self-portrait with Reich and Riley (and Chopin is there too)'.

Ex. 3.7 Ligeti, 'Désordre', *Études*

Messiaen's 'personnages rythmiques'

We saw in Chapter 2 how the Russian music of Stravinsky had a profound impact on Messiaen, a fact evident not just from the music itself but from the many references to Stravinsky, especially to rhythmic procedures, in Messiaen's theoretical writings. We saw how, in Messiaen's works of the 1960s in particular, their boldly innovative block and verse–refrain structures, their interest in new kinds of non-narrative, non-linear time, their localised rhythmic working, and not least 'a sort of progression by means of accumulation', were indebted to Stravinsky. This last feature often resulted in layering – for instance, the superimposition of (melodically differentiated) lines, variously derived from Gregorian chant, Indian music and birdsong, in *Et expecto resurrectionem mortuorum*. But there are also examples in Messiaen of a layering which is primarily rhythmic. Some of the most extreme examples are to be found in *Chronochromie*. The two Strophes, for example, demonstrate a rhythmic layering which is in part brought about by what Messiaen indicates in the preface to the score as the superimposition of 'interversions' of a durational series: 'The temporal or rhythmic material employs 32 different durations, treated in symmetrical interversions, always interverted in the same order. The 36 permutations thus obtained are heard either alone and fragmentarily, or superimposed three by three.'[49] The duration of each of the Strophes is determined on each occasion by the simultaneous presentation of these three last-mentioned interversions (in strings and untuned percussion) while other 'free' strata of birdsong are further superimposed in wind and tuned percussion. Given the non-directed nature of the sequence of chords of the interversions, and of the many birdsong fragments, the overall result, while highly rhythmicised (and indeed rhythmically 'controlled' by the interversions) is decidedly 'static'. Each Strophe comes to an end solely because the underlying interversions have run their course. As Paul Griffiths puts it, they represent 'segments of time given a single colour, since perpetual change gives the impression of constancy'.[50]

The most extreme example of layering in this work is to be found in the Épôde. There is no obvious structuring using the durational interversional series here. Rather, as Messiaen states in the score, 'the Épôde is a counterpoint of 18 real voices' (solo strings), that is, there are for the most part no subsidiary voices; each voice counts – though in order to avoid 'the impression of an inextricable mass with a single intensity', Messiaen specifies that certain voices periodically emerge 'in full light' and then return 'to the shadows'. Each voice is that of a specified French birdsong and each has a specific rhythmic character (distinctly ornithological 'personnages rythmiques'). Once all eighteen voices have entered, and with the exception of a sudden breaking off and recommencement of the music with some new birdsongs at the halfway point, the character of the music remains unchanged from start to finish. Though there are connections across the voices (many songsters of the same species are singing simultaneously – for instance, there are six blackbirds), and though each voice in itself involves a high degree of repetition (some lines are more obviously repetitious than others – the blackbirds seem quite free whereas the high reiterated Es of the 'fauvette babillarde' (second violin 4) are a fixed feature of each recurrence), the rhythmic differentiation between layers is absolute. No voices ever work together rhythmically, except coincidentally. There is at any moment a wide variety of rational and irrational subdivisions (from quavers to sextuplet demi-semiquavers) of the notional quaver beat, though it is interesting that Messiaen hardly ever groups or ties across the beat, implying an underlying (albeit unheard) metre. The result is a babble of voices, an extraordinary dawn chorus. The concept of the simultaneous sounding of musical motifs that are connected but not temporally coordinated is an obvious Stravinskian one. It is here, however, quite different from virtually anything Stravinsky ever produced – a music (despite the constant activity) of seeming absolute stasis. The Épôde is virtually without form and takes on a meaning only because of the context of its placement within the formally organised overall structure. Though more than any other composer this century Stravinsky has been by turns credited and accused of 'inventing' static music, never – even in extreme moments such as the layered structure of the first of the *Three Pieces* or the polyphonic webs of the serial works – is his music ever as static as this.

For a more varied complexity of structuring by means of the layering of rhythmic patterns and durational sequences, we need to look back to the *Turangalîla* Symphony. Messiaen discussed aspects of his work in specific relation to *The Rite of Spring* (for example, the treatment of the six 'personnages rythmiques' in the fifth movement, 'Joie du sang des étoiles', is derived from his understanding of the 'Danse sacrale'[51]), but in fact the influence of *The Rite* is subtly felt everywhere in *Turangalîla*. Paul Griffiths perceptively sums this up:

> the Stravinsky of *The Rite of Spring* . . . offered much more than a model for
> rhythmic characters. Indeed, the *Turangalîla-symphonie* comes nearer than
> any other successor to Stravinsky's penetration to the barbaric through
> sophisticated means, his imagery of the machine as mediation between the
> modern and the archaic, the individual and the general. Like Stravinsky's,
> Messiaen's machines are usually rhythmic, but they can also be actual, for it

Ex. 3.8 Comparison of opening melodies of Messiaen, 'Turangalîla 1',
Turangalîla-Symphonie, and Stravinsky, *The Rite of Spring*

is a machine instrument, the ondes martenot, that gives the work its most
human voice, its most distinctive colour and the means by which it sings of
the most universal human experience, that of love, in a manner all its own.[52]

And, though Griffiths does not mention it, his account also suggests other
parallels with Stravinsky's aesthetic as expressed in *The Nightingale*, where
the 'natural' and the 'mechanical' are in conflict, where a machine is perceived to sing more beautifully than the real thing.

The third movement, 'Turangalîla 1', is of particular interest as it
evinces striking parallels with the Introduction to Part 1 of *The Rite*.[53]
There is a strong resemblance between the two openings: solo woodwind
instruments in the same register playing a limited, repeating but varied
melodic motif. Ex. 3.8 shows the obvious rhythmic and rhetorical correspondences between the melodic openings. In bar 2 of *The Rite*, the
melody is joined by the horn outlining a chromatic segment (C♯–D–C♯),
while in 'Turangalîla 1' the unfolding of the melody is punctuated by a
vertically-presented chromatic segment (G–G♯–A) in the vibraphone;
note that the first compressed reprise of the *Rite*'s opening melody (at fig.
1[+3]) is similarly accompanied by a horizontal chromatic trichord in both
clarinet 2 and bass clarinet 1. At fig. 1, Stravinsky's melody spawns a subsidiary line – a chromatic descent in clarinet 1 traversing the entire
octave from the horn's c♯, to the c♯ below (doubled a fifth below by the
bass clarinet); at Messiaen's fig. 1, his melody also spawns a subsidiary
descending chromatic line (solo pizzicato double bass) which begins on
c♯ and then descends through nearly two octaves to the E at the bottom of
its range.

In terms of their general aesthetic intentions, these two works
have much in common (though, of course, their differences are also
significant). Both have an underlying non-narrative programme. Both

make much of the idea of play: Messiaen gives one of the meanings of the Sanskrit 'Lîla' as play 'in the sense of the divine action upon the cosmos, the play of creation, of destruction, of reconstruction, the play of life and death'.[54] Stravinsky's various accounts of the scenario of the first part of *The Rite* mention spring games of abduction, a 'khorovod' game of cities, and so on. As a whole, *Turangalîla* is for Messiaen 'all at once love song, hymn to joy, time, movement, rhythm, life and death'. Compare this with Stravinsky's scenario: 'In *The Rite of Spring* I wished to express the sublime upsurge of self-renewing nature: the total pantheistic upsurge of the universal sap . . . The annual cycle of forces that are reborn and that fall again to nature's breast is consummated in its fundamental rhythms.'[55]

The overall shape of Messiaen's movement bears at least a passing resemblance to Stravinsky's Introduction. As we saw above, Boulez identifies three 'principal motifs' associated with the first three 'phases' of the Introduction, which are later superimposed before being cut off to allow a simplified return to the opening music, which in turn leads to the next section, 'Les augures printaniers'. Messiaen similarly introduces three main themes (at the beginning, at fig. 2 and at fig. 6) which form the substance of his movement, before superimposing them, only to be cut off for a simplified return to the opening music, which in turn leads directly to the start of the next movement, 'Chant d'amour 2'. In both works, the divisions between sections are not clear-cut as there is much sharing of material – thus, Griffiths's summary of the structure of Messiaen's movement as a simple ABABA does not do justice to the subtlety of the transformation and combination of themes (for example, the appearance of the third theme at fig. 6 is accompanied by the chromatic pizzicato double bass subsidiary motif associated with the first theme; the reappearance of the first theme at fig. 8 is accompanied by the subsidiary semiquaver stratum that had appeared with the third theme – all of which serves to confirm the freedom of vertical association possible in a structure such as this built from layers).

'Turangalîla 1', especially its opening, thus constitutes a fascinating reworking of the elements of Stravinsky's Introduction; indeed, given the significance of *The Rite* for Messiaen, his rewriting could well be understood to be a creative *mis*-reading of his illustrious precursor. Following Kevin Korsyn's lead in applying Harold Bloom's revisionary ratios, we might express the relationship between the first section of Messiaen's third movement and the first phase of Stravinsky's Introduction as an example of *tessera* or 'antithetical completion', allied by Bloom to the rhetorical trope of synecdoche. Korsyn quotes Bloom:

A poet antithetically 'completes' his precursor, by so reading the parent-poem as to retain its terms, but to mean them in another sense, as if the precursor has failed to go far enough. . . . In the *tessera*, the later poet provides what his imagination tells him would complete the otherwise 'truncated' precursor poem and poet.[56]

Messiaen clearly retains Stravinsky's terms. But in what sense is 'Turangalîla 1' a completion of the *Rite*'s Introduction? One answer may lie in the climactic section of Messiaen's movement (figs. 8–13), where nearly all the motifs are superimposed to create a polyrhythmic passage which parallels Stravinsky's climax at figs. 10–12 of *The Rite*. Both musics break off, regaining their opening gestures to signal the conclusion of the section/movement. However, there are many more component elements to Messiaen's climax, the differences between layers (harmonically, if not rhythmically) are more marked, the control of the repetition of the motifs is more precisely ordered. The underlying metre is barely able to contain such heterogeneous voices. The whole passage is much longer than Stravinsky's (implying that the precursor work was somehow 'truncated'?) and Messiaen has pushed further ideas that were perhaps not exploited to their fullest extent in *The Rite*. However the parallelisms between the two works are interpreted, and whether or not 'Turangalîla 1' was a conscious rewriting of Stravinsky's Introduction, it is undeniable that, as Griffiths surmised, *The Rite* offered *Turangalîla* much more than a mere model for rhythmic characters.

Three specific 'personnages rythmiques' nonetheless make themselves heard in this movement (constituting a fourth, entirely rhythmic, theme), and they conform precisely to Messiaen's prescript that one should increase, one should decrease, and one should remain unchanged.[57] This process is initiated at fig. 6 and then continues, regardless of other formal boundaries, to the end of the movement. The bass drum begins by sounding a pair of semiquavers, whose duration is augmented by one semiquaver on each subsequent appearance – quaver, dotted quaver, crotchet, etc. – reaching a pair of minims (eight semiquavers), after which the process goes into reverse; conversely, the maracas begin with a pair of minims, whose duration is successively diminished by one semiquaver going as far as a pair of semiquavers, at which point augmentation begins. The wood block beats out an insistent, unchanging pattern of 2–1–1–1–2 semiquavers. In practice, the only rhythmic personality to be heard is the fixed identity of the wood block, as the other 'characters' are swamped by the rest of the music. What Messiaen has done here is to rationalise less formal processes of rhythmic augmentation and diminution found in Stravinsky (Stravinsky surely never does anything this predictable?) and

Fig. 3.1 Messiaen, 'Turangalîla 1': durational patterns (figs. 8–13, strings)

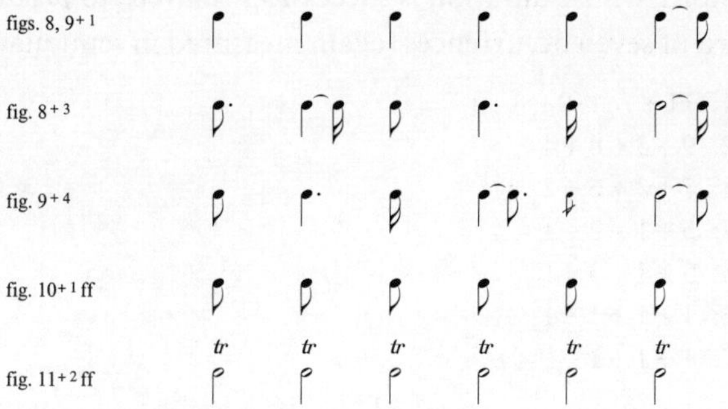

incorporates them into the movement as a complement to other formalised rhythmic processes, as one rhythmic layer among a number.

Another such layer occurs in the strings throughout the climactic section. A sequence (literally, a linear intervallic pattern) of six chords (a cousin, perhaps, of the 'statue theme') is presented first in even crotchets and then its durations are subjected on subsequent appearances to a simultaneous combination of diminutions and augmentations (see Fig. 3.1). If we represent the first appearance in semiquavers as 4–4–4–4–4–(6), the next durational sequence can be seen to be the result of the alternate subtraction of 1 from 4 and the addition of 1 to 4, namely 3–5–2–6–1–(9), a process continued in the fourth sequence, i.e. 2–6–1–7–0–(10), after which it reverts to sequences of equal note values, as in the first sequence. Earlier in the movement (figs. 4–6), the restatement of the first theme (violin 1, trumpets, ondes) is punctuated by a group of repeating events which expand on subsequent appearances. Thus the durations of a sequence of four horn and woodwind plus percussion chords at fig. 4 are augmented by the addition of a quaver on each occasion, resulting in the following pattern (measured in semiquaver units):

1: $1 + 5 + 2 + 6$
2: $3 + 7 + 4 + 8$
3: $5 + 9 + 6 + 10$
4: $7 + 11 + 8 + (10)$

This is joined by a repeating piano motif (not dissimilar to the 'flower theme') plus percussion, which is augmented in a similar manner by the addition of a quaver. By contrast, and simultaneously with the above expanding patterns, a sequence of four chords in the strings (from fig. 4, possibly a variant of the 'chord theme') is successively diminished by the subtraction of a quaver unit from the duration of each chord (excepting the last chord, whose duration is successively halved) to produce the following pattern of seven occurrences (again measured in semiquaver units):

1: $11 + 7 + 10 + 8$
2: $9 + 5 + 8 + 4$
3: $7 + 3 + 6 + 2$
4: $5 + 1 + 2 + 1$
5: $3 + 1 + 3 + 1$
6: $1 + 1 + 1 + 1$
7: $1 + 1 + 1$

The only other superimposed layer remains essentially immobile. It is a variant of the chromatic descending subsidiary theme in the piccolo (now spanning only a major third, with each quaver subdivided into three reiterated triplet semiquavers), accompanied by a new rising arpeggio motif in the bass clarinet, and joined at fig. 5 by the original subsidiary theme on the double bass, now 'syncopated' in places. Thus, in practice, the entire passage from fig. 4 to fig. 6 is constructed from three layered groups of 'personnages rythmiques', one expanding, one contracting, one fixed, in the presence of the reprised first theme. The set of percussive rhythmic personalities then follows immediately at fig. 6. Though the structure by layering is most obvious in the climactic section from fig. 8, it is clear that *every* section of this movement is constructed from layers whose primary identity is, usually, rhythmic. It is through the application of common rhythmic/durational procedures to diverse musical materials that Messiaen is able to contain otherwise seemingly disconnected – though simultaneously presented – ideas. The precedents are to be found in *The Rite of Spring*; Messiaen elevates Stravinsky's general rhythmic practice into a rational constructive principle. He is thus able to build a rich structure out of ordered repetitions but over which he nonetheless retains a degree of flexibility in order to prevent the music reverting to the 'purely' mechanistic. This is man-made music (even the ondes Martenot requires an expressive human operator!); the polyrhythmic schemes are just another example of Messiaen's sense of 'play' in this work, and express through time and number a transcendence, 'a joy that is superhuman, overflowing, blinding, unlimited'.[58]

From 'Danse de la terre' to *Earth Dances*

Messiaen's re-reading of *The Rite* in *Turangalîla* forms an important link in Stravinsky's modernist chain. For Birtwistle, hearing Messiaen's work was a decisive moment:

I went to London with Sandy [Alexander] Goehr to hear his father do *Turangalîla Symphony*. . . . As we got there [to stage level] they were doing the movement that begins with pure [*sic*] percussion ['Développement de l'amour']. That was an absolute magical moment for me. At that point, there was a one-to-one relationship with what I had imagined, and I saw it was possible.[59]

Turangalîla has played its part in widening further the complex web of direct and indirect influences of *The Rite*. Some of the possibilities it suggested were realised much later in Birtwistle's orchestral work, *Earth Dances*, a work which, ever since its first performance in London on 14 March 1986, has frequently been compared with *The Rite of Spring*. Nicholas Kenyon, writing in the *Observer*, began the trend:

Out of a primeval rumble, like a far-off echo of 'The Rite of Spring', a jangle of tambourine initiates a stuttering, angular dance. . . . In two especially long and awesome build-ups . . . the spectre of Stravinsky's 'Rite' comes ever closer, only to recede in an entirely original complex of disintegrating sound. . . . It is a desolate, disturbing rite of spring for this decade.[60]

Following a series of performances by Christoph von Dohnányi and the Cleveland Orchestra in 1994, Andrew Clements, in the *Guardian*, reaffirmed the Stravinsky parallel alongside that of two of Varèse's large orchestral works which, as we saw in Chapter 2, Stravinsky himself considered to be in 'the shadow of *Le Sacre*':

Earth Dances emerged sounding more like Stravinsky or Varèse than could possibly have been imagined. . . . [B]ehind Earth Dances' massive terraces of sound . . . lies the examples of Amériques and Arcana.[61]

And, once the journalistic convenience (cliché?) of the alignment of Birtwistle with *The Rite* had taken hold (convenient because, by associating Birtwistle with what is generally perceived as the most iconoclastic work of the century, it perpetuates his 'enfant terrible' image, something which the British press – even, perhaps, the composer himself – seems reluctant to relinquish), the analogies proliferated:

Compared with the music for the Oracle of the Dead [Act 2 of *The Mask of Orpheus*], *The Rite of Spring* is merely sophisticated folk music.[62]

[*Carmen arcadiae mechanicae perpetuum*] . . . whose machine-like patterns were juxtaposed several times over and finally galvanised into a climactic ritual dance. It was rather like the Rite of Spring in miniature, something which seemed evident also in the character of its scoring.[63]

this [*Endless Parade*] is primeval music, as earthy as Stravinsky's Rite of Spring, yet like the Rite constantly giving you amid the violence visions of beauty, of sensuousness even.[64]

But, as with all clichés, there is a core of truth, and there are, at the very least, superficial parallels between the two large orchestral works – not just in shared titles but, as the critics were quick to point out, in their structures built from small repeating fragments, in their extraordinarily imaginative orchestration, in the primordial, elemental rhythmic power of their wholes (their '*stikhiya*'). More particularly, the layering we have identified as characteristic of *The Rite* is a fundamental aspect of the structure of *Earth Dances*, a fact that suggested the geological metaphor of Birtwistle's title and his discussion of its independent musical layers as 'strata'.

There are, according to the composer, as many as six separate strata characterised by their 'intervallic hierarchy', as well as their register, and distinguished by their rhythms.[65] The origins of such thinking lie in the major ensemble work whose composition preceded *Earth Dances*: *Secret Theatre*. We shall see in Chapter 4 how *Secret Theatre* is structured from two layers designated 'cantus' and 'continuum' which 'change at the same time'; Birtwistle has suggested that *Earth Dances* grew out of this, and proposed that the relationship between the increased number of layers in *Earth Dances* might be more 'contrapuntal'.[66] In practice, the six strata are rarely explicitly present simultaneously but periodically come to the surface – 'layers are overlaid like geological strata which one after another erupt and push their way towards the light. It is as though an earthquake were in progress.'[67] This account is telling. It parallels Messiaen's description, quoted above, of the emergence 'in full light' and the return 'to the shadows' of layers in the 'Épôde' of *Chronochromie*. It also calls to mind, once again, Cone's account of a different kind of 'stratification' in the *Symphonies of Wind Instruments*: it is as if, though unheard ('underground'), each stratum continues to change, shift, develop in the light of the audible 'surface' music, so that when it reemerges we hear it from a different perspective – a new kind of inter-lock. It is through these continually shifting relationships between strata that it might be said that the 'earth dances'. But, as was the case with Varèse, the consequences of these processes for the work's overall form are such that the form becomes hard to grasp (a 'resultant', to use Varèse's word) – a labyrinth, perhaps, in which we continually re-encounter familiar objects but from which there is not necessarily an escape. Despite the eschewal of symphonic argument, *Earth Dances*, following Stravinsky's example, is able to build a vast non-narrative, non-linear structure from the considered assembly of its carefully defined constitu-ent parts. Peter Heyworth throws up his arms at the possibility of an analytical interpretation:

What is it, I ask myself, that holds these weird and wonderful events together? What leads the ear and mind from one thing to the next? In 'Earth Dances', in particular, one can point to ostinatos and fragments of material that recur like colours in a brick wall. But in the final resort one can only, rather lamely, say that Birtwistle's music is motivated by its inner life.[68]

But, though its structure conforms to no known formal given, it is possible to try to articulate why so many critics and listeners sense a 'rightness' to the work's shape – which must surely have something to do not only with our interest in each moment as it passes but also with the timing of these events, the movement towards and away from defining moments. Arnold Whittall interprets it as 'a dialogue between assertion and reassertion of focus, on the one hand, and music whose character and tension are defined by the absence of focus [on the other] – an absence which yields, not negative incoherence, but positive challenge to the force of gravity itself'.[69]

Let us examine the 'inner life' of one passage that bears more than a passing resemblance to *The Rite* and is clearly constructed from Heyworth's ostinatos and fragments of material. Boulez wrote of the 'Glorification de l'élue' that 'the architecture . . . is determined by its rhythm [; . . .] the "form" depends at least as much on structural rhythmic figures of some complexity as on straightforward harmonic relations'.[70] In the same way the organisation of this passage of *Earth Dances*, it would seem, is rhythmic. Figure 3.2 shows the organisation of the dominant 'rhythmic' stratum from fig. 35, which is self-evidently built from Stravinsky-like near-exact repetitions of tiny rhythmic cells. Further 'substrata' are cumulatively added (at fig. 35^{+5} and fig. 35^{+8}), while at fig. 36^{+1} a fragment of a potential new stratum in the woodwind (strongly reminiscent of the rapid, rising wind figures in the first part of the 'Glorification' and similarly accompanied by pounding drum strokes) 'erupts' from and interrupts the established stratum, with which it then alternates, later (after fig. 37) opening out into a more sustained, cantus-like stratum. The overall result is a music which is built from the repetition of static elements yet which is never quite the same on any two occasions (as Boulez shows is also true of the continual recombining of rhythmic cells in the opening of the 'Glorification'). The same is true of the various interlocking appearances of this stratum throughout the work – always different yet recognisably the same. Though Fig. 3.2 shows how it consists of a number of interacting rhythmic strands, it does not give the entire picture: there is another independent layer in the violins and violas which forms a more sustained cantus in opposition to the continuum of the rhythmic stratum. This cantus is registrally distinct from the continuum: it seems to begin in the registral gap (a–e´) between strands of the continuum, and presents a

Fig. 3.2 Birtwistle, *Earth Dances*, rhythmic stratum (fig. 35)

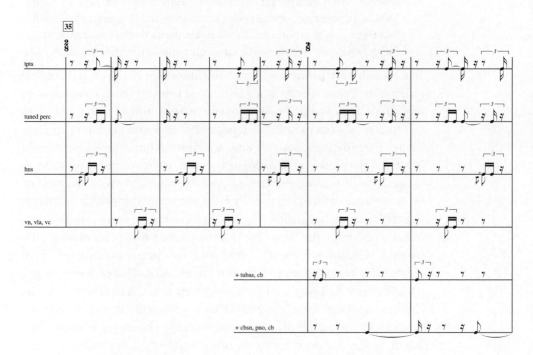

heterophonous melody which is essentially linear in concept (its peak notes rise progressively to the climactic a″ in the upper violins just before fig. 37) and which is rhythmically freer. There also seems to be one further stratum in cellos and basses whose separate identity is uncertain but which appears to mediate between cantus and continuum. It begins with the long held notes characteristic of the cantus but then responds to the rhythms of the double bassoon, piano and other double basses (fig. 35^{+5}) and later with the untuned percussion (fig. 36^{+1}). In its low register, instrumentation and intervallic profile, this is evidently a brief reemergence of the music heard at the very outset of the work.

There are a number of important referential motifs which punctuate the course of *Earth Dances*, the most prominent of which is the D–F motif which had played such a significant role in articulating the structure of *Secret Theatre* (and at the same register: d′–f′). One might speculate as to the origins of this motif, and of the associated focus on D. Might it have been absorbed/appropriated by Birtwistle from *The Rite* where it plays a periodic but important referential role? A prophetic D♭/D–F motif prefaces the 'Danse de la terre', which concludes Part 1 (Ex. 3.9), and is a recurrent presence in the climactic 'Danse sacrale' – see, for example, the

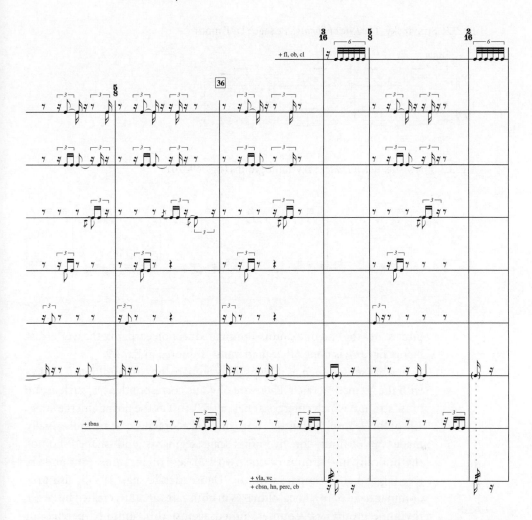

repeating D–F motif in double basses at figs. 146–9 of the opening 'refrain', and the focal sustained Ds of the second 'verse' at figs. 174–84, interrupted by a brief snatch of the 'refrain' at its original transposition (figs. 180–81), including the D–F bass motif. Whittall, for one, has proposed that 'Birtwistle's D evokes Stravinsky'.[71] Whatever its origins, it is undeniable that D provides focus while the D–F motif initiates beginnings and signals endings and other important moments. Most obviously (and in further support of the *Rite* connection) it dominates the landscape at the work's monumental climax, which in its rhythmic energy strongly corresponds to the 'Danse sacrale', beginning on D with the emerging cantus just before fig. 65 and culminating with definitive statements of D–F at figs. 77/78. By the end, as in *Secret Theatre*, this motif is virtually all that remains. It is also of interest here to note that an extended form of the motif, D–F–C♯, which

Ex. 3.9 Stravinsky, *The Rite of Spring*, 'Le sage': D–F motif

NB the D♮, and not the D♭, is accented.

Fig. 3.3 Birtwistle, *Earth Dances*: rhythmic groups (figs. 69–70)

punctuates the end of a cantus-dominated section earlier in the work (just before fig. 31), is none other than motif 's' quoted in Ex. 3.9.

In what senses, then, is it helpful to compare the climax of *Earth Dances* with the 'Danse sacrale'? There are obvious correspondences, such as the brass stratum which emerges at figs. 69–70, just as the horns emerge at fig. 193 of the 'Danse'. Birtwistle's horn lines, like Stravinsky's, are individually made up of four- or five-note scale segments and shaped homo-rhythmically into groups of one, two and, less often, three, four and six (see Fig. 3.3 and compare with the 'Danse sacrale', figs. 193–5, also pre-dominantly in 3/16). Local climaxes in both cases are thus created by larger rhythmic groupings. Counterpointed against this, untuned percussion and lower strings articulate a different pattern of paired events, usually in the brass's 'gaps' (rests), to generate a more complex overall rhythmic pattern, just as the percussion and bass instruments in the 'Danse' provide a counterpointed A–C pair. Birtwistle's rhythmically mobile, limited 'melodies' are thus clearly Stravinskian in origin.

But '*Rite*-spotting' of this kind, while diverting, reveals little more than the obvious fact that Birtwistle's musical language is indebted to Stravinsky. The cataclysmic section of *Earth Dances* is, in structure, more closely related to the polyrhythmic layering of the 'Danse de la terre'[72] and, as Clements suggested, the superimposition here of strata exposed separately earlier in the piece bears an equally strong resemblance to the climactic coming together of blocks of materials at the end of Varèse's *Amériques*. Birtwistle's difference from both Stravinsky and Varèse is that he is able to build his climax over a much longer span,[73] not just through the cumulation of materials but also by controlling the speed of rhythmic activity – follow, for example, the decreasing gaps between the placement of even demi-semiquaver xylophone figurations (significantly highlighting the D–F motif in a different register) which propel the music inexorably forwards (in this respect, the increasing density of repetitions of small motifs bears comparison with the closing thirty bars of the 'Danse sacrale'). What begins as an implied background pulse against which the rhythmic identities of the different strata are counterpointed eventually forces its way into the foreground so that, from around fig. 75, *all* the strata are in some way subsumed into the omnipresent demi-semiquavers. The return to the focal pitches of D and F signals arrival but, I would argue, rhythm is nonetheless the 'principal structural agent' of this climax. The only other comparable climax in Birtwistle is to be found in Act 2 of *The Mask of Orpheus*. There should be little doubt that, for decades, *The Rite* has continued to cast its distinctive shadow firmly over Birtwistle.

'Metric modulation'

Proportional tempi are nothing new. The mensurational innovations of the ars nova, for example, were concerned precisely with the ratios between notes of different durations (at different levels described as 'mood', 'time' and 'prolation') and led to the introduction of mensuration signs or time signatures. The principal structural force of the music of de Vitry's contemporaries was rhythmic. Having lost such a structural sense of rhythm during the tonal era, it should hardly surprise us that many twentieth-century composers, Stravinsky included, have looked back to earlier music for models (see, for instance, the 'game' Stravinsky plays with the French dances and the number 12 in *Agon*). At the same time as Stravinsky was working on *Agon* and Stockhausen on *Gruppen*, Peter Maxwell Davies produced an orchestral work called *Prolation* (1957–8) based explicitly on medieval mensurational techniques. Though, as David Epstein has attempted to demonstrate in his intriguingly titled *Shaping Time*, implied proportional tempi are significant in a range of tonal examples from Mozart to Mahler,[74] it is in the twentieth century that proportional tempi have become a primary structural element. The prime exemplar, the 'real breakthrough piece',[75] is the *Symphonies of Wind Instruments*, where particular musical ideas are identified with specific tempi and where the ratios between those tempi become a crucial structural feature: specifically, metronome marks of crotchet = 72, 108 and 144, that is, tempi in a ratio of 2:3:4. In a work constructed of discontinuous musical blocks, such proportional tempi articulate that discontinuity while at the same time expressing a relationship between the elements (Kramer, as we saw in Chapter 2, has gone further and shown how the 3:2 tempo ratio of the first part of the *Symphonies* has wider manifestations for the durations of sections). The emergence of the third tempo only in the second part is further evidence to support an argument that divides the work into two distinct parts (Taruskin identifies Tempo III with the 'Kanon' or strophic hymn that occurs in the second section of the *panikhida*). The legacy of the *Symphonies of Wind Instruments*, among other of Stravinsky's works, is, according to Kramer, 'that carefully controlled durations can have perceivable effect and that they can generate a form'.[76]

For Carter, the notion of proportional tempi, or what he more dynamically interprets as the principle of 'metric modulation', is used as Stravinsky had done in the *Symphonies*, 'both as a mode of proceeding smoothly or abruptly from one speed to another and as a formal device to isolate one section from another'.

> If you listen to or look at any part of the first or last movement of my *First String Quartet*, you will find that there is a constant change of pulse. This is caused by an overlapping of speeds. . . . The structure of such speeds is correlated throughout the work and gives the impression of varying rates of flux and change of material and character.[77]

Here are two examples from that work that show the subtlety with which Carter brings about metric change. Ex. 3.10a is taken from the last movement and shows how the music is able to move smoothly from crotchet = 96 in 2/4 to crotchet = 120 in 3/4. First there is a gradual acceleration from crotchets to quintuplet semiquavers and then, by keeping a basic unit of measurement the same but changing the time signature, or vice versa, the shift is effected. Ex. 3.10b, from the first movement, shows the overlapping of speeds Carter refers to – a crotchet beat in the viola at b. 157 is subdivided into quintuplet semiquavers, which then becomes the basic five-semiquaver group in a 15/16 bar, while the dotted quaver beat in the cello remains constant, and so on.

The First Quartet was a turning-point in Carter's development. Though the new ideas presented in the quartet would be elaborated in far more complex ways in later works, his basic techniques were established there and, in principle at least, remained consistent. Griffiths sums up the significance of the quartet:

> In its objectivity, and in its dancing rhythms, the First Quartet may still be Stravinskian, but it was also the first work in which Carter placed himself

Ex. 3.10a Carter, First String Quartet, final movement (bb. 126–37)

Ex. 3.10b Carter, First String Quartet, first movement (bb. 157–68)

within the context of a wider divergence of modern masters: Ives, Debussy (whose *Jeux* and orchestral *Images* provided nearer examples of multiple tempos under supreme control), Schoenberg.[78]

One of Carter's most important contributions to the music of the second half of the century has been his sophisticated on-going exploration of the relationship between rhythm, metre and tempo, and of their involvement with other aspects of musical structure, a refinement *through his music itself* of Stravinsky's blunt distinction between 'ontological' and 'psychological' time. It was an effort, as he said himself, 'to find a more significant temporal thought' than had hitherto been the case, 'a desire to find a new flow of musical thought and expression'.[79] Though in various ways Stravinsky suggested the possibilities, Carter has developed his rhythmic innovations with an unparalleled rigour and depth.

'Rhythmic energy is the hallmark of Tippett's style', writes Ian Kemp.[80] His rhythmic language is clearly derived from Stravinskian practice, as well as from other complementary sources such as jazz, Elizabethan music and the poetry of Gerald Manley Hopkins. Characteristic features of syncopation, 'additive' and 'sprung' rhythms, irregular stresses, rhythmic ostinatos, rhythmic polyphony etc., can all, at least in part, be traced to Stravinsky – and are certainly evident in his most overtly Stravinskian work, the Second Symphony. The polyrhythmic momentum established at the opening is generally representative, with its pounding quaver pulse in the lower strings (outlining a C major triad), the anticipatory quaver beat in the horn fanfare (outlining a D major triad) and a cross-accented line in the violins joining at fig. 1. The *Symphony in Three Movements* was a strong model, though it is interesting to note how Tippett transforms Stravinsky's violent conflicts into something more obviously connected (apparent even in the diatonic opposition of C and D compared with Stravinsky's harder-edged octatonic G–D♭ opposition). The block structures initiated by *King Priam* suggested a concern for relational tempi too. Kemp gives a useful example from the Concerto for Orchestra[81] which seems to parallel Carter's metric modulations, while the 2:3 ratio of the two tempi of Part 1 of the Third Symphony ('Arrest', crotchet = 88; 'Movement', crotchet = 132) invokes Stravinsky (note the superimposition of the tempi with two different time signatures at fig. 87). Nonetheless, though in general terms Tippett adopts Stravinskian ways, the differences are also significant. Kemp attempts to define the 'organic' nature of Tippett's rhythms, by which he seems to suggest that, despite the many radical aspects of Tippett's musical aesthetic, there is in practice a desire to maintain a continuity with earlier traditions (not least of the eighteenth and nineteenth centuries), an unwillingness irrevocably to challenge conventional musical continuities: his rhythms do not 'lead to new concepts of musical form: they revitalize the old ones'.[82] Tippett's balancing of the progressive and the traditional results in a unique interpretation of (Stravinskian) modernism, and, as such, stands at the head of a line of British composers of his generation for whom the more superficial harmonic and rhythmic aspects of Stravinsky's neoclassical style were something to be absorbed into music that was, on the whole, reactionary in terms of form and expression: for example, Walton (born 1902), Lennox Berkeley (born 1903, studied with Boulanger), Britten (born 1913), and even a later generation of composers (many of whom studied with Berkeley at the Royal Academy), such as William Mathias (born 1934), whose 'Stravinskyisms' were more likely acquired via the influence of Tippett and Britten.[83] Similar observations could arguably be made for that generation of American composers who grew up with Copland (born 1900), many of whom learnt about Stravinsky from Boulanger.

For Birtwistle, born in the same year as Mathias, the lessons of Stravinsky's modernism are much more deeply incorporated and reworked. In much of his music of the later 1970s and early 1980s, a concern with pulse is preeminent, partly as a consequence of his work in the theatre and of a desire to coordinate music and movement more precisely. In Chapter 2 we saw how, in *Carmen arcadiae mechanicae perpetuum*, the successive opposition of pulses ('six musical mechanisms . . . juxtaposed . . . without any form of transition') was reinforced by tempo relations which were insignificant in the sense that they did not effect any kind of perceivable connection. By contrast, transitions between different pulses are a structural feature of *Carmen*'s companion piece, *Silbury Air* (also written in 1977), Birtwistle's most elaborate exploration of pulse. The score is prefaced by a 'pulse labyrinth' (Fig. 3.4) which controls the changes of metre and tempo in the piece and ensures smooth 'metric modulation' throughout (though, typically, the scheme breaks down at certain points, or at least the composer chooses to override it). The result is a fascinating polyphony in which a variety of shifting pulses are superimposed, layered (that is, where *differences* are maintained), but also in which there is a perceivable relationship between pulses, both vertically and in terms of horizontal transitions (that is, where some element is held *in common*). The pulse labyrinth, like Carter's metric modulations, ensures a consistent balancing of such difference and similarity, 'varying rates of flux and change of material and character'.[84] As so often in Birtwistle, the same basic musical objects are constantly being viewed from new perspectives (the cyclic returns to

Fig. 3.4 Birtwistle, *Silbury Air*, preface (pulse labyrinth)

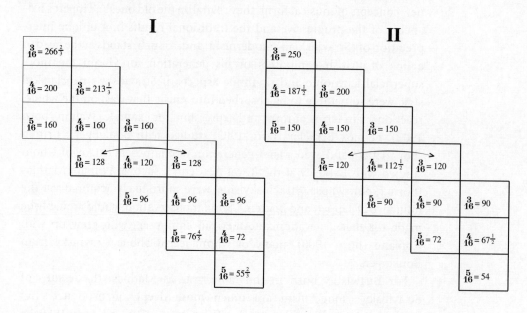

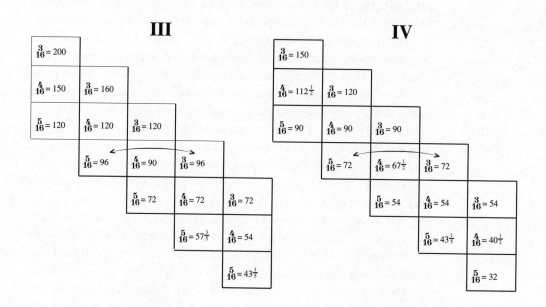

the focal pulsed E of the opening, for example, are always at a different speed).

There are many important works and composers that this overview has ignored. The *stikhiya* of much of the music of Xenakis – especially in elemental works for percussion such as the extraordinary *Pléïades* (1978) – is clearly descended from *The Rite*. The rhythmic complexity of works as diverse as Boulez's *Le Marteau sans maître* and Ferneyhough's *Time and Motion Studies*, while of the 'Darmstadt generation' with origins more in Schoenberg's modernism than Stravinsky's, is at the very least Stravinskian in its self-conscious engagement with time itself (Griffiths makes Ferneyhough connect in a fascinating way with both Stravinsky and Birtwistle).[85] And, at the other extreme, the stasis, the *nepodvizhnost'*, of so much recent music, whether the 'oriental' time of Takemitsu, or the 'spiritual' time of Pärt, or the 'processed' time of Reich, continues to participate in the reevaluation of musical temporality initiated by Stravinsky. Though for some composers since World War 2 – Messiaen, Carter and Birtwistle preeminent among them – Stravinsky's modernist legacy has informed and been transformed by every aspect of their music, Taruskin's general assertion would nonetheless still seem to hold true. Stravinsky and *The Rite* continue to hypnotise, inspire and compel all who come into contact with them: the Legend of Stravinsky the Rhythmic Innovator is alive and well.

4 Ritual theatres

Stravinsky's theatres

> I can take any empty space and call it a bare stage. A man walks across this empty space whilst someone else is watching him, and this is all that is needed for an act of theatre to be engaged.

In his brilliant and thought-provoking book of 1968, *The Empty Space*, the English theatre director Peter Brook identifies four distinct categories of theatre: a Deadly Theatre, a Holy Theatre, a Rough Theatre and an Immediate Theatre.[1] Throughout his career, Stravinsky engaged with all four types, sometimes singly, sometimes in combination. Brook bluntly defines Deadly Theatre as 'bad theatre', one concerned with the unthinking repetition of well-tried formulae: 'A deadly director is a director who brings no challenge to the conditioned reflexes that every department [direction, design, music, etc.] must contain.'[2] Stravinsky was intimately familiar with the well-tried formulae, the conditioned reflexes of his musical heritage, and in the neoclassical pieces he worked with them in many ways. From *Pulcinella* onwards Stravinsky has re-presented familiar musical conventions in order that he can challenge and subvert them. In *The Rake's Progress*, for example, he works with the conventions of eighteenth- and nineteenth-century opera and theatre – formal set pieces, musical gestures, tonal procedures – but placing them in quite new contexts. On the one hand, this could well help to account for the popularity of *The Rake's Progress* among (on the whole) highly reactionary opera audiences: on one level, the work fulfils the conventional expectations of its audiences (reinforced by the institutions which support it) – 'the comedy of verbal and musical manners of one's first impression', as Stephen Walsh puts it[3] – and in that sense its use of dead formulae has deadly consequences. On the other hand, it is clear that this is not the only level on which the work operates – if it were mere Mozart pastiche, it could hardly sustain itself. Below the surface there is something quite different. In Stravinsky's hands, the Deadly becomes the Immediate (that is, a vital, 'necessary theatre, one in which there is only a practical difference between actor and audience, not a fundamental one'[4]). The use, for instance, of the eighteenth-century device of the Epilogue, stepping out of character and in front of the curtain to point out the work's 'moral', is a brilliant touch

132

and stands for so much of the musical as well as dramatic masking and unmasking that takes place during the course of the work:

> Let Baba warn the ladies:
> You will find out soon or later
>   That, good or bad,
>   All men are mad;
> All they say or do is theatre.

In this sense, the procedures of Stravinsky (and his librettists, Auden and Kallman) are not so far removed from Brecht's technique of *Verfremdung*, or alienation, an aspect of his epic theatre where he lulls the audience into a false sense of security (fulfilling the deadly expectations of his bourgeois audiences) before abruptly interrupting or switching (immediacy) in order to make the audience acutely and actively aware of the conventions of the theatre, in order to avoid deadliness. As Jonathan Jeremiah Peacham states at the outset of *The Threepenny Opera*:

> Something new is needed. My business is too hard, for my business is arous-
> ing human sympathy. There are a few things that stir men's souls, just a few,
> but the trouble is that after repeated use they lose their effect. Because man
> has the abominable gift of being able to deaden his feelings at will . . .[5]

The immediacy of much of Brecht's theatre (and, indeed, of the music that his collaborators, notably Weill, produced for it) results from his involvement with another of Brook's categories: Rough Theatre, that is, popular, folk and street theatre, circus, pantomime and cabaret. Such Rough Theatre was clearly of fundamental importance to Stravinsky too: puppetry and the *commedia dell'arte* (*Petrushka, Pulcinella*), Russian itinerant folk entertainers (*Renard, The Soldier's Tale*), rustic Russian rituals (*Les Noces*). Its roughness once again results in an immediacy lacking from more formal, institutionalised kinds of theatre and opera. It is characterised by, *inter alia*, a boldness and directness of presentation, a breakdown of the distinction between actors and audience (the audience are active participants in much folk theatre) and a utilisation of a wide range of performing spaces (certainly not dedicated theatres), often open-air, and rooted in the community; it dispenses with the parapherna-lia of formal theatre, working with the minimum of props, costumes, sets and so on; it is usually ritualised and stylised in presentation; and actors, singers, dancers and musicians are all in constant view. In other words, Rough Theatre represents a continuity with a much older tradition of pre-literate theatre such as the Ancient Greek Dionysian rites or the medieval English mystery plays. An interest in such theatre was endemic in the earlier years of the twentieth century, as was a looking outwards to oriental theatre, particularly from Indonesia and Japan. Artaud, Brecht, Cocteau, Jarry, Meyerhold, Pirandello, to name but a few, were all engaged with exploring new kinds of immediate, non-naturalistic, non-narrative theatre by drawing, in part, on ancient, folk and non-Western sources.[6] Stravinsky's collaboration with Cocteau is especially significant. But it is probably *The Soldier's Tale* that best demonstrates his engagement with Rough Theatre and helps to account for the subsequent influence of this work.

Adorno had once championed *The Soldier's Tale*. As Max Paddison reminds us, in 1932 Adorno had regarded it as among Stravinsky's 'best and most exposed works', allowing it 'a certain "logical consistence" in its critical, ironic and dialectical relation to society'.[7] By the late 1940s, however, in *Philosophy of Modern Music*, Adorno had altered his position, using *The Soldier's Tale* as a prime example of Stravinsky's regressive 'infantilism' and now denying its dialectical aspects. Though he gives Stravinsky credit for his critical use of jazz elements by which he 'reveals, by means of distortion, the shabby and worn-out aspects of a dance music . . . now given in completely to the demands of the market',[8] Adorno nonetheless argues that '[t]here is hardly a schizophrenic mechanism . . . which does not find therein a highly valid equivalent. The negative objectivity of the work of art recalls in itself the phenomenon of regression.'[9] In Paddison's gloss on this passage, he confirms Adorno's view that 'the Subject regresses to the repetitive behaviour of the infantile state, and to notions of the archaic and the primitive "beyond history"'.[10] In Chapter 1 we explored some of the reasons for this stance of Adorno (to be followed up in Chapter 7). It should be clear (historically) why he regarded the collective aspects and objective presentation of Stravinsky's ideas as regressive, and if we remember how he asserts Stravinsky's position dialectically in relation to Schoenberg, his 'cultural blindness', as Paddison describes it, becomes evident. Paddison argues that

> those elements of which Adorno is so highly critical in Stravinsky's music, and which he regards as regressive . . . are precisely those features which distinguish the music of many non-European cultures from the tradition of European Classical and Romantic music. . . . In what Adorno criticizes as a lack of a sense of the historical dimension of the material, and also as a lack of creativity, can be seen from another perspective in fact as exactly what distinguishes Stravinsky in this century.[11]

It is those objective features of Stravinsky's 'rough' music theatre, rooted in a collective heritage, that constitute its originality and its influence.

The aspects of *The Soldier's Tale* that identify it unequivocally as Rough Theatre are obvious enough. In *Expositions and Developments*, Stravinsky tells Craft that he had been considering writing a 'dramatic spectacle for a *théâtre ambulant*' for some time[12] – though, equally, during the 'shoe-string economics' of World War 1, writing a theatre piece for severely reduced forces, independent of the machinery of the established theatre, seemed a necessity if it was to be performed at all (in fact its first – highly successful – performance took place in a small Victorian theatre in Lausanne). Being scored for three speakers, a dancer and seven instrumentalists, all of whom are present in the performing space all of the time, and its subject matter being focused on an 'ordinary' soldier, the work's 'rough' credentials as theatre with origins far from the bourgeois theatre are readily apparent. Rough Theatre, as Brook defines it, 'deals with men's actions, . . . it is down to earth and direct . . . [and, unlike the Holy Theatre] it admits wickedness and laughter'.[13] This is clearly true of *The Soldier's Tale.*

The origins of the story are to be found in one of Afanasiev's tales, translated (with Stravinsky's assistance) and moulded into a libretto by C. F. Ramuz. In 1918 a story about a soldier and the devil, however much rooted in a folk past, could only have been interpreted in the light of developments of the time: '*Histoire du soldat* remains my one stage work with a contemporary reference.'[14] Its other immediately apparent contemporary element, to which we have seen Adorno's attention was drawn, is its 'jazz' content. Stravinsky describes his discovery of American jazz at this time as 'a very important event' in his life.[15] It influenced, he argues, his choice of instruments, opting for 'high' and 'low' in each category: violin and double bass, clarinet and bassoon (instead of saxophone), cornet and trombone, and percussion. In practice, despite his claim that these instruments are 'jazz legitimates', his band seems far less like a jazz combo than, say, Walton's slightly later *Pierrot lunaire* parody, *Façade* (1920–21), which is scored for flute/piccolo, clarinet/bass clarinet, saxophone, trumpet, percussion, cello and speaker. The fact is, it was not the actual sound of jazz that had had a profound impact on Stravinsky because, as he admits, he had never actually heard any jazz at that point, his knowledge being derived entirely from sheet music copies which Ansermet had brought with him from America: 'I borrowed its rhythmic style not as played, but as written.'[16] In a sense, then, just as the pared-down instrumentation immediately suggests that Stravinsky is moving away from his nineteenth-century Russian orchestral patrimony, so the incorporation of all sorts of popular musics into the score of *The Soldier's Tale* indicates the beginnings of neoclassicism. His distanced reworking of ragtime sits alongside an eclectic mix of dances (a tango and a waltz), a 'Royal March' which alludes to nineteenth-century opera and two pseudo-Lutheran chorales, and in many senses offers as much a critique of his materials as he was to present two years later in *Pulcinella*. Furthermore, this eclecticism (there is no pretence at unity) of material, which serves to undermine narrative continuity, and the use of popular as well as folk music further reinforce the directness, the roughness of the work.

The apparent contemporaneity suggested by the character of the soldier and the jazz is offset by the way in which the tale is presented. Just as Stravinsky appears to distance himself from the jazz elements he uses (he 'reinvents' ragtime in the same way he was, in subsequent neoclassical works, to 'reinvent the past'), so the audience is made to distance itself from the subject matter. This is achieved by the use of the narrator, a device 'adopted to satisfy the need for a two-way go-between; that is, for someone who is an illusionist interpreter between the characters themselves, as well as a commentator between the stage and the audience'.[17] The device is not new. The chorus in Attic tragedy, for example, served just this function, as both an active participant in the unfolding of the drama and a commentator who could stand back from events and interpret them for the audience. In *The Birth of Tragedy* (1872), Nietzsche recalls that it was Schiller who suggested that the chorus was 'a living wall that tragedy constructs around itself in order to close itself off from the world of reality and to preserve its ideal domain and its poetical freedom. . . . The introduction of the chorus, says Schiller, is the decisive step by which war is declared openly and honorably against all naturalism in art.'[18] So it is with the introduction of the narrator into *The Soldier's Tale* – and, even more obviously, as will be seen below, in *Oedipus rex*. Nietzsche's discussion of tragedy took place at a time when contemporary art was concerned with what he describes as 'the region of wax-work cabinets',[19] that is, the Romantic preoccupation with naturalism and realism. And it was similarly against such naturalist traditions that so many early modernists turned, looking, as we have seen, beyond Western culture and to pre-naturalistic forms as sources for their new art. This is surely one of the reasons for the prevalence of Ancient Greek themes in so much (broadly defined neoclassical) work around the 1920s, as exemplified in the work of such key figures as Cocteau, Satie, Poulenc, Milhaud, Stravinsky, Eliot, Joyce and Yeats. Though the fragmentary, multiple texture of classical allusions in T. S. Eliot's *The Waste Land* (1922) is a landmark in the development of modernism, a work first published in the same year offers another example of a wonderful coming together of the high-minded classical, the bawdy *commedia dell'arte* and the colourfully exotic. Edith Sitwell's *Façade*:

Popular Song

Lily O'Grady,
Silly and shady,
Longing to be
A lazy lady,
Walked by the cupolas, gables in the
Lake's Georgian stables,
In a fairy tale like the heat intense,
And the mists in the woods when across the fence
The children gathering strawberries
Are changed by the heat into negresses,
Though their fair hair
Shines there
Like gold-haired planets, Calliope, Io,
Pomona, Antiope, Echo, and Clio . . .

Sitwell's poetry seems to share something of the 'objective' Stravinskian spirit through its disrupted attempts at narrative where, when spoken rhythmically, the exciting rhythmic and metrical patterns of the words dominate their sense. Its eclecticism, too, is striking. When performed with Walton's score, infused as it is with allusions to all sorts of popular music, such a sense is reinforced.

In performances (at dramatic festivals) of tragedies, such as Aeschylus's *Oresteia* plays, the chorus would have been made up of ordinary citizens. Commenting on the design of Greek theatres, Nietzsche observes that 'there was at bottom no opposition between public and chorus'. He continues:

> A public of spectators as we know it was unknown to the Greeks: in their theaters the terraced structure of concentric arcs made it possible for everybody to actually overlook the whole world of culture around him and to imagine, in absorbed contemplation, that he himself was a chorist.[20]

It is important to note that, though the chorus represented some kind of collective voice, it was not necessarily presented as collective speech or singing – individuals spoke from within the chorus in the first person singular, principally the chorus leader or 'Choregos' figure. The wearing of masks, however, reinforced the collective identity. Here again we find a fascinating convergence of concerns of the early modernists: masks were one of the elements of stylisation common to Greek theatre, Japanese Noh drama and puppetry. And Brecht's alienation technique too, though not literally involving masks, is a prime example of playing with the metaphorical masks of convention.

The narrator in *The Soldier's Tale* fulfils the role of the chorus. His most important function is one of distancing the audience from the tale, that is, in making it clear, as does Baba at the end of *The Rake's Progress*, that they are witnesses to and participants in an act of theatre. As a member of the audience at a *Festspielhaus* performance of *The Ring*, you ease yourself into seats in a darkened auditorium; the source of the orchestral sounds is hidden from view, as is all the machinery by which the stage effects are brought about (assuming Wagner's production specifications are observed). Giants, dragons, swimming Rhinemaidens, magic fire and the destruction of Valhalla are all meant to be believable: as a passive spectator, you must, in Coleridge's famous phrase, suspend your disbelief. As a member of the audience at a performance of *The Soldier's Tale*, you are involved from the start because you share the performing space, you witness the costume changes, you can see the musicians at work – you respond, as Stravinsky wanted, as much to 'the scrape of the violin and the punctuation of the drums'[21] as to the music itself. And, as in Stravinsky's earlier piece of rough folk theatre derived from Afanasiev, *Renard* (1916), instrumental role-play is important – here the identification of the violin with the soldier's soul and the drums with 'diablerie'. Though a narrative is presented, the very presence of the alienating narrator allows for the disruption and fragmentation of that narrative: hence, the musical 'collage'. Hence, too, the sense that the audience is as much participating in a ritual as observing a play. And, of course, in works where there is no attempt at presenting a narrative, this sense of ritual is all the more heightened – pre-eminently in *Les Noces*.[22] This is where Rough Theatre merges with Holy Theatre.

The Soldier's Tale has been an important point of origination for the development of much twentieth-century music theatre. Along with that other crucial work for ensemble and narrator, *Pierrot lunaire* (which Stravinsky famously described as the 'solar plexus as well as the mind of early twentieth-century music'[23]), whose latent expressionist theatre has influenced post-World War 2 composers in so many ways, *The Soldier's Tale* paved the way for a new wave of music theatre, from the overtly 'rough' undertakings of such works as Birtwistle's *Down by the Greenwood Side* (1968–9), Maxwell Davies's *Le Jongleur de Notre Dame* (1978) and *The Lighthouse* (1979) and Mark-Anthony Turnage's *Greek* (1986–8), the anti-opera, nonsense theatre of Ligeti's *Aventures* (1962) and *Nouvelles aventures* (1965), and even the instrumental role-play of Stockhausen's monumental *Licht* (1977–). The possible reasons for the renewal of interest in Stravinsky's theatre in the 1960s in particular will be explored below, though it is interesting to observe how this coincides, in Europe especially, with the growing impact of the experimentalism of Cage and other Americans, for whom theatre was an ineluctable aspect of any and every musical performance. This context notwithstanding, the particular influence of Stravinsky's rough, 'objective', non-narrative theatre, often involving instrumental role-play, was undeniably broad.

Brook's other category of theatre, which can be seen to have an important bearing on the way in which we might understand Stravinsky's theatre, is that of the Holy Theatre – or, slightly more long-windedly, the 'Theatre of the Invisible-Made-Visible'. The theatre, he argues – and we might easily add the concert platform – 'is the last forum where idealism is still an open question: many audiences all over the world will answer positively from their own experience that they have seen the face of the invisible through an experience on the stage that transcended their experience in life'.[24] Interestingly for our purposes here, one of the first examples he gives of a work that can achieve this, that can fire 'the spirit' and give 'a reminder that daily drabness is not necessarily all', is *Oedipus*. Brook gives Artaud's 'Theatre of Cruelty', alongside Happenings and the work of Samuel Beckett, as twentieth-century examples of Holy Theatre. Artaud's theory of the theatre shares many aspects with the Rough Theatre: for example, his interest in Balinese theatre, his prescription (in the 'First Manifesto of the Theatre of Cruelty', which was included in his 1938 collection *The Theatre and its Double*) that stage and auditorium should be abandoned to enable direct contact between actors and audience, his rejection of narrative, realistic theatre. But Artaud also proposed moving away from a theatre dependent on text and towards one more concerned with myth, ritual and magic, with something metaphysical, sublime: 'Instead of harking back to texts regarded as sacred and definite, we must first break theatre's subjugation to the text and rediscover the idea of a kind of unique language somewhere in between gesture and thought'.[25] Balinese theatrical productions offered Artaud an important model because there 'is something of a religious ritual ceremony about them, in the sense that they eradicate any idea of pretence, a ridiculous imitation of real life, from the spectator's mind'.[26] A holy theatre, by Brook's definition, 'not only presents the invisible but also offers conditions that make its perception possible'.[27]

This ritual dimension clearly underlies many of Stravinsky's works – and not necessarily only those written for the theatre: we saw in Chapter 2, for instance, how it is possible to read the first of the *Three Pieces for String Quartet* as a kind of latent drama, and that ritualistic – even holy – concerns are also a part of the structure of the *Symphonies of Wind Instruments*. Such ritual is at its most obvious in major stage works spanning his entire creative life: *The Rite of Spring*, *Les Noces*, *Oedipus rex*,

Agon, The Flood. Ritual is concerned with the expression of the collective, of the community; as in ancient ceremonies and acts of religious worship, it transcends the mundane through repeated and repetitive actions; it is symbolic rather than representational; it is stylised and is often associated with a special place and language separate from the everyday. For these reasons, ritual is not primarily concerned with linear time or narratives and it cannot represent contemporary events. Myth (broadly defined) thus becomes an important part of many rituals because it represents a collective heritage – indeed, for Jung, myths and their archetypal characters are nothing less than a direct expression of the collective unconscious. Stravinsky's well-known musical characteristics – crudely put – of repeating rhythms, regular pulse, ostinatos, static pedal points, symmetries, limited melodies and non-developmental structures are ideally matched to the presentation of ritual. And, as we have seen, this constituted more than enough evidence for Adorno to condemn Stravinsky as a regressive primitive, as guilty of infantilism, concerned with 'self-elimination, unconscious dexterity, and adjustment to the blind totality'.[28] But once again this is a further indication of Adorno's 'cultural blindness': the involvement of Stravinsky with collective ritual was as much a consequence of his Russianness as was the attitude of Schoenberg (who entrusted 'himself openly to the aesthetic principle of individuation') the historical product of the post-Beethoven Austro-German tradition. Adorno believed the composer's role was to move beyond music's primitive, magical, ritualistic origins, 'to "grasp" and to place all sounds into an order, and to reduce the magic essence of music to human logic'.[29] While Stravinsky's music embodies a submission to 'natural' phenomena, Schoenberg's music, in Adorno's view, represents a more advanced stage, namely the domination of nature, something that has been longed for, he argues, since the beginning of the bourgeois era.

But if Stravinsky's work were only mere magic – no better than some sort of shamanistic incantation or the worst excesses of the latest club techno music (to which the collective response in the 1990s has been enhanced by mass 'recreational' drug-taking) – it would certainly not have Brook's 'holy' characteristics. The ways in which the 'invisible is made visible' in his non-narrative theatre are many-levelled and correspond with the complex non-developmental nature of his music. Nowhere is this more obvious than in *Oedipus rex*. The means by which Stravinsky and Cocteau constructed a stylised theatre of 'monumental aspect' have been widely discussed. They embraced Schiller's introduction of the chorus as an 'open and honourable' declaration of war against all naturalism and took it one stage further. Most obviously, the chorus and the protagonists sing in Latin, immediately distancing them from the audience. Stravinsky's statuesque chorus of tenors and basses, masked and in costume and ranked in full view at the front of the stage, comments on the action. But in a sense the 'true' chorus (a Choregos figure) is the speaker, detached from the drama and introducing the work's events in the language of the audience (he 'expresses himself like a conférencier, presenting the story with a detached voice'). Wearing evening dress and standing in front of the proscenium, he appears as both one of the audience and an intermediary between auditorium and stage. Indeed, some producers of this work (David Alden at English National Opera, for example) have gone further in representing 'audience as chorist' by placing the chorus, also costumed in evening dress, in the audience (though why a modern-day audience should be speaking Latin is somewhat baffling). Other aspects of production specified in the preface to the score serve to reinforce the work's stylisation: bold, rough and two-dimensional décor, the use of masks, a stylised acting style where only arms and heads move. The conflict between speaker and actors/singers, which severely disrupts narrative continuity and naturalistic representation, is matched by the music which, as a self-confessed *Merzbild*, enhances the disruption of any sense of linear unfolding of plot or argument. Even though individual moments, such as Jocasta's Act 2 aria (by adopting the rhetoric of nineteenth-century opera), might seem to invite narrative interpretation – even a kind of 'naturalistic' expressivity with which the audience might begin to identify – they are not connected with other moments in the work, each of which is individually characterised, so that the musical whole takes on a static aspect in keeping with the work's professed monumentality. Just as the structure of the plot is overtly signalled by the speaker, so through various devices of repetition the music signals its own functions as structural punctuation and frame (that is, it is quite clearly not some sort of emotional prop or merely a backdrop for the stage characters). This is music theatre as ritual where indeed the music *is* the ritual (this is what defines it as 'holy').

Take, for example, the Epilogue (beginning at fig. 170). It begins with a familiar signal (role-play), a fanfare for four trumpets which interrupts and is interrupted by the speaker and which announces the arrival of the messenger. But, like the fanfare at the start of *The Rake's Progress* which proclaims little more than 'on va commençer', this fanfare proclaims the structural fact that, as the speaker spells out for us, 'Ensuite c'est l'épilogue'. What ensues is a sequence of four eight-bar refrains for the messenger ('Divum Jocastae caput mortuum!') alternating with verses for the chorus (the only interruption to the pattern is at fig. 192, 'Aspikite fores').

The messenger disappears, Oedipus reappears, and the chorus signals closure ('Ekke! Regum Oedipoda') with a return to the music of the very opening of the work. It is fitting that *Oedipus rex* should finish with the simplest of the ostinatos (repeated Gs and B♭s) that have not only punctuated the course of the work (and also relate to its putative system of tonal centres) but that, in their very stasis, symbolise both the work's essentially non-linear character and the fact that, as a ritual, a definitive ending is impossible.

Stravinsky's reluctance to commit himself to the nature of the genre of *Oedipus Rex* – he designates it an 'opera-oratorio' – is telling,[30] and indicates in part why it is such a radical and influential work. In its 'objective' mode of delivery, its dispassionate presentation of the facts of the Oedipus story, its focus more on music than plot (it could not, in fact, be otherwise because the speaker has already told us what is going to happen before it happens), it is clearly in the tradition of the oratorio. Yet it is also a work which is concerned explicitly with the nature of ritual itself, with role-play, with a formality and stylisation characteristic of opera, and which therefore belongs absolutely on the stage. Its significance as a reevaluation of what music theatre was capable of should not be underestimated. Even if subsequent composers of music theatre works may not have been directly influenced by *Oedipus rex*, its novel attitude to the roles played by music in the theatre paved the way, as will be discussed in the second part of this chapter, for a rich variety of experiments which have culminated in some of the most important musical statements of the second half of the twentieth century.

Music theatre since the Second World War

The resurgence of interest in theatre among composers in the 1960s is a fascinating phenomenon. Opera had been disregarded by the avant-garde since World War 2, and continued, for the most part, to be so throughout the 1960s. Boulez's celebrated rallying cry that all opera houses should be burned, and Ligeti's comment that 'I cannot, will not compose a traditional "opera"'[31] are symptomatic of wider attitudes. There were, of course, important operas written in the thirty-five years following the end of the War – preeminently *The Rake's Progress*, but also all Britten's operas (from *Peter Grimes* in 1945 to *Death in Venice* in 1973) and, for example, a more conventional work by Henze (*The Bassarids* of 1965, to a text by the librettists of *The Rake's Progress*) and, perhaps surprisingly, Maxwell Davies (*Taverner* of 1962–8). Though they engage with the operatic tradition in different ways, these works can nonetheless be considered 'traditional' operas because their (apparent) continuity with the operatic past is more obvious than their discontinuity.

Paul Griffiths sums up the position of the avant-garde with customary conciseness: 'In the 1950s, when attention was generally fixed on musical fundamentals, few young composers wanted to work in the theatre.'[32] Opera and its institutions were perceived as the domain of the reactionary, and as the past was being rejected ('History as it is made by great composers is not a history of conservation but of destruction – even while cherishing what has been destroyed'[33]) so the operatic genre as a whole was discarded by the younger generation. The experiments taking place in Paris and Darmstadt involving both the will to control (integral serialism) and the deployment of a new-found formal freedom (aleatoricism), not to mention the challenges to the entire European tradition being mounted by John Cage and his followers, left little room for a genre rooted in tonality and concerned, in general, with the presentation of a linear narrative (with the notable exception of such key works as *Wozzeck*, *Lulu* and *Moses und Aron*). However, this is not to say that composers abandoned entirely the notion of theatre. One of Cage's most important lessons to his contemporaries was that all music-making was concerned with theatre: *4′33″* (1952) places the theatricality of performance in the foreground and draws the audience's attention to the fact that any concert is a kind of Holy Theatre (it takes place in a dedicated space with its own costumes and rituals), though equally Cage challenges an audience to recognise how 'deadly' the ritual of concert life had become. *4′33″* is a limited kind of Happening; Cage himself had initiated other Happenings in the early 1950s with his colleagues at Black Mountain College, most notably Robert Rauschenberg, Jasper Johns, Merce Cunningham and David Tudor. The Happening, a performance art that crossed and challenged disciplinary boundaries, was a piece of total theatre that had a profound impact on the way many artists and musicians thought. The work, in America, of La Monte Young and the Fluxus movement, and Harry Partch, and, in Europe, of Bussotti, Kagel, Ligeti, the Stockhausen of the late 1960s onwards, H. K. Gruber, even – arguably – the *Polytopes* and *Diatope* of Xenakis, all owe a debt to Cage and contributed to the 'development' of the Happenings. As in *4′33″*, 'music' (as the sonic phenomenon we might conventionally recognise) is conspicuously absent, even if the 'pieces' are realised by musicians: La Monte Young, for example, in a series of pieces dating from 1960 called simply *Composition*, and Stockhausen in *Aus den sieben Tagen* (1968) resorted to scores consisting merely of sets of (wildly impractical) instructions, while Kagel's *Der Atem* (1970) depicts a wind player caring for his instrument and only rarely actually playing it.

Although the high modernism of the 1950s had generally precluded an overt engagement with theatre the situation began to change around 1960. New kinds of operas were produced in the 1960s and 1970s that demonstrated an engagement with the concerns of a Cageian theatricality but incorporated them into a more 'composerly' kind of drama, a total theatre that attempted to articulate new kinds of narratives. One reason for this was a desire to engage overtly with the politics of the left: Nono's *Intolleranza* (1960) and Zimmermann's *Die Soldaten* (1958–64), for example, challenged the conventional narrative lines of bourgeois opera by inventing a multiple theatre that employs film and electronic tape to extend the bounds of the drama (in Zimmermann's case, it came from a desire to demonstrate the 'sphericality of time', the simultaneous presence of past, present and future). Henze, in another political opera, *We Come to the River* (1974–6), attempted similar things. Berio, too, in the provocatively titled *Opera* (1970), subverted some of the expectations its title might suggest (itself a decidedly 'Stravinskian' act), a tendency which culminated in the monumental achievement of the fragmented, anti-narrative structure of *La vera storia* (1977–81).

What was happening on the stage of the opera house reflected a broader engagement with theatre by composers outside the opera house. The reasons for this may well, in part, have had something to do with a renewed interest in communication – both integral serialism (formalism at its most extreme) and electronic music (which did not require any visible performers) failed to engage with an audience much wider than one of composers, performers and delegates at the specialist summer schools. The wish to communicate political messages necessitated a return to the institutions if not the conventions of the operatic theatre (even Brecht realised that you could not destroy bourgeois theatre; you had to use it as a vehicle for change). Similarly, composers began to recognise that not only was a musical performance inherently theatrical but that, by engaging with the Rough and the Holy Theatres, they could once again involve audiences in the performance of new work, while at the same time freeing themselves from the necessity of conventional narrative story-telling. One model was *Pierrot lunaire*, whose latent theatricality, flexible ensemble, formal organisation and expressionistic directness offered possibilities that were taken up by many, most notably Maxwell Davies in such pieces as *Revelation and Fall* (1965–6), *Eight Songs for a Mad King* (1969), *Miss Donnithorne's Maggot* (1974) and *The Medium* (1981), and, to a lesser extent, Birtwistle in *Punch and Judy* and *Monodrama* (1967, subsequently withdrawn), as well as Henze in his politically explicit music theatre works such as *El Cimarrón* (1969–70) and *Der langwierige Weg in die Wohnung der Natascha*

Ungeheuer (1971). In the case of the latter, the *Pierrot* quintet is used to symbolise the 'old sick bourgeoisie', to which a brass quintet, jazz group ('the expression of a false Utopia'[34]), Hammond organ, percussionist and tape (playing, among other sounds, snippets of Verdi's *Aïda*) are added. Such music theatre appears to bring together in an interesting way (and not without precedent in *Pierrot* itself) the traditions of expressionism with the 'objectivity', the alienation of neoclassicism.

On the whole, the *Pierrot* model offered composers the opportunity to explore individual character, often individuals *in extremis*, where inner conflict or mental torment is stylised in such a way as to confront an audience directly (Immediate Theatre), paralleled by the break-up in its narrative structure (in, for instance, *Eight Songs for a Mad King*, a prime example of such music theatre, the disturbed King interacts with caged instrumentalists, with a wide range of fragmentary musical *objets trouvés*, and with the audience). An alternative model was suggested by Stravinsky. His 'objective', non-narrative theatre, his interest more in the collective than in the individual, and his concern for the covert drama of instrumental role-play, have had immense consequences for composers since 1960. It did not offer many opportunities for character exploration or a platform for political debate; rather, it concerned itself with myth and ritual. The legacy of the rough folk theatre of *Renard* and *The Soldier's Tale*, combined with a continuing interest in non-Western theatre, can be observed in many smaller-scale music theatre pieces, from Birtwistle's *Bow Down* (1970) and Stockhausen's *Musik im Bauch* (1974–5) to Judith Weir's *A Night at the Chinese Opera* (1987). Arguably, even Britten responded to this trend (he had always admired *Oedipus Rex*) when, in the 1960s, he suspended his production of works for the opera house in favour of the church parables, which combined the medieval liturgical dramas and mystery plays with Noh drama to produce a fascinating fusion of the Rough and the Holy – principally in the ritualised *Curlew River* of 1964, based on the Japanese *Sumidagawa* play, and displaying such 'rough' characteristics as itinerant musicians, stylised delivery (a tenor takes the leading role of the Madwoman) and a greater than usual prominence given to untuned percussion.

More recently, the Holy Theatre has moved back into the opera house and has brought about a renewal and redefinition of opera (though, of course, the expressionist tradition also persists). Opera began as a stylised entertainment (Monteverdi, Lully, Handel, Gluck . . .) and it was only in the nineteenth century, when grand opera and music drama took on some of the naturalistic characteristics of contemporary literature, that the genre came to be associated with musical and emotional excess. Since

1970, having experimented on a small scale with non-narrative music theatre and having learnt all sorts of lessons from Cage, composers returned to the opera house, but to an earlier stylised kind of theatre, recognising the ritualised conventions associated with opera (that opera can, in fact, never be naturalistic). In addition, the modern opera house offered the technical facilities for a new, integrated music theatre. The consequence has been many ritual works for the opera house such as Philip Glass's trilogy, *Einstein on the Beach* (1975, produced in collaboration with the radical American director and designer, Robert Wilson), *Satyagraha* (1980) and *Akhnaten* (1984). Robert Wilson also collaborated with Louis Andriessen on *De Materie* (1985–8), an extraordinarily eclectic (and decidedly non-narrative) stage work whose texts include a seventeenth-century treatise on shipbuilding, the visions of Hadewijch and the reminiscences of Marie Curie. Andriessen's opera, *Rosa* (1994, after Peter Greenaway's 'horse drama'), while being concerned in part with the genre of opera itself, equally distances itself from the narrative conventions of that genre. And in his operas, John Adams attempts a coming-together of his 'distanced', repetitive post-minimal music and the immediacy of 'realistic' contemporary subject-matter: *Nixon in China* (1987), *The Death of Klinghoffer* (1990) and the quirkily titled 'song play', *I Was Looking at the Ceiling and Then I Saw the Sky* (1995), on the subject of the most recent San Francisco earthquake. Stockhausen's remarkable on-going *Licht* cycle, on which he first began work in 1977, is clearly an outcome, writ large, of his interest in ritual theatre explored in the 1960s and 1970s, while Birtwistle's monumental *The Mask of Orpheus* (1973–5, 1981–4, first performed 1986) fuses music, song, drama, myth, mime and electronics in vast, ritual cycles of death and renewal. As if to confirm this new-found confidence of composers in the possibilities of opera, Messiaen, at the age of nearly seventy, began work on his first and only stage work, *Saint François d'Assise* (1975–83), a series of eight 'Franciscan scenes' lasting more than four hours. Here again we are offered not a narrative opera (as in the Glass, Stockhausen and Birtwistle examples, Messiaen is not primarily concerned with story-telling) but a ritual meditation – in this case, an explicitly religious one, a truly holy theatre – perhaps not significantly different from his other 'rituals' such as *Turangalîla*, *Et expecto* or *La Transfiguration*. Though he cites *Pelléas et Mélisande* and *Boris Godunov* as significant (operatic) influences, these 'scenes from a saint's life' (a drama of emotions, not action) might equally well have *Les Noces* as a precursor. Certainly the extended kinds of non-linear time explored in all these ritual stage works owe much to the innovations of Stravinsky earlier in the century.

Ex. 4.1 Maxwell Davies, *Vesalii icones*, No. 8 ('St. Veronica Wipes his Face') (opening)

The Stravinskian theatrical legacy was in evidence not just on the opera stage. While Maxwell Davies's *Eight Songs for a Mad King* clearly grew out of *Pierrot lunaire*, his next theatre work, *Vesalii icones* (1969), though sharing the formalism of *Pierrot*'s structure (its fourteen movements take as their starting point the superimposition of Vesalius's drawings of the human body on the fourteen Stations of the Cross), its interaction of dancer, solo cellist and ensemble appears to be indebted at least as much to *The Soldier's Tale* and *Agon*. We are now in a more ritualised world (each movement begins with the turning of a bell wheel) and, instead of investigating character, the work (like so many of Maxwell Davies's works of this period) is concerned with the theme of betrayal – specifically, the betrayal of Christ and of spiritual thought throughout the ages. Parody, again a common feature of his works of this time, is used here to powerful effect: an expression of doubt, derision and hypocrisy. This is seen at its most hard-hitting in No. 8 ('St Veronica Wipes his Face'), which is not merely a collage of found musical fragments; these objects are distorted to confuse any sense of what is musically (and spiritually) real. The movement begins, for example, with a quotation in the cello from Maxwell Davies's own motet *Ecce manus tradentis* (1964, a work which similarly deals with the betrayal of Christ by Judas) but distorted by the nineteenth-century drawing-room style of the piano accompaniment, 'an inflated plainsong fragment in a musical style which suggests a Victorian daguerreotype'[35] (see Ex. 4.1). Other distortions occur during the course of the movement, including the bending of the *Ecce manus* material 'to resemble a Schenkerian analysis [of the scherzo from Beethoven's Fifth Symphony], but instead of stripping off layers of music to expose ultimately a "common" skeleton below, the "skeleton" is heard first and levels are added'.[36] At the end of the movement, we are presented with a musical 'daguerreotype': the opening bars are replayed on a poor quality tape recorder. In the sixth movement, 'The Mocking of Christ', it is an out-of-tune piano, played by the dancer, which distorts a Victorian hymn-tune ('a musical style which I consider almost the ultimate blasphemy'[37]), later transformed into a 1920s foxtrot. In all these cases, it is difficult to discern what is musically 'true' – just as we cannot see the 'reality', Davies seems to be saying, of the reproduction of Christ's face on St Veronica's cloth, for the centuries of accumulated interpretation. This culminates in the last movement with the resurrection, not of Christ but of the Antichrist, again accompanied by a foxtrot: 'It is a matter of distinguishing the false from the real . . . one should not be taken in by appearances.'[38]

The parallels with *The Soldier's Tale* are striking. Van den Toorn's account is pertinent here: 'Under both the "Russian" and neoclassical labels, often [Stravinsky composed] a kind of mock ritual: a cool, crisp, brittle mechanization of the musical manners or conventions – and hence, presumably, of the underlying beliefs, sanctities, and spiritualities – of bygone or nearly bygone eras.'[39] This is partly Maxwell Davies's intention. And similarly Maxwell Davies's dictum for *Vesalii icones* – 'one should not be taken in by appearances' – might equally well stand for *The Soldier's Tale*. Among other things, the two works share the triumph of the Devil/Antichrist, the ironic transformation of religious choral songs, and the incorporation of twentieth-century popular music. Most significant is the direct participation of instrumentalists in the theatre itself: just as in *The Soldier's Tale* possession of the violin is equated with possession of the soldier's soul, so in *Vesalii icones* the cellist takes on a number of different roles, ranging from the Flagellator to St Veronica. The cellist is required to sit apart from the rest of the ensemble, close to the dancer, and so becomes an intermediary rather like Stravinsky's narrator, while the dancer interacts with the musicians through such means as playing the piano and tapping out rhythms which are then taken up by the ensemble. Though a different kind of theatre, the parallels with *Agon* are also not without interest, a formal, multi-movement work (another kind of 'mock ritual' – literally, a 'competition') which involves the coming together of dance, an eclectic range of musical allusions from the Renaissance to the contemporary, and employing the self-confessed inflections of 'blues and boogie-woogie'.

A more recent work that also explores, in quite a different way, aspects of religious life and heritage from different perspectives (namely that of Jews, Muslims and modern-day Americans), and whose origins in the ritual tableaux of *Les Noces* and *Oedipus rex* are clear, is Steve Reich's *The Cave* (1990–93). Written in collaboration with the video artist Beryl Korot, this 'video-theatre' work began as a series of video interviews with representatives from the different cultures regarding their interpretation of figures and events common to all the traditions: Abraham/Ibrahim, Sarah etc. The pitch/rhythmic profile of their words then becomes the starting-point for repeating melodies for an ensemble of instrumentalists and singers (a technique developed in *Different Trains* of 1988 and continued in *City Life* of 1994–5 and the *Three Tales* (in progress)) whose music, in performance, is coordinated with the interview fragments on large video screens. As well as involving the rhythmic typing of text on to the screens (to be sung homophonically by the chorus acting as narrator) the work requires movement of the performers about the performing space (which, in its first performances, took place on a specially designed set which incorporated the screens). Reich regards *The Cave* as a kind of 'video opera'. It offers a large-scale ritual experience, enhanced by his typically repetitive and highly rhythmic music. In common with the music theatre of a figure such as Birtwistle, it is not anti-narrative but, rather, attempts to examine the richness of a number of narratives from a variety of per-spectives (Biblical, Koranic and contemporary American academic) without necessarily reconciling them – indeed, the rapid cross-cutting of materials in Part 3 would seem to mitigate against such a 'synthesis'. Whether or not this is 'opera' is a moot point; what should be clear from the above account, however, is the ritual, dramatic origins of *The Cave* in a work such as *Les Noces*.

The link between *Les Noces* and *Oedipus rex*, at one end of the century, and *The Cave*, at the other, might be understood to be achieved via ritual works for the concert hall which do *not* involve any obvious theatre (other than the theatre of performance itself) but which still clearly have their roots in Stravinsky's music. The drama, the ceremonial, in these cases is derived from the internal structure of the music, often involving a high degree of repetition, and from the implied roles played by instruments within that structure – such as we have seen on a number of occasions lie at the heart of such works as *Three Pieces for String Quartet* and the *Symphonies of Wind Instruments*. Much of the music of Messiaen falls into this category, and not only because there is a Christian subtext to all his works. Preeminent among them, as we saw in Chapter 2, is *Et expecto resur-rectionem mortuorum* for wind and percussion, a monumental though non-specific religious ceremony (enhanced by the Biblical quotations that preface each movement and the use in some movements of transformed Easter plainchants). This is non-narrative, non-developmental music in the extreme which articulates a kind of non-linear time through its ritual repetitions, its bold block structure and its ceremonial use of percussion (which 'reinforces the grandeur of the Symbols and the reverence of the Holy by terrible fortissimos and mysterious resonances'[40]). The final movement ('And I heard the voice of a great multitude') consists of a long, slow, seemingly undirected melody, like a kind of chorale. This melody is sometimes in unison/octaves, sometimes 'harmonised', an alternation which, despite the lack of obvious repetitions in the melody itself (unlike the corresponding melody of the first movement), gives the effect of verses and refrains. The melody is accompanied throughout by percussion, most notably the repeated semiquavers on the gongs whose regular pulsations simultaneously mark the passage of time and, through their very repetitiveness, suggest a much larger (timeless) continuity. The parallels with another ritual concert work written ten years later by one of Messiaen's pupils – Boulez's *Rituel* – are striking. It shares with *Et expecto* a repetitive, ritual character which, in the work's dedication to the memory of Bruno Maderna, Boulez describes as an 'imaginary ceremony':

> Perpetual alternation:
>
> A sort of verse and response for an
> imaginary ceremony.
>
> A ceremony of remembrance – whence these
> numerous returns to the same
> formulae, while changing profile
> and perspective.
>
> Ceremony of extinction, the ritual
> of disappearance and survival:
> in this way are images imprinted on
> the musical memory –
> present/absent, imprinted on uncertainty.[41]

The 'perpetual alternation' of 'verse and response', which clearly brings *Rituel* into line with Messiaen and Stravinsky, is brought about by alternating conducted, odd-numbered refrains with unconducted, much freer, even-numbered verses. The ensemble (whose placement on the platform, as in *Et expecto*, is specified in the score) consists of eight distinct instrumental groups, each with associated percussion. As in the Messiaen, much of the musical material is melodic, sometimes presented as a monody, sometimes 'harmonised', and is punctuated by the regular pulsation of the percussion. Unlike the Messiaen, however, the music here is not continuous but is written in short 'bursts' (or 'éclats', cf. *Éclat/Multiples*) so that the silences or sustained notes between groups further contribute to its ritualised character. There is also a kind of role-play to the extent that, in the odd-numbered sections, the conclusion of a sustained note or chord is signalled by a short note or group of notes. Coincidentally, the modal material from which *Rituel* and the last movement of *Et expecto* are built is

Ex. 4.2a Boulez, *Rituel,* basic seven-note mode

Ex. 4.2b Messiaen, *Et expecto resurrectionem mortuorum*, first movement, opening mode

(unison instruments)

very similar: *Rituel*'s material is derived entirely from a seven-note mode (Ex. 4.2a: 0125678 [D,E♭,E,F,A♭,A,B♭]) while the opening repeated section of *Et expecto* is also built from only seven notes (Ex. 4.2b: 0124567 [G,A♭,A,B,C,C♯,D]). While it could be argued that there is a ritual dimension to many of Boulez's works, from the 'orientalism' of *Le Marteau sans maître* to the Varèse-like spatial interaction of natural and computer-controlled sounds in *Répons,* the overt ceremonial of *Rituel* is unique in Boulez. The simplicity of its musical building blocks and its formal execution immediately suggests parallels with Messiaen and draws our attention to the different kind of time being articulated – Boulez's 'ceremony of remembrance' with its 'returns to the same formulae, while changing profile and perspective'. An explicitly Stravinskian credo and atmosphere (perhaps more 'objective' than Messiaen's). Interestingly, the matrix from which *Rituel* is derived is itself derived from the matrix of *...explosante-fixe ...*, which was begun as a tribute on the death of Stravinsky in 1971 (its focal E♭ is an 'Es' for 'Stravinsky').

Both Messiaen and Boulez, like Stravinsky and Debussy before them, have drawn on Asian culture, from which aspects of their rituals are derived; for many twentieth-century American composers, especially those of the experimental tradition, Eastern aesthetics were immensely alluring as a means of renewing *Western* concert life while avoiding *European* models (*every* Cage performance, it could be argued, is not just theatre but ritual). But even for mainstream European modernists such as Xenakis, the musics of Arabia, India, Indonesia and Japan have had a profound impact, and the resulting music, while sharing little of the expected gentleness and serenity of much oriental art, nonetheless has a clearly ritualistic dimension through its repetitions, silences and stylised gestures – most notably in solo percussion works such as *Psappha* (1975) and *Rebonds* (1988). For composers of Asian origin who have attempted to fuse Eastern and Western traditions, such ritual is a given. The music of the

Japanese Toru Takemitsu, for example, expresses a non-directed sort of time – and it is interesting in this context to read Griffiths arguing that much of Takemitsu's later music 'is close to Messiaen, though with a gentler, more yielding character'.[42] The Chinese Tan Dun has moved, in his two works titled 'orchestral theatre', from an implicit 'holy' ritual to incorporating aspects of 'rough' theatre: *Orchestral Theatre I: Xun* (1990) involves the murmuring, shouting, chanting and singing of the orchestral players, while in *Orchestral Theatre II: Re* (1993) the audience is invited to participate in the singing.

Much mention has already been made of instrumental role-play in Stravinsky. In certain works, such as *The Soldier's Tale* and *Renard*, instruments take on specific characters. Stravinsky was not the only composer to think in this way. Quite independently, Charles Ives had used instruments to play clear roles, most famously the trumpet 'questioner' and flute 'respondents' in *The Unanswered Question*, but also in the 'Discussions' and 'Arguments' of his Second String Quartet (1911–13), in which the second violin acts out the imaginary character of 'Rollo', the staid voice of tradition. Ives described it as a 'S.Q. for 4 men – who converse, discuss, argue (in re "politick"), fight, shake hands, shut up – then walk up the mountain-side to view the firmament'.[43] For Elliott Carter, a key figure in 'discovering' and promoting Ives's music after World War 2, the Second Quartet is an important model, and aspects of its role-play can be discerned in many of his works where oppositions between instruments are 'dramatised' within the confines of a purely musical structure. In Carter's own Second String Quartet, the four instruments are clearly characterised as four separate strands which remain distinct in the first half but which interact in different ways in most of the second half: 'each instrument is like a character in an opera made up primarily of "quartets"'.[44] In Carter's Third String Quartet (1971) the instruments are organised as two opposed duos of violin 1 and cello against violin 2 and viola where (Stravinskian) dramatic contrasts of 'change' and 'continuity' are primary. Here and elsewhere, Carter uses register, interval and tempo (often resulting in Ivesian/Stravinskian simultaneous stratification) in order to distinguish between roles (though other aspects of his music suggest a closer affinity to the 'expressionist' stratum of modernism). In more recent works, he has become much more specific about the importance to him of 'play' – even in the very titles of *Gra* (1993, Polish for 'game') and 'Partita' (1993, the first part of the *Symphonia* trilogy, a title Carter translates from the Italian as 'game'). In the Clarinet Concerto (1996), this play takes on a literally dramatic dimension when Carter invites the soloist to move nearer to each of the five instrumental groups as it engages with them, and to the conductor when engaging with the entire orchestra (immediately suggesting resonances with Boulez's earlier *Domaines* – see below). Thea Musgrave had done similar things in her Clarinet Concerto (1968).

Role-play of a different kind can also be found in certain concert works which enact a specific but abstract drama. A prime example is Birtwistle's *Tragoedia* (literally 'goat dance') of 1965, which is modelled on the formal structure of Ancient Greek tragedy. It is intended to 'bridge the gap between "absolute music" and theatre music',[45] and each section of the work takes its title from the constituent elements of tragedy as defined in general by Aristotle: prologue, parados, episodion I (strophe/antistrophe), stasimon, episodion II (strophe/ antistrophe) and exodos. The overall formal layout is symmetrical. Concentric layers are arranged outwards from the stasimon, the 'central static pillar', and often involve verse–refrain patterns. The work's scoring reinforces the idea of a drama: there is a clear conflict between instrumental groups (wind quintet and string quartet with harp as mediating 'continuo') and within groups (the cello and horn – the 'odd men out', as Birtwistle describes them – who 'act as individual opponents within the conflict'[46]). Its formal organisation, its symmetries and its repetitions lend a highly stylised, ritualised character to the work, and yet the conflicts of its musical unfolding also guarantee it an immediacy, a directness; rather like Greek tragedy itself, the work's formalism contains and controls (albeit only barely) its passionate subject matter. It was then only a small step for Birtwistle to an overt engagement with theatre: all of the music of *Tragoedia* is incorporated into his first 'opera', *Punch and Judy* (a 'tragical comedy or a comical tragedy'). But a number of later works also concern themselves with instrumental role-play (discussed below), the most obvious being *For O, for O, the Hobby-Horse is Forgot* (1976) for six percussionists, whose title is taken from *Hamlet* and in which two players are denoted 'King' and 'Queen' while the other four take on the role of 'Chorus'.

Messiaen adopts the structure of Greek choral odes in certain of his works, first seen in 'Le Chocard des alpes' from *Catalogue d'oiseaux* (1956–8). *Chronochromie* is structured in seven large sections which Messiaen labels introduction, strophe I, antistrophe I, strophe II, antistrophe II, épôde and coda. And he describes the structure of specific movements from *Des Canyons aux étoiles* (1971–4) in similar terms: both movement 5 ('Cedar Breaks et le don de la crainte') and movement 7 ('Bryce Canyon et les rochers rouge-orange') are organised into a strophe, two antistrophes, an épôde and a coda. The reasons for adopting these labels are not so obviously dramatic as in the case of Birtwistle. Here it seems to be another way of organising large-scale oppositions and

repetitions of blocks of musical material that might otherwise be understood to be self-contained – as, for example, in the way Stravinsky organises the sequence of independent dances in *Agon*. Just as the Prelude and
Interludes in *Agon* punctuate the arrangement of the dances while at the
same time displaying a degree of 'interlock' (that is, the repetitions are
never the same),[47] so in *Chronochromie* the opposition of strophes and
antistrophes is balanced by the variation of these sections across their
repetitions. In general, the strophes and épôde are characterised by a
continuous complex counterpoint of superimposed lines (verses) while
the antistrophes are characterised by juxtaposed, vertically-coordinated
blocks (refrains); introduction and coda provide a frame. There is a ritual
drama of oppositions at work in *Chronochromie* and, like Birtwistle,
Messiaen was drawn to the abstract structure of Greek drama as a means of
ordering those oppositions.

With hindsight, it can be seen that the logical consequence of this abstract
interest in theatre and drama within the context of ritualised works for the
concert hall was a direct engagement with theatre, not in order to return to
the presentation of a narrative, but to make explicit the dramatic nature of
the organisation of musical materials. Thus emerged in the 1960s a kind of
music theatre which has come to be known as 'instrumental theatre'. Such
music theatre is categorically different from Cage's concert works because,
in the case of Cage, the theatre stemmed from the inherent theatricality of
musical performance, whereas instrumental theatre stemmed, on the
whole, from the structure of the music itself. Once again, it can be seen that
the ritualised role-play found in Stravinsky led the way.

The first significant instance of such instrumental theatre is to be found
in Berio's *Circles* (1960) for female singer, harpist and two percussionists.
The work uses three poems by e e cummings, arranged in such a way as to
produce the (circular) pattern ABCB′A′, to which the instrumental writing
responds accordingly. The singer, however, operates according to a
different structure: as the work unfolds, she becomes more involved, more
closely integrated with what the instrumentalists are doing, eventually
being required to clap and take up percussion instruments herself. This
changing musical relationship is dramatised by her movements – she
moves physically closer to the players at the same time as her musical
proximity develops. (What is interesting structurally here is the dramatic
balancing of circle (instruments) and line (singer) which, as we shall see in
Chapter 6, was an on-going concern of Stravinsky in his neoclassical
works.) Berio has commented on a number of occasions that the relationship between voice and instruments in this work is often complex, so some

sort of visual coordination is required – thus the singer uses gestures to keep the ensemble together. As in Stockhausen's later *Inori* (1973–4), these movements then become a gestural parameter in their own right.

Though Berio would certainly have been familiar with Cage's work since his first visit to the USA in 1950 and his attendance at Darmstadt – indeed, *Circles* was written in America and first performed at Tanglewood – it should be clear that the singer's theatrical response to issues of musical structure makes *Circles* a significantly new work in the development of post-War music theatre. Berio's contribution to many different aspects of (a highly politicised) music theatre throughout the 1960s is noteworthy – the diffusion of the speaking chorus into the audience in *Passaggio* (1963) in order to abuse the solitary woman on the stage, the dramatic interaction of music, text and electronics in *Laborintus II* (1965), the challenge to bourgeois conventions in *Opera*. One series of works, begun by Berio in the late 1950s with *Sequenza I* for flute (1958), is perhaps a little more obviously Cageian, not only in its adoption of proportional notation and other novel graphics, but also in the fact that it does play with the drama of virtuosic performance. *Sequenza III* (1965–6) for solo female voice, written, like *Circles*, for the extraordinary voice of Cathy Berberian, might in some respects be understood as a continuation of the concerns of Cage's *Aria* for solo voice (1958, also written for Berberian) in the variety of 'voices' it expects of its performer. But whereas Cage's work seems primarily to be about the humorous confrontation of different singing styles and traditions, *Sequenza III* publicly explores and dramatises the psychology of the performer to produce a work that is as theatrical as it is musical. While the solitary female here might suggest resonances with the expressionist world of *Erwartung*, the Stravinskian notion of 'instrumental' role-play is also being explored and extended.

Sequenza V (1966) for solo trombone is also a dramatic study in the psychology of the performer. Dedicated to the memory of 'Grock the clown', it picks up on Stravinsky's concerns with 'rough' theatre, with *commedia dell'arte* figures and with masks. Certain gestures are notated in the score (such as the picking up and putting down of the instrument) and the player is required to sing, speak and breathe audibly through the trombone. The work is in two sections. Section A (played standing up) is concerned with masks: of the clown, of the performer, of the music itself. Voice and trombone imitate each other and the section moves through the word's constituent phonemes towards the articulation of the question 'Why?'. Its pitch structure is tightly organised and the arrival at the question 'Why?' coincides with the revelation of the final pitch class of

Ex. 4.3 Berio, *Sequenza V*, section A

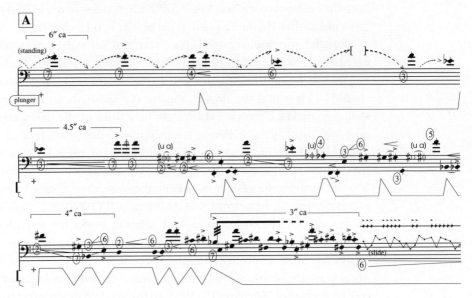

the total chromatic (the instrument's lowest note, a pedal B♭) (Ex. 4.3). In section B (with the performer seated) some of the masks are lifted in an attempt to answer this question. A 'performance' now takes place and the performer is able to sing lines independently of those of the trombone. Its organisation gives the impression of being freer, almost an improvisation. Yet this freedom seems to prevent the performer from answering the question, and ultimately silences him completely: the word disintegrates back into its phonemes so that, at the last, the trombonist removes the trombone from his lips. Once the performer's mask (the trombone) is taken away, he is unable to communicate anything at all. In *Sequenza V*, then, the role-play of instrument and instrumentalist becomes the very substance of the work. It is a powerful study in the nature of musical communication, or perhaps more accurately a study in our *inability* to communicate with each other. Just as Beckett's *Waiting for Godot* (1952), in keeping with so much of the contemporary 'Theatre of the Absurd', is an exploration of the purposelessness of existence – where two clowns wait for something that never happens – so in *Sequenza V*, Berio (who was intimately familiar with Beckett's works) formulates an unanswerable question and seems to be suggesting that a musical performance can communicate nothing other than its own purposelessness – though perhaps at the same time, through

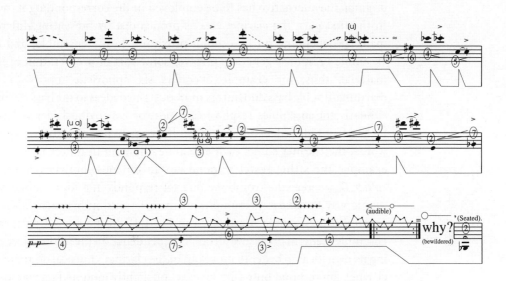

the clown, he also invites us to laugh at ourselves. Stravinsky's 'objectivity' and Berio's 'absurdity', both dramatised through the use of masks and clowns, appear to have much in common.

Boulez has made one foray into instrumental theatre with his *Domaines* (1961–8) for solo clarinet and six instrumental ensembles (the original version was for solo clarinet alone). Like Berio's *Circles*, the soloist moves about the platform in direct response to issues within the work's musical structure: 'It could be played without moving about, but this would give a false perspective of a piece that actually has a very clear tendency to individualise its various component parts.'[48] The domains of the title are the 'fields of action' within which both soloist and ensembles operate (melodic, harmonic, spatial etc.). The soloist interacts, in turn, with each of the six ensembles; the ensembles only ever interact with the clarinettist, never with each other. Moreover, the mobility of form with which Boulez had been preoccupied ever since his Third Piano Sonata here takes on a (limited) theatrical dimension. The work is in two parts: *original* and *miroir*. In the first part, the soloist plays six *cahiers-originals*, in any order, moving towards the corresponding ensemble, which then responds with its own music; once all six *originals* have been played, the *miroir* sequence begins, now with the ensembles leading and the soloist responding.

Within each of the solo *cahiers* there are a further six elements, which can be played in one of two different orderings (whichever is chosen in the *original*, the alternative has to be employed in the corresponding *miroir*). In the first part, the clarinet acts as protagonist by presenting different material depending on its timbral proximity to the ensemble, and the ensemble's response generally involves some sort of proliferation of that material: thus, for example, it offers six aphoristic motifs to the marimba/double bass duo but six more sustained ideas to the bass clarinet; similarly, the ensembles' responses are more or less obviously derived from the clarinet's ideas depending on their instrumental constitution. In other words, the clarinet enters each ensemble's domain in different ways: for example, the string sextet responds in an obvious motivic manner to *cahier B*, whereas the trombone quartet responds in a more subtle harmonic way to *cahier A* (examples of the relationship between *cahier A-original* and ensemble A are given in Ex. 4.4). In the second part, each ensemble seems to break away from its dependence on the soloist, developing its own ideas in order to move out of the clarinet's musical domain; the clarinet can respond only with an exact or slightly modified retrograde of its *cahier-original*. As their musical relationship has changed, the clarinet is required to move out of that group's physical domain and into the next. Though an effective abstract ritual, Boulez himself acknowledged a certain 'lack of perspective' in *Domaines*: 'this symmetrical arrangement of visits to the instrumental groups is too audible'.[49] We continue to await the promised revision.

One of the most sustained and committed contributions to instrumental theatre has been made by Birtwistle. We have already seen that, by the late 1960s, he had explored a range of kinds of music theatre from the latent, abstract drama of *Tragoedia* to the stylised Greek drama of the withdrawn *Monodrama* and the 'rough' theatre of both *Punch and Judy* and *Down by the Greenwood Side*. In 1968–9 he produced a landmark work in instrumental theatre, *Verses for Ensembles*, which made theatrically explicit the dramatic oppositions of many of his earlier works as far back as *Refrains and Choruses* (1957). Subsequent important contributions to the genre include *Secret Theatre* and *Ritual Fragment* (1990), as well as other works where both a spatial drama (*Five Distances for Five Instruments* (1992), where the players stand as far apart as possible as a consequence of their very different musical material) and instrumental role-play (*The Cry of Anubis* (1995), where the solo tuba takes on the role of the mythical jackal-headed creature) are of importance.

In Chapter 2 I alluded to the fact that *Verses for Ensembles*, though not

Ex. 4.4 Boulez, *Domaines*: comparison of solo and ensemble material in *cahier A-original*

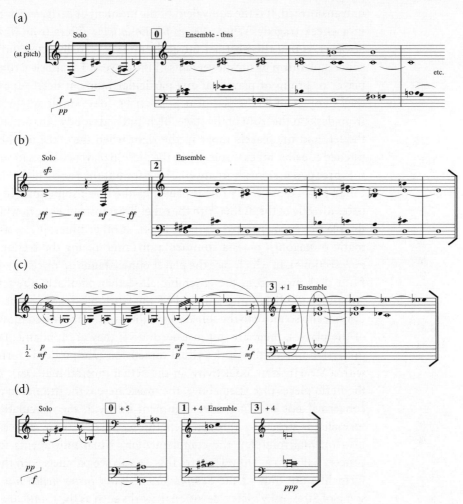

explicitly structured according to the categories of Greek tragedy, nonetheless has an overall form remarkably close to that of *Tragoedia*.[50] At the heart of the work are two 'episodes' built almost entirely of abruptly juxtaposed musical blocks, with the exception of the two trumpets, who become musically and physically liberated from the rest of the ensemble (they move to the back of the platform). Unusually for Birtwistle, the second episode is an exact repeat of the first. These episodes stand either side of a central 'stasimon', made up of a series of much freer solo wood-wind verses over a kind of horn ground, separated by brass 'ritornelli' or refrains/choruses. The stasimon, as in *Tragoedia*, marks the work's turning point, after which previously exposed material is 'revisited', either exactly or transformed. It is the equivalent of the moment of *peripeteia* or reversal in a Greek tragedy. Where *Verses for Ensembles* differs from *Tragoedia*, however, is that this abstract musical drama is actually acted out on the concert platform by the movements of the players. The musical role of any player or group of players at any particular moment determines where they sit or stand on the platform. Solo verses, for example, are performed from desks at the front of the stage; high-pitched woodwinds are seated on the left and the players move to the right when they take up their low-pitched cousins, for example, when the piccolo player changes to alto flute; the three percussionists occupy one level for untuned and a higher level for tuned percussion. A key role is played by the horn: sometimes it participates directly in the drama with the other brass instruments, in which case the player remains seated with the brass; at other times, it acts as a dramatic protagonist or as a commentator (announcing the beginnings of new sections), in which case the player either stands up or else moves to a front desk away from the ensemble altogether. Similarly, the trumpets announce the beginning and end of the work by standing 'outside the drama', and so move to the solo desks at the front. The stylised movements of the players, then, are not just decorative; they are fundamental to an understanding of the work's ritual dimension (and, indeed, correspond with a Stravinskian 'objectivity' in the actual musical material). As with the Berio pieces discussed above, the music here *is* the drama. In a music concerned not with narrative argument but with the articulation of a formalised structure through repetition, verse–refrain patterns and instrumental role-play, the complementary ritual movements turn the concert hall into a 'Holy Theatre'. It is easy to see parallels with the ritual formality, not only of the *Symphonies of Wind Instruments*, but also of some of Stravinsky's later 'devotional' works such as the *Canticum sacrum* (1955), *Threni* (1958) and *Requiem Canticles* (1966). In *Verses for Ensembles* it is perhaps not too far-fetched to regard the stage as a kind of church with the ranks of players in the choir, 'lessons' read from the front lecterns and musicians calling antiphonally from the galleries behind.

As suggested by its title, the drama of Birtwistle's next important work of instrumental theatre, *Secret Theatre*, is less overt. Written immediately after the completion of two major works for the stage – *The Mask of Orpheus* and *Yan Tan Tethera* – it is prefaced by lines from Robert Graves's poem of the same name which do little more than hint at what might be the work's 'subject matter'. The relatively simple opposition of verse and refrain in *Verses for Ensembles* has developed here into a more subtle distinction between what Birtwistle designates 'Cantus' and 'Continuum', a distinction which is again realised theatrically: the Continuum is seated in a semi-circle at the front of the platform from which players move to stand at desks behind when taking the role of Cantus ('we mount the stage as though at random', as the Graves poem expresses it). Again unlike Birtwistle's works of the 1960s, *Secret Theatre* is not concerned with the stark opposition between Cantus and Continuum (though that is actually how it begins), but explores a fluid and continuously changing relationship between the two groups which is articulated physically by the players' movements. As Arnold Whittall has commented, it 'evokes the private celebrations of human love rather than the public rituals of epic drama'.[51] The Cantus is essentially linear (indeed, being present virtually from the start, it suggests the somewhat un-Stravinskian idea of an 'endless melody'), the Continuum circular, but these roles shift: Cantus-like ideas appear from within the Continuum; both Cantus and Continuum share the presentation of an important D–F motif which punctuates the course of the work. Ex. 4.5a shows a clear distinction between simple, repeating patterns in the Continuum (note the D–F–[G♭] motif in the xylophone) and a flowing, heterophonous melody in the Cantus, while Ex. 4.5b shows a clear exchange of roles between Cantus and Continuum in the context of the D–F motif. Indeed, it is *only* this D–F motif which is left in the Continuum at the end of the work ('Lost to the outraged, humming auditorium', according to Graves's poem), suggesting another dramatic distinction between the Continuum as audience (collective) and the Cantus as actor/soloist (individual). Thus, though the meaning of the players' movements is often difficult to discern, it is clear that they are a direct consequence of shifting musical roles. *Secret Theatre* enacts an intimate ritual by means of a highly sophisticated kind of musico-dramatic role-play.

The theatre of *Ritual Fragment* is more obvious. The work's fourteen players are seated in a semi-circle and, during the course of the piece, ten of them cross the platform in turn, to occupy a solo position at the front before returning to the ensemble (each taking the place vacated by the next soloist). The other four instruments (bass drum, piano, cello, double bass) remain immobile and form a continuo group, helping to accompany and link the solos and to signal moments of structural importance. Like so many ancient rites, this ritual begins with a 'call to order' from the drum. Its brief (ritual) fragment, together with the trochaic pattern on the piano which always follows it, periodically punctuates the unfolding of the 'drama'. The first solo instrument (trumpet) quickly moves to the front of the stage and initiates a melodic procession which continues virtually uninterrupted to the end of the work. Like *Secret Theatre* before it, *Ritual Fragment* is concerned with a continuous musical line, though, whereas

Ex. 4.5a Birtwistle, *Secret Theatre* (figs. 39–40⁺²)

* at this point, flute and oboe
may exchange parts if necessary

the soloists in *Secret Theatre* articulated a single melody heterophonically, *Ritual Fragment* presents a heterogeneous sequence of discrete melodic fragments. Each solo melody has its own timbre and tempo, and is identified by a short motif (which can also occur independently of the solo). When not playing the role of soloist (Cantus/protagonist), each instrumentalist moves back into the ensemble to become accompanist (Continuum/chorus). Sometimes they take their material directly from the solo line as a kind of commentary on it; at other times they paint a new landscape of pedals and ostinatos. Occasionally they take a more active role in order to make a transition from one solo to the next. At the end of the work, there is a ceremonial 'roll call' of the principal motivic fragments in the presence of a long pedal D (a pitch which has served as a recurrent point of reference throughout) when the flute, the final soloist, reiterates its motif no fewer than nine times to which, in turn, each of the other solo instruments responds. Yet this is no climactic synthesis; though the fragments have (motivic) elements in common, they nevertheless remain independent of one another. Their proximity here merely signals that the ritual has come to a temporary halt. As the final violin D disappears into the distance, we are left in the knowledge that, like all rituals, it will continue on another day, in another place – we have been party to only a fragment of something much larger. It is the 'Theatre of the Invisible-Made-Visible'.

From *Renard* and *The Soldier's Tale* to *The Mask of Orpheus* and *Ritual Fragment* may seem a long journey, and it certainly cannot be claimed that Stravinsky's models have necessarily had a direct impact on all subsequent non-narrative music theatre. Nonetheless, it should be evident that Stravinsky's attitude to the theatre – his interest in folk and popular entertainments, in puppets and masks, in Ancient and Oriental theatres, in myth, in formalised, stylised modes of presentation – was not only in tune with contemporary developments in the theatre (Cocteau, Meyerhold, Brecht, Artaud, Pirandello), but also established an innovative climate within which composers could work. Furthermore, the non-developmental character of much of his instrumental music – exploiting as it did block forms, verse–refrain patterns, repetition – articulated new kinds of time, thus establishing a ritualised music in which instrumental role-play could be explored. The 'rough', rustic entertainment of *Renard*, the 'holy' ritual of the *Symphonies of Wind Instruments*, and their fusion in the ritualised theatre of works as diverse as *The Rite of Spring*, *The Soldier's Tale*, *Oedipus rex* and *Agon*, have had, I would argue, a profound impact on the development of a variety of kinds of music theatre since World War 2. These, combined with

Ex. 4.5b Birtwistle, *Secret Theatre* (figs. 66–8)

the radical challenges offered by Cage in the 1950s and 1960s, have resulted in a fascinatingly diverse culture where ritualised, non-narrative theatre has flourished in the opera house, where action has entered the concert hall, and where it has become possible to address through music and theatre a wealth of subject matters from the pastoral to the political, from the mythical to the contemporary, from the spiritual to the comical. The prospect at the turn of the millennium of new and challenging works for the opera house from important Stravinsky successors including Andriessen, Birtwistle, Carter (his first stage work), Tan Dun and Turnage would seem to suggest that Stravinsky's theatrical legacy is alive and well.

5 Minimal developments

The opening of Steve Reich's *City Life* (1994–5) offers exceptionally clear evidence of the way in which Stravinsky's works continue to resonate through the music of our own time (see Ex. 5.1a). In this case, echoes of the final chorale from the *Symphonies of Wind Instruments* are barely disguised. The homophonic scoring; the parallel motion of chords; the alternation of bars of 2/4 and 3/4 and the use of crotchet rests to disrupt downbeats; the mainly stepwise melodic motion (especially at the end where, in both cases, there is contrary stepwise motion between uppermost and lowermost voices, the former rising to the highest melodic pitch, the latter falling to the lowest bass note – excepting doublings); the exclusively diatonic harmony – even shared harmonies (Reich opens with a form of set 5-35, which is precisely the set formed by the chord which, from fig. 71 onwards, initiates each of the final phrases of Stravinsky's chorale; Ex. 5.1b). All these features indicate that, without doubt, Reich has here directly appropriated Stravinsky's famous chorale. Minimal development of materials inherited from Stravinsky, one might almost say. There are differences, of course. Reich's 'chorale' is less obviously triadic than Stravinsky's and less clearly 'directed' towards its conclusion, principally because its rhetorical role in the work is quite different from Stravinsky's. Indeed, what Reich does here might be understood more generally to be symptomatic of the use to which Stravinsky has been put by many minimal composers – Stravinsky's ending is turned into a new beginning (which also throws a different light on the open-ended, 'unending' character of the *Symphonies* as discussed in Chapter 2).

There are other Stravinskian aspects to *City Life*. For example, the first main harmonic shift, which occurs at b. 71, is from the exclusively diatonic context of the opening to an exclusively octatonic one – van den Toorn's Collection III (A,A♯,C,C♯,D♯,E,F♯,G) (see Ex. 5.1c). This, combined with its syncopations, invokes a 'jazz topic', such coming together of 'high' and 'low' not only recalling Stravinsky but being a defining characteristic of much minimal music. Elsewhere, rhythms involving syncopations, the combination of rational and irrational divisions of the beat, and irregular metres look back to *Petrushka* and *The Rite* – though repeated regularly and incessantly in a way rarely found in Stravinsky. One further aspect of

Ex. 5.1a Reich, *City Life*, first movement (opening)

Ex. 5.1b Stravinsky, *Symphonies of Wind Instruments* (final phrase)

Ex. 5.1c Reich, *City Life*, first movement (bb. 83–5, pianos only)

the work, which links it to the 'machine aesthetic' that has come to be identified, at least in part, with Stravinsky's modernism, is its use of sampled city sounds – snatches of conversations, doors slamming, bus and subway air blowing, car motors and tooting horns. As in *Different Trains* and *The Cave*, however, these sounds are not just used as pure found objects (an exercise in Futurist *musique concrète*) but are incorporated into the substance of the music as melodic and rhythmic patterns, to become a musical celebration of the sounds of the modern city. It is this incorporation, this 'making one's own', that is so Stravinskian about Reich's attitude here.

Reich's minimalism grew directly out of post-World War 2 American experimentalism. Though Cage suggested the possibility of a music built from the simplest means, as indeed had Satie before him in the extraordinary *Vexations*, minimalism's founding father is generally considered to be La Monte Young who, influenced by Indian teaching, explored the musical (and environmental) consequences of very slow, repetitive music. Terry Riley, a member of Young's group, the Theatre of Eternal Music, produced his influential *In C* in 1964, which seemed to encapsulate Young's ideas in a slowly evolving music which employed improvisation, repeating modal patterns and drones within a constant pulse, and led the way to the production of a minimalist, static, non-developmental music concerned with paring down Western music to its essential elements. As with Cage, such music formed in part a critique of the received Western (European) tradition. Like Reich and Glass, all these composers were inspired by non-Western musical practices. Reich studied African drumming and the Balinese gamelan, with their emphases on repeating rhythmic structures and layered patterns; Glass studied with Ravi Shankar. The other principal arena for experiment was the electronic studio: one particularly important 'discovery' was Reich's 'phasing' of tape loops, as in *It's Gonna Rain* (1965), a technique which has become an omnipresent feature of all his subsequent music. Intersection with the vibrant American rock music of the 1960s also had its impact on the emergence of minimalism. Yet, despite all this, the music Reich and Glass produced also paralleled Stravinsky's music in fascinating ways: in its modal/diatonic aspects, in its emphasis on rhythmic process, its stasis, its attitude to repetition, its balancing of 'high' and 'low' art. The 'primitivisms', the 'orientalisms', the objectivity of minimalism clearly share a line with Stravinsky's modernism. Andriessen and Schönberger strongly identify it with Stravinsky:

> precisely because of the monotonous repetition of 'continually the same' and 'continually slightly different', these bars [from the 'Pas d'action' from *Orpheus*] are a prophetic premonition of (and, at the same time, put into

Ex. 5.2a Reich, *Music for Pieces of Wood* (opening)

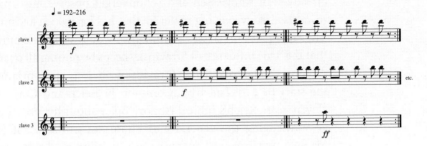

Ex. 5.2b Glass, *Music in Similar Motion*

perspective) the music that Steve Reich and his followers would write twenty years later. Random becomes 'process' and pandiatonicism changed into arpeggiating modal chords.[1]

For example, the basic rhythmic pattern of Reich's *Music for Pieces of Wood*, while also being highly characteristic of patterns in Ghanaian drumming, is Stravinskian in its use of a subtractive/additive process and in its symmetry, as well as the subsequent superimposition of (metrically) varied forms of itself (layering/phasing) and in the use of cross accents (Ex. 5.2a). The 'objectivity', too, of a process which, once set in train, will work itself out, has Stravinskian overtones. Glass's *Music in Similar Motion* (1969) has similarly Stravinskian traits of additive melodies within an essentially static, repetitive context (Ex. 5.2b).

In the 1970s the music of Reich and Glass gradually divested itself of its experimental status. Abstract works (betrayed by their titles) such as Reich's *Six Pianos* (1973) and *Music for Eighteen Musicians* (1974–6), and Glass's *Music in Twelve Parts* (1971–4) and the best-selling album *Glassworks* became 'classics', and, especially in Reich's case, as the music became more 'composerly', the more Stravinskian its preoccupations also seemed to become: a non-directed music built from short, rhythmically distinctive, layered motifs, constantly varied. In the later 1970s, both Reich and Glass began to turn away from abstraction, at their best matching the non-developmental, repetitive nature of their music to non-narrative ritual presentations, such as in Glass's opera trilogy – *Einstein on the Beach*, *Satyagraha* and *Akhnaten* – and his film soundtrack *Koyaamisqatsi* (1982), and in Reich's *Tehillim* (1981) and *The Cave*. It is not, then, just aspects of Stravinsky's rhythmic practices, or even his use of diatonic harmony, that has had an impact on the working of the minimalists; it is, as we have already seen Andriessen and Schönberger observe, his 'specific attitude towards already existing material' that has been such an influential force. The emergence of 'classic' minimalism would seem to confirm their view that the 'true influence of Stravinsky keeps beginning all over again'.[2]

Thus, though paralleling Stravinsky, obvious appropriations such as at the start of *City Life* are uncommon in Reich and Glass. John Adams, eleven years Reich's junior, is more open about his use of Stravinsky, in acknowledging the general and important influence of Stravinsky on his own music as well as, on occasions, alluding directly to Stravinsky's works. Though Adams did engage with (Cageian) experiment as a student, his music more generally belongs with that of so-called post-minimalists who have followed Reich and Glass. If it has any use, such a label perhaps indicates the fact that minimalism is now a stylistic (and, just as significant, commercial) fact, a broadly recognised *lingua franca* that has shed its origins in the experimental tradition. Adams, like his younger American successors, writes for established symphony orches-tras, opera houses and ensembles, not, as did first-generation minimal-ists, for home-grown experimental ensembles associated exclusively with 'their' composer's music (Steve Reich and Musicians, the Philip Glass Ensemble, etc.). Given, then, that he is working from within rather than outside established musical institutions, it is perhaps inevitable that Adams's focus should be on the 'mainstream' of Western art and popular musics: more than Reich and Glass, Adams engages directly (and perhaps anxiously) with his precursors. This is self-evident in the *Grand Pianola Music* (1982), whose very title alludes obliquely to Stravinsky, and which is written as something of an (Ivesian) homage to Adams's own musical heritage, including marching bands, Beethoven, gospel music, even Philip Glass, as well as many snatches of Stravinsky. The glittering orchestration of this, as with so many of Adams's works, becomes an end in itself – Adorno's 'fetishism of the means', which he identified with Stravinsky's *Rite* but which is also a typical characteristic of commercial music – a part of the work's obvious entertainment character. Listen beyond its surface appeal and, like much of Ives, it does not really seem to cohere; as listeners we are encouraged to focus on the moment (such as the comical minimalist treatment of the opening bars of the 'Hammer-klavier' Sonata), and as such this music seems to represent an extreme instance of Stravinskian *drobnost'* but where the sum makes for *less* than its constituent parts. It is perhaps a telling comment on the way we listen now: Adams is throwing back at us the fact that, in a digital age when any music from any culture or era can be sampled and employed in countless new contexts, listeners find it hard to hear music as more than a mere string of isolated moments. This is just one aspect of its *post*modernity, which I discuss below.

Hypostatised Stravinsky is very much in evidence in two short orchestral show pieces (dubbed 'fanfares'): *Tromba lontana* and *Short Ride in a Fast Machine* (both 1986). Both are dominated by a *Petrushka*-like oscillating ostinato heard at the outside; both layer ostinatos which move simultaneously at different speeds. Particularly in *Short Ride*, it can be seen how a 'typical' Stravinskian moment is extended into an entire piece. Adams's opening oscillating ostinato uses *at pitch* a subset (D,E,A) of *Petrushka*'s opening four pitch classes (D,E,G,A)(4-23), similarly scored (Stravinsky: clarinets and horns; Adams: clarinets and 'brass' preset on the synthesisers). Adams's articulates this ostinato almost identically to Stravinsky's violins and later harp, at fig. 2. Stravinsky's opening 'fanfare' in the flutes uses his ostinato's tetrachord horizontally, making a feature of interval class 5; Adams's fanfare (trumpets) also employs his ostinato's trichord, making a feature of interval class 5. A little later, Adams introduces another layer, a descending, sextuplet flute/piccolo flourish, made up of 4-23 (D,E,G,A) which is a virtual imitation of the triplet figuration that forms the second component of Stravinsky's flute fanfare (see Ex. 5.3). Unlike Stravinsky, who very quickly interrupts his 'static' block with others, Adams's material forms just about the entire substance of his work. Because the material thus remains 'fixed', the focus is thrown, as in much minimal music, on to the vitality of its rhythmic procedures and the changes in texture/orchestration. It is not meant to be heard ironically – that is, as a Stravinsky moment stretched over four minutes – but the origins of Adams's language lie undoubtedly in *Petrushka*. It is arguable that such 'hypostatisation' of past music could only be possible in a post-modern culture dominated by (and dependent on) commerce. But in another sense this can be seen as just another manifestation of an American love affair with Stravinsky's diatonicism, rhythms and repetitions, one that goes back at least as far as Copland. Adams is nothing if not an *American* composer.

Adams has admitted to 'the particular influence of Stravinsky' in his orchestral work *Fearful Symmetries* (1988).[3] There is certainly a mechanical aspect to this work, an incessant motoric pulse, and many of its rhythmic details – syncopations, punctuating off-beat chords, rhythmic ostinatos, cross-beat phrasing, and so on – are clearly Stravinskian in origin (though this much is true for countless works this century). In many ways, it 'sounds' less like Stravinsky than *Fast Ride* does, but closer examination reveals all sorts of Stravinskian turns. Adams's opera, *Nixon*

Ex. 5.3 Comparison of openings of Adams, *Short Ride in a Fast Machine*, and Stravinsky, *Petrushka*

in China, whose composition immediately preceded *Fearful Symmetries*, renewed his interest in the 'joy of making many events coexist effortlessly',[4] and in *Fearful Symmetries* motifs (usually distinguished rhythmically) are cumulatively superimposed to give a sense of forward motion – though the 'effortlessness' of the combination often results in a music with fewer internal conflicts than one finds in, say, the layers of *The Rite of Spring*. Elsewhere, the music can be more homophonic, such as the extraordinary accelerating rising chromatic passages – which seem decidedly un-Stravinskian, comically out of place, like some undigested chunk of a Romantic symphony. These and other build-ups are often – Stravinsky-like – cut off in order that the music can begin to 'accumulate' over again, giving the impression that overall the piece proceeds as series of large-scale upbeats (but whose associated downbeats never arrive). Certainly, though the constant pulsation of the music suggests a degree of continuity across the work, the form is as block-like as anything found in Stravinsky, each block being in essence internally 'static' except for the sense of directedness generated by the progressive accumulation of superimposed motifs. This music makes a feature of the absence of transition.

Adams also absorbs the sounds and gestures of popular American music into the work's material – dance patterns, boogie-woogie riffs, big-band orchestrations, and so on. One recurring section with a boogie-woogie bass line (e.g. bb. 196–213) calls to mind a very specific Stravinsky moment: the octatonic 'jazz-like' block at figs. 7–13 of the *Symphony in Three Movements* (discussed in Chapter 6), which alternates two forms of 4-27 holding G–B♭ invariant over a 'walking bass'. Adams similarly alternates two tetrachords holding G and Bb invariant over a 'walking bass', outlining alternately G–B♭–D and G–B♭–E♭ (later transposed up a major sixth). Indeed, ostinatos made from the alternation of pairs of notes or chords are highly characteristic of Adams and can be seen to spring from Stravinsky's so-called 'accordion' oscillations, such as in the first tableau of *Petrushka*. And the alternation of arpeggiated chords is more generally a stylistic feature of much minimal music, especially that of Glass, echoes of whose music can also be heard in *Fearful Symmetries* (for instance, the passage beginning at b. 658).

The most striking Stravinskian feature of much of Adams's music is its 'objectivity'. Adams acknowledges this in some of his pieces (what he calls 'the Trickster – the garish, ironic wild card'[5]) but more generally his works seem to be self-consciously 'music about music', even, as is certainly the case with *Grand Pianola Music*, 'music about other music'. As Adorno accused Stravinsky's music of depersonalisation, so we find in many of Adams's works not only a sense of depersonalisation, the rejection of expression, but also a playfulness, a sense of irony, an eclecticism. This is certainly what suggests a reading of Adams (and his successors) in postmodern terms, a music which almost seems to represent

> the end . . . of style, in the sense of the unique and the personal . . . As for expression and feelings or emotions, the liberation, in contemporary society, from the older *anomie* of the centered subject may also mean not merely a liberation from anxiety but a liberation from every other kind of feeling as well, since there is no longer a self present to do the feeling. This is not to say that the cultural products of the postmodern era are utterly devoid of feeling, but rather that such feelings – which it may be better and more accurate, following J.-F. Lyotard, to call 'intensities' – are now free-floating and impersonal and tend to be dominated by a peculiar kind of euphoria . . .[6]

Such euphoria, a constantly exaggerated elation, a sense almost of existing in the present only, is characteristic of Adams, and to a lesser degree of Reich and Glass. Fredric Jameson writes of the 'exhilaration of these new

Ex. 5.4 Torke, *Adjustable Wrench* (opening)

surfaces' in postmodern architecture, but the same could equally be written of Adams, and, indeed, of Reich's *City Life*, in which 'urban squalor can be a delight to the eyes [and ears] when expressed in commodification, and how an unparalleled quantum leap in the alienation of daily life in the city can now be experienced in the form of a strange new hallucinatory exhilaration'. These are, for Jameson, key aspects of postmodernity: 'the waning of the great high modernist thematics of time and temporality, the elegiac mysteries of *durée* and memory'.[7] Certainly Adams's music tends to inhabit the 'synchronic' rather than the 'diachronic' and so becomes as much concerned with space as with time (hence the importance of orchestration in his music). In the postmodern, 'the past itself has disappeared (along with the well-known "sense of the past" or historicity and collective memory)'[8] so that Beethoven, gospel music, Stravinsky, jazz can all appear in Adams's work with equanimity and without any sense of contradiction. The next stage, the elevation of pastiche to compositional *desideratum*, has already been realised by Michael Torke in, for example, the Beethovenian *Ash* (1989). Stravinsky was never a *pasticheur*. There is a clear distinction between his (modernist) use of the past – where history still operates, where a critical distance between present and past is still maintained (however precariously) – and these postmodern practices. Though the origins of such thinking may usefully be identified in Stravinsky's modernism – as Jameson and Watkins, among others, have done – this does not turn Stravinsky into a postmodernist. What is interesting is how Stravinskian features identified with as iconoclastic a work as *The Rite of Spring* have been absorbed into a music that now has a wider international popularity and commercial viability than any new music has ever had.

The music of Torke typifies that of the younger generation of post-minimalists who are as familiar with popular music as they are Stravinsky, and for whom the minimal 'style' is already a given. An intriguing fusion of these elements has now taken place, exemplified by the opening of Torke's *The Yellow Pages* (1985), which alludes directly to the spirit of Stravinsky, not least in the way in which it absorbs a pop bass line (from Chaka Kahn) into its own ostinato. The basic material of *Adjustable Wrench* (1987) (see Ex. 5.4) could be a syncopated Stravinsky-like folk melody, a four-bar pop phrase or a typical minimalist motif; its subsequent working suggests that it is perhaps all three simultaneously. Certainly the restless energy of this music is derived equally from pop and rock music and from an understanding of Stravinsky. This is also true of the music of many younger European post-minimalists, especially those from Britain and the Netherlands, where American developments have been most readily received; two notable examples are Steve Martland and Graham Fitkin.

Martland and Fitkin, along with many other young British composers, studied at The Hague with Louis Andriessen. The European response to American minimalism has been, on the whole, a creative one.[9] Although initially it might seem that Andriessen's music is little different from that of his American counterparts – anti-Romantic, highly rhythmicised, jazz-inspired, repetitious, colourful – it quickly becomes apparent that its aesthetic is quite different. For a start, Andriessen engages directly with politics, with the role of music and musicians in society, in contrast to the clinical, clean objectivity of much American minimalism of the 60s and 70s, which appeared to be offering an escape from its contemporary world. For another, he openly acknowledges the fact that Stravinsky is one of the principal driving forces behind his music. Take, for instance, *Hoketus* (1975–7). It has a roughness quite absent from the smooth lines and transitions of most American minimal music, a physicality associated with rock (what Andriessen calls 'downtown' music). Its harmonic resources are categorically *un*-diatonic, hard-edged; its scoring is for jazz/pop musicians. Its additive rhythmic processes are obviously Stravinskian but its ritualistic focus *entirely* on rhythm is more minimalist (as well as, interestingly, invoking medieval precedents; Ex. 5.5). However, the piece also seems to be offering a critique of that minimalism. 'One of the limits of the little groups of Steve Reich and Phil Glass is that you have long forms but not large forms.'[10] In *Hoketus*, the (Stravinskian) manner in which the motifs are varied is constantly shifting so that there is a tangible sense of movement across the larger span – which is simply not the case in music which merely works its way through a process. The 'Danse sacrale' is an obvious model. American post-minimalists have also attempted to engage in this way with *The Rite* but with very different results. Michael Gordon's *Love Bead*, premiered at the 1997 Proms and influenced by Andriessen, has an obviously rough, urbanised, rock character. This music, too, is built from insistent repeating rhythms organised in small blocks, and continually evokes the sound-world of *The Rite*, but somehow its absolute directness, its incessant (and loud) repetitions, blunt the kind of critique initiated by Andriessen's work.

Andriessen's *De Staat* (1972–6) is, according to the composer, 'a contribution to the discussion about the place of music in politics',[11] and to this

Ex. 5.5 Andriessen, *Hoketus* (opening)

end sets excerpts from Plato's *Republic*. But, for our purposes here, it is also a fascinating contribution to the reworking of the Stravinsky legacy for the later twentieth century. It is scored for groups of four instruments (and, appropriately, employs predominantly tetrachords throughout) arranged 'confrontationally' on the concert platform, immediately emphasising the ritual aspect of the work. In so many ways, *De Staat* boldly 'steals' Stravinskian materials, especially from *The Rite*, but places them in new contexts: harmonies (unlike American minimalism, employing both the diatonic and the more chromatic), rhythmic/metric patterns, block organ-isation, even reaching a climax with the familiar 'chorale' (fig. 45) whose oscillating seconds ape Stravinsky but whose harmony is more strident. Many 'moments' from *The Rite* can be identified, and provide the material for entire blocks in Andriessen's work, as, for example, at figs. 19–20, which are clearly built from an imitation of a few bars of the 'Jeu du rapt' (Ex. 5.6).

De Staat's first block (beginning to fig. 3), scored for the double reed quartet of oboes and cor anglais, is entirely static harmonically, being con-structed from just one tetrachord (B,C,E,F). Voices move mostly together, sometimes in contrary, sometimes in similar motion, though such non-directed movement is twice suspended by a punctuating cadence, whose stepwise contrary motion of outer voices once again suggests Stravinsky, and by an imitative central passage (fig. 1). The time signature changes fre-quently to challenge any sense of metric regularity within a constant quaver pulse. Additive patterns abound but these have a 'random' charac-ter about them: there is certainly no sense of a Reichian process in opera-tion. Thus, there is very much a Stravinskian sense here of motion within stasis, though this also invokes the gamelan (not least through its use of a quasi-Balinese scale segment; Ex. 5.7a). The next two blocks (figs. 3–4 and 4–5) have a denser, more chromatic harmonic content and suggest a greater sense of movement within each block through the progressive addition of pitch classes and 'melodic motion' to peak notes of increasing height (Ex. 5.7b). The block that then takes over at fig. 5 returns to a static tetrachordal harmony (D,E,G♯,A) whose exact bar-by-bar repetitions give it, for the first time, more the character of a classic American minimal work. The way in which the four pitch classes are rhythmically layered also parallels the Reich of such contemporaneous works as *Music for Mallet Instruments, Voices and Organ* (1973). And so the characterisation and differentiation of successive blocks continues. Coherence of the whole is brought about in part by means of a kind of interlock between blocks (but not the obvious cross-strata continuities of the *Symphonies of Wind Instruments*), a playing with degrees of similarity and difference between blocks in the short and longer term.

Ex. 5.6 Andriessen, *De Staat* (figs. 19–20)

What is so fascinating about *De Staat* is the way in which Andriessen is able to take so many ideas from *The Rite of Spring* and build from them something distinctly new, distinctly his own, which fuses Stravinsky, rock and minimalism in a coherent way to explicit expressive ends. This may be 'music about other music', but the sources are transformed (there is clearly a new *attitude* towards already existent material here), and this distinguishes Andriessen from the more commercially-minded 'irony' of Adams and Torke (and, for that matter, Nyman). *De Staat* may be 'minimalist' in its repetitions and even in some of its gestures, but in every other respect it is decidedly different from its American complements –

representing a European engagement with and transformation of tradition, perhaps, as distinct from an American attempt to invent new ones.

In this context it is worth mentioning a work that received its première in Amsterdam in 1995. If evidence were still needed of the continuing obsession with Stravinsky, especially in the Netherlands, then *Bending the Bone* by the Dutch composer, Henk van der Meulen, provides it convincingly. In part, of course, this Stravinsky obsession springs from Andriessen, whose influence on Dutch musical life should not be underestimated,[12] and certainly the general language of van der Meulen's piece – with its blend of 'high' and 'low', its aggressive dissonance, its insistent

rhythms – owes much to the Andriessen of *De Staat*. But the eponymous 'bone' is the *Symphonies of Wind Instruments*, whose rhetorical outline van der Meulen follows in general, even as far as a slow, chorale-like ending. Stravinsky's work is bent, twisted, troped, as if it were somehow being viewed through a large distorting mirror. Direct quotations and their re-reading sound simultaneously, as if it were impossible fully to incorporate Stravinsky's material into the new. The work appears almost to dramatise what has happened to Stravinsky in the late twentieth century: it is an extraordinary fact that composers, even at the century's end, are still (anxiously) trying to come to terms with the enormity of Stravinsky's achievement and influence.

Even for Andriessen, there are some works where this anxiety of

Stravinskian influence manifests itself, where the persistent presence of Stravinsky is so strong that it seems to debilitate original expression, and a sense of renewal is lost. *M is for Man, Music, Mozart* was originally written as the soundtrack to a Peter Greenaway film of the same name, commissioned by the BBC for the 1991 Mozart Bicentenary, and is explicitly concerned with the anxiety of influence. The work is about the omnipresence of Mozart, about the reception of his music now, about the values his work has come to symbolise for our late twentieth-century culture. In 'Instrumental I',[13] Andriessen directly invokes the presence of Mozart with quotations of the incipits of the A minor and C major piano sonatas, K.310 and K.545. He acknowledges the on-going relevance of Mozart to composers today inasmuch as the quotations become a part of the substance of the movement – the opening six bars employ 'sequential' writing which appears to lead to and absorb the A minor sonata; the repeated figurations (themselves now a cliché of minimalism) comfortably take up the repeated left-hand chords of the Mozart accompaniment almost as if the Andriessen had been written before the Mozart. The actual quotation is mediated through Andriessen's twentieth-century ears – extra doublings, changes in harmony, scoring for jazz instruments, and so forth. The later K.545 quotation (known to all good European children who have learnt to play the piano) is treated with an even heavier irony – now only the melody is left, played far too *dolce* on the alto saxophone. Mozart is thus fragmented, fetishised, just as he has been by bourgeois culture. But so are more general Classical gestures, such as the opening sequences (more like Schubert than Mozart), which are taken out of context, implying a tonal function but not conforming to tonal voice leading (dissonances resolve to dissonances). Stravinsky had done this, preeminently in *The Rake's Progress*. What Andriessen has learnt from Stravinsky is how to cut himself off from the past while alluding to it to create something new: 'Stravinsky's influence can be seen . . . in a specific *attitude* towards already existent material.' Andriessen is able to distance himself from his Mozart materials because he was never, he claims, that close to them: 'Early bop and cool jazz have also influenced me very strongly, much more than Mozart, Bach, and Brahms.'[14] But his relationship with *Stravinsky* is, of course, of a different order. Looking at the overt way in which Andriessen appropriates Mozart might help us to understand the much more covert ways in which he works with Stravinsky.

Inevitably a work such as this, scored for a jazz ensemble and deeply imbued with the harmonic and rhythmic language of jazz, invokes the *Ebony Concerto* as model. More specifically, the opening of Stravinsky's *Concerto*, involving the metric dislocation of alternating melodic whole tones, 'harmonised' homophonically for brass then saxophones, is

Ex. 5.7a Andriessen, *De Staat* (opening)

directly imitated by Andriessen (see, for instance, the first two bars of Ex. 5.8a). But, as Stravinsky might have said, *Le Sacre* also casts its shadow. For example, there is a clear allusion to the 'Jeu du rapt' (Ex. 5.8a and b): the same tetrachord (4-27), transposed down a fifth, in the same scoring, with a similar continuation (diatonic like the *Ebony Concerto* rather than chromatic like *The Rite*), and even Stravinsky's perfect fifth horn-call figure, similarly transposed, is present in the bass. These fifths continue insistently (through repetition a Stravinskian figure becomes a minimalist device), becoming a diminished fifth which then leads to a more veiled allusion to the 'Évocation des ancêtres' (Ex. 5.8c and d). Many other Stravinsky 'moments' can also be identified. Andriessen seems to be playing a ritual game of abduction ('jeu du rapt') with his 'already existing musical materials' by means of the 'évocation des ancêtres', the evocation of his own illustrious ancestors. At least, this is the case with Mozart. But how are we to interpret the Stravinskian references? Are we meant to hear them, as we do the Mozart sonatas, as Stravinsky quotations, or has Andriessen lived so close to Stravinsky for so long that his own music sometimes becomes little more than an unconscious assemblage of found Stravinskian objects? '[T]o say that a piece of music sounds like Stravinsky every once in a while does not really say much.'[15] There is no evidence of any distance here, of an 'attitude' towards his Stravinskian material. In Stravinsky's neoclassicism, according to Andriessen, '[r]enewal is concealed in the old';[16] such renewal seems absent here. What we have instead is an illustration of what has happened more generally to Stravinsky in the hands of many minimalists (though rarely, it should be admitted, in Andriessen): the uncritical fetishisation of Stravinskian moments. As Bloom might understand it, we see here the

Ex. 5.7b Andriessen, *De Staat* (figs. 3–4)

Ex. 5.8a Andriessen, *M is for Man, Music, Mozart*, 'Instrumental I' (fig. 7)

Ex. 5.8b Stravinsky, *The Rite of Spring*, 'Jeu du rapt'

Ex. 5.8c Andriessen, *M is for Man, Music, Mozart*, 'Instrumental I' (fig. 9)

revisionary ratio of *kenosis*, that is, the fragmentation and reordering of the precursor, allied to the rhetorical trope of metonymy and, significantly, to the psychic defence of regression. It is perhaps ironic that a work which began as an attempt to interpret what *Mozart* has come to mean in our fragmented, postmodern culture, ends up becoming also an unwitting assessment of the *Stravinsky* legacy.

Ex. 5.8d Stravinsky, *The Rite of Spring*, 'Évocation des ancêtres'

PART II

Stravinsky Reheard

6 A fresh look at Stravinsky analysis

Back in 1989, Fred Lerdahl described a phenomenon he understood to be characteristic of musical modernism in general: 'coherence in the face of no theory', something which he regarded as nothing less than the 'theorist's nightmare'.[1] Such a view is implicit in the unitary approaches to the analysis of the music of the twentieth century propounded by so many influential theorists who, following Schoenberg's lead, established theory as an independent discipline in American universities after World War 2: Salzer, Babbitt, Forte, Perle, Lewin, Cone, Berger, among others. Forte's *The Structure of Atonal Music* (1973), despite the many subsequent revisions to and adaptations of the theory, has remained a paradigm. It attempted to do for 'atonality' what Schenker had done for tonality, that is, to offer a single theory which could account for connections both between all elements within a specified atonal work and between members of a recognised canon of atonal masterpieces: 'Any composition that exhibits the structural characteristics that are discussed [in *The Structure of Atonal Music*], *and that exhibits them throughout*, may be regarded as atonal.'[2] This desire to demonstrate connectedness (without necessarily precluding 'multiple meaning'), stemming from the two dominant theoretical traditions of Schenker on the one hand and twelve-note theory on the other, was everywhere apparent after the War, whether in the mathematical rigour of Babbitt and Lewin, the contrapuntal logic of Salzer, or the motivic thoroughness of Perle. Where the identity of the music was deemed to be 'problematic' – and attention was, for the most part, focused on the so-called 'transitional' music of early modernism – the 'theorist's nightmare' was overcome by broadening the scope of received models: the work of Katz, Salzer, Travis, Morgan, Baker, Straus and others, in extending the precepts of Schenkerian voice leading to accommodate the music of Schoenberg, Debussy, Skryabin and Stravinsky, is significant in this regard. In other words, though the modernism of such music seemed radically and variously to challenge the nineteenth-century ideal of the unified musical work, theory took a contrary reactionary stance by generally insisting on reinstating the primacy of connecting processes in that music (even in the absence of hierarchies) in order to assert its coherence.

Some of this theoretical work attempted to give a fuller picture of early modern music by amalgamating seemingly mutually exclusive tonal and non-tonal approaches. Baker's seminal analysis of Skryabin's *Enigme*, Op. 52, No. 2, for example, combines voice-leading and set-theoretic techniques to show that 'tonal forces . . . are responsible in large part for the overall coherence' of the piece without denying the structural role played by whole-tone configurations and complementary pitch-class sets.[3] Straus has attempted to demonstrate how a non-tonal configuration (a prominent foreground pitch-class set) can be 'prolonged' across much larger spans of music. And Lerdahl's 'listener-based theory of atonal music' also incorporates Schenkerian and set-theoretic perspectives, while taking into account the ways in which listeners 'predict heard hierarchical structures' from 'particular musical surfaces', in order to show once again that the music is 'able to convey intuitions of elaboration and linear connection that are fundamental to any understanding of the piece(s)'.[4]

Stravinsky's neoclassical works have presented particular analytical problems. Some writers have blithely ignored the deep contradictions of the neoclassical style and considered its tonality in terms little different from those appropriate for Mozart. Take, as just one example, Paul Griffiths's study of *The Rake's Progress*, which routinely discusses the opera's structures in terms of keys – keys which though thoroughly compromised in the music remain unchallenged in the analytical account. The opening Act 1 duet and trio is predominantly 'in A major' according to Griffiths, even though the number contains not a single unadulterated root position triad in A.[5] Schenker-derived readings by, among others, Katz and Salzer, have proved more successful because at the very least they have shown how Stravinsky's practices differ from classical tonal voice leading through such means as the 'polychord' and the 'contrapuntal-structural chord'.[6] Forte has generally left the neoclassical works well alone because they clearly do not exhibit those structural characteristics consistent with an atonal reading. And, aside from Taruskin's projection of Stravinsky's Russian origins into the neoclassical works, alongside a number of important investigations by, for example, Hyde, Kielian-Gilbert and Rogers,[7] the only other major study to have grappled substantially with the contradictions of the style is that of van den Toorn. He attempts a fascinating balancing act between, on the one hand, the discovery of quasi-functional 'tonics' and 'dominants' and, on the other, the music's essentially modal harmonic context.[8] More problematically, Joseph Straus has tried to show that what he segments as a significant foreground harmonic and melodic component – in the case of his analysis of the *Symphonies of Wind Instruments*, the pitch-class set 4-11 – also controls the music at the deepest level.[9] Unfortunately, however, he cannot fully let go of his strict Schenkerian upbringing and so is not prepared to allow this idea its structural weight: the background is not diatonic and therefore the 'descent cannot be considered prolongational'.[10]

Beyond America rather different perspectives are to be found. Some theorists and analysts, though equally well versed in the received theoretical traditions, have nonetheless proved themselves less slavishly beholden to those traditions and their associated synthesising/unifying tendencies. For example, in a provoking analysis of Tippett, Derrick Puffett adopts a Schenkerian methodology in order to demonstrate both the tonal limits of the movement under scrutiny and the limits of the analytical techniques themselves:

> What is the value of such an analysis? Precious little, if it is judged by the conclusiveness of its results. Tippett's fugue has been shown to be, if not beyond analysis (other methods may be more successful), then at least, and predictably, beyond Schenker. Yet perhaps the very inconclusiveness of the analysis is its best achievement.[11]

Far from being horrified by this 'nightmare' of the failure of theory, Puffett draws from his results positive conclusions about the nature of Tippett's musical language:

> a certain amount of tension between the various musical elements – harmony, counterpoint, and the like – is inevitable in a more modern piece, and . . . such a tension, far from being something to be regretted, should be valued as a source of satisfaction.[12]

This view chimes well with Whittall's 'modernist analysis', honed in part on the music of Tippett, which is highly alert to the competing tendencies in such music.

In the last few years, the American School of Unitary Theory and Analysis has come under increasingly fierce attack from within the academy itself. The 'new musicology' (so-called), an interdisciplinary movement taking its cues from critical theory, feminism and other spheres of modernist thought, has condemned post-War theoretical and analytical practices as 'conservative, elitist, specialist, insular, narrow, closed, masculinist, formalist, positivist, "technical", dry, objective and mechanical'.[13] Spearheaded by Kerman and Treitler, others such as McClary, Abbate and Laurence Kramer have been quick to join the fight. The formalists' first response was to stand their ground. Pieter van den Toorn has mounted perhaps the most sustained defence of 'autonomous' analysis, and Stravinsky's octatonic structures are once again deployed in support of his argument. While he acknowledges that '[a]n appropriate framework for Stravinsky's music, one that can transcend pluralism and address that sense of a distinctive musical presence on which there has always been such insistence, is elusive', in practice he asserts his and other theorists' right to live out their desire 'to familiarize themselves with the workings of musical structures' by means of consistent and coherent theoretical practices.[14] Puffett's view from across the Atlantic is a little more accommodating:

> ... there is no less need for precision, or exactitude, in analysis than there was before... Analysis, in other words, needs to maintain its own internal logic, its aims and its sense of purpose – which may be described as formalist aims and purposes, in the best sense of the word. This does not mean that analysts can afford to ignore everything else that is going on in the world.[15]

Puffett, then, admits to the need for an awareness of context (to avoid the pitfalls of what Jim Samson has described as American empiricist 'clean, efficient analytical techniques, unpolluted by troublesome issues of context or mediation'[16]). Craig Ayrey sums up this shift in thinking:

> the siege of analysis produced a sea-change in the way the discipline was viewed by its practitioners: the 'positivistic' blindness to aporia was relieved, and the concreteness of 'over-determined' theory fractured. As Puffett indicates, the critical legacy presented a methodological problem for analysts: how to achieve the Barthesian 'loosening' of theory while preserving, *faute de mieux*, analytical tools and procedures that remained of unrivalled efficiency and refinement.[17]

When the sea changes it is dangerous to be caught with your head in the sand. The new musicology may not have converted all 'power analysts'[18] into born-again feminists, but there is a distinct rethinking taking place within formalist quarters. There is, for example, a definite tendency among many of the contributors to – of all unlikely things – Forte's recent *Festschrift* to allow for pluralism, to admit to the possibility of the inadequacy of the unitary view.[19] As we have already seen, Whittall, the only contributor from outside North America, continues to shout out loud his plea for an appropriately modernist aesthetics. And a younger generation of theorists (not represented in the Forte *Festschrift*), such as Kevin Korsyn and Richard Cohn, have set a strong example for the ways in which interdisciplinary concerns can successfully be incorporated into rigorous analysis. But even van den Toorn is also now prepared to admit that '[w]hile the impression gained of such an analysis [of the *Symphony in Three Movements*] is likely to be one of nonorganicism, there are ... few alternatives'.[20] Straus puts it more strongly: the admission of the possibility of 'error' from this formerly orthodox Schenkerian represents a highly significant shift in the direction of pluralistic thinking, an admission (in the face of the challenges of Kerman, Street and Abbate) that unity is not everything, an acknowledgement even of the potential for a genuinely 'modernist analysis':

I think that analysts of twentieth-century music may have spent too much time seeking a single vantage point from which to hear a piece whole, as an integral organism with all its detail functioning in the service of the central idea . . . But atonal voice leading, and atonal structure more generally, is more diverse, multivalent, and discontinuous than some of us may initially have thought or wished were the case. I think the time has now come to embrace the multiplicity and diversity of atonal music, to accept the tensions and discontinuities that form part of our listening experience, and to reflect them in our theoretical models.[21]

Stravinsky's neoclassical music presents particularly interesting challenges to the analyst. Its re-engagement with tonality, its adoption of the materials and structures of the music of the past, has often diverted analysts (and listeners) from other aspects of the music. In particular, 'synthesising' views concordant with the apparent surface continuities have tended to cover over deeper discontinuities, and so undermine the radicalism of much of the music of the 1930s and 1940s. As long ago as 1957, one American writer recognised the inappropriateness of readings of Stravinsky's neoclassicism in conventional terms. He was the (Stravinsky-influenced) composer, Roger Sessions:

For in spite of its apparent break with everything that bore the imprint of 'modernism' in the nineteen-twenties, and in spite of Stravinsky's very conscious and even outspoken development of impulses derived from certain styles of the past, in his music the familiar concepts have taken on quite different meanings. Tonality, diatonicism, chord-structure – even harmony, rhythm, expressivity – have quite another meaning for him than they had for Haydn or Brahms; and *it is futile to apply to his music the analytical criteria which are valid for theirs.*[22]

What follows aims to take a fresh look at the analysis of Stravinsky's neoclassical works in an attempt to investigate the 'modernity' of his 'antimodernism', and to test Carter's proposition that 'all the brief, almost discrete fragments, however roughly they connect with each other, end up by producing a work that holds together in a very new and telling way'.[23] In the light of the myriad uses to which Stravinsky's music has been put, it would seem unlikely that its import should hang on just a small handful of much-analysed works (*Petrushka*, *The Rite of Spring*, the *Symphonies of Wind Instruments*). Composers have long heard what analysts have been deaf to: the radical nature, the committed modernism, of *all* Stravinsky's output, not least the neoclassical works. If Stravinsky's legacy to the twentieth century (and beyond) is to be fully evaluated, then an analytical rehearing of his neoclassical works is long overdue.

Two case studies in neoclassicism

Symphony in C

The Symphony in C has had a fairly extensive critical discussion. Edward Cone's 1963 article on the 'uses of convention' is still of value, and in recent years accounts of the work by Paul Johnson, Joseph Straus and Stephen Walsh, among others, have all offered new perspectives.[24] One reason for this abundance of discussions may be the traditional impression given by the work, making it easier for critics to relate it to known models of symphonies and works in C. Indeed, Stravinsky himself fuelled such speculations by admitting to having on his desk copies of symphonies by Haydn and Beethoven, as well as Tchaikovsky's First Symphony, while he was writing the first two movements (composed in France in 1939).[25] The third and fourth movements (composed in Boston and California in 1940) are, it is claimed, more 'American': the composer acknowledged that certain passages might not have occurred to him before he had known the 'neon glitter of Los Angeles's boulevards from a speeding automobile',[26] and Walsh too describes the later movements as evoking 'fleetingly the scurry and glitter of celluloid America'.[27] The work was an American commission – for the fiftieth anniversary of the Chicago Symphony Orchestra – and its apparently traditional structure may well be as a result of this. As Walsh again comments: 'of all Stravinsky's 1930s scores it is the one which most obviously fits into a conventional celebration within the institutional life of a conservative culture.'[28]

This raises a number of interesting questions. Was Stravinsky constrained by the circumstances of the commission? Did he feel the need to kowtow to the conservative tastes and expectations of an American subscription audience? Contemporaneously with the symphonic activities of Shostakovich (but under very different circumstances), Stravinsky was commissioned to write a symphony which, on the surface, conformed to a general understanding of what a 'good', 'accessible' symphonic work should be, that is, something with traditional and recognisable formal outlines and an essentially triadic basis to the musical language. But appearances can be deceptive. A rehearing of the Symphony in C suggests that, beneath the surface, things are very different.

A further aspect of the 'institutional life of a conservative culture' to which Walsh referred is that of the academy. One reason why the work has been so widely and well received critically may be that it is eminently 'analysable', that is, it 'fits' into a conservative theoretical tradition. Analytical techniques – of form, at least – appropriate to eighteenth- and nineteenth-century symphonic music appear to work equally well for the

Symphony in C. For example, Eric Walter White provides us with a Toveyesque 'analytical note' which examines the motivic organisation of the work in terms of the B–C–G motto with which it opens;[29] Roman Vlad, too, highlights this motif's contribution towards ensuring 'the substantial unity of the work';[30] and Francis Routh asserts that 'the first two movements are comparatively orthodox in structure and tonality'.[31] The culture gave its approval to the work because it represented a 'conventional celebration' of tonal coherence and thematic unity.

Stravinsky himself, however, expressed dissatisfaction with such responses:

> critics (who must earn their livelihood) will find a great deal of nothing to say – factitious comparisons to other music, profound observations on the diatonicism and the use of fugato, on the existence of a suite-of-dances in the third movement, on flirtations with ballet everywhere. But anyone who had failed to notice as much would require a very different sort of commentary . . .[32]

In contrast to White, Vlad and Routh, more recent analysts have challenged the ability of conventional theory to account fully for the structure of the Symphony in C. For them, and still for us today, the work itself challenges tradition in two principal respects: first, the ways in which the Symphony is a symphony; and second, if it is in C, the kind of C it is in. One early commentator on these issues was the conductor, Ernest Ansermet, who took a negatively critical view of Stravinsky's achievement. White quotes Ansermet at length on the 'dialectic of symphonic form': 'the Allegro of the Symphony in C is no more than the portrait of a symphonic allegro', judges Ansermet, because, in White's words, 'its form is static and its motives fail to grow in meaning'.[33] Ansermet has identified a crucial structural feature of the first movement, but implicitly to condemn it for not being a Beethoven symphony is a miscalculation. As in so many of his other neoclassical works, Stravinsky is taking material from classical models and placing it in new contexts, working with it in different ways. It is not merely a poorly executed exercise in pastiche. Walsh cites a similar argument from a contemporary British symphonist: '[its motivicism] guarantees unity, but it perhaps does not guarantee that cogency of argument without which, according to Robert Simpson, a symphony cannot properly be so called.'[34]

Joseph Straus, in his chapter on sonata forms, like Charles Rosen before him, distinguishes between eighteenth- and nineteenth-century forms of sonata structure. Twentieth-century composers who have adopted a nineteenth-century outlook, he argues, have written uninteresting sonatas

because 'the sonata form floats upon the musical surface, a mere arrangement of themes lacking in real connection to the harmonic structure
beneath'. Certain twentieth-century sonata movements, however, and the
first movement of the Symphony in C is one such, have grappled structurally with the eighteenth-century concept 'where the thematic organization deeply implicates the underlying harmonic organization'.[35] This
might suggest an unwelcome retreat to a nineteenth-century organicist
view, and the covert synthesising tendency in Straus's work is undeniable
(his 'cherished' reverence towards a strictly Schenkerian understanding of
prolongation betrays a more orthodox approach to analysis than the
potentially radical agenda of *Remaking the Past* implies). Though Straus
acknowledges that, in the twentieth century, a nineteenth-century notion
of organicism is no longer possible, he nevertheless insists that '[e]ven in
the strongest and most interesting twentieth-century sonatas, the fit
between the form and the deeper levels of harmonic structure is never
seamless'.[36] I find this assertion faintly ridiculous, just as Stravinsky was
amused by critics who made 'factitious comparisons to other music'.
Straus is telling us that this work is not a symphony in the same way as a
symphony by Haydn or Beethoven – this was Schenker's mistake with
regard to Stravinsky. Fortunately, Straus does not draw the same conclusion as Schenker. His analysis discusses the various polarities of the music
in a positive way, while the language of 'undercutting' and 'undermining'
tonal structures in his prefatory remarks is fortunately not borne out by
the conclusion that 'Stravinsky's tonal polarity is powerful enough to
endow the traditional form with new meaning'.[37] Throughout his book,
Straus's actual analyses are more convincing than the scepticism embodied
in his theoretical discussions. Bloom's Oedipal anxiety of influence, the
subject of the book, would appear to operate more strongly on Straus (the
inescapable dominance of the Schenkerian father figure) than it does on
Stravinsky, who is able to use, adapt or reject the music of his forebears
freely and creatively.

The tradition of discussing Stravinsky's music in terms of (atonal)
pitch-class collections, initiated by Arthur Berger and continued in
different ways by Forte and van den Toorn, is followed by Paul Johnson in
his examination of the Symphony in C. Johnson's contention is that deep
level harmonic consistency exists in much of Stravinsky's music as a result
of the presence of two collections: the octatonic and what he calls the
eight-note diatonic collections (0,1,2,3,5,7,8,10). In the case of the use of
the latter, major third relationships tend to predominate and often the referential sonority (or 'tonic') that characterises these works is a (0,4,7,11)
tetrachord, e.g. C–E–G–B, 'delineating a polarity between triads a major

Ex. 6.1 Joseph Straus's analysis of Stravinsky, Symphony in C, first movement
(Exs. 5.2 and 5.6 from *Remaking the Past*)

(a)

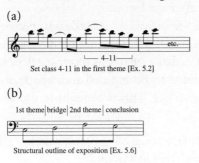

Set class 4-11 in the first theme [Ex. 5.2]

(b)

1st theme│bridge│2nd theme│conclusion

Structural outline of exposition [Ex. 5.6]

third apart'.[38] The polarity between C and E is, of course, fundamental to
the first movement of the Symphony. Most interesting about Johnson's
essay, though, is his attempt to show how the (0,4,7,11) tetrachord on C is
prolonged linearly. Straus, too, has discussed the possibility of the prolongation of pitch-class sets that occur frequently on the surface of the
music,[39] and in the case of the Symphony in C it is, he argues, the unfolding of set-class 4-11 that governs the structure of the exposition while at
the same time preserving the 'balance' between C and E – or, rather, a move
from the dominance of one to the dominance of the other (Ex. 6.1).[40]

The question of the prolongation of a referential sonority is both an
attractive and a problematic one. The attraction is that it is a convenient
way of getting to grips with obvious aspects of linearity in the music. The
principal problems (certainly in Straus's work) are twofold. The first is a
technical issue of what might loosely be termed segmentation, i.e. the basis
on which selection is made of the referential sonority that is to be prolonged. Are there any rules governing its size, e.g. are three-note or nine-
note sonorities equally viable, or is there some unstated preference for
four-note collections? Is statistical frequency of occurrence the preferred
rule of selection? How are we expected to decide and/or mediate between
two equally likely readings (such as between Johnson's prolongation of
4-26 and Straus's of 4-11)?

The second problem has to do with the synthesising tendency of such
prolongational readings. There is always, I would argue, a substantive
tension between harmony and voice leading in neoclassical Stravinsky.
When a motivic element becomes the basis for middleground structural
(i.e. harmonic) motion, that opposition is minimised: it is almost as if the
referential sonority becomes a substitute for the triad – certainly an
implicit assumption in Johnson's work. How does the balance between C
and E that is thus demonstrated differ from the balancing of tonic and

dominant in classical music? The 'fit between form and the deeper levels of harmonic structure' here may not be 'seamless', but neither is this always the case even in classical sonata forms.

One further difficulty with Straus's analysis is its perspective. We might assume, because of the thrust of his theoretical discussion, that his intention is essentially poietic, that is, that he is trying to tell us something about the way in which the music was composed and, maybe, the 'anxious' state of the mind of the composer. This is brought to our attention by such statements as:

> The first movement of the Symphony in C is Stravinsky's most profound attempt to grapple with the sonata form . . .

> Although the traditional formal outline remains intact in the Symphony in C, beneath it Stravinsky explores new musical imperatives.[41]

And yet the analytical techniques Straus employs would seem, at times, to show more concern for the way in which the musical structure is perceived. The model (though never explicitly invoked) is less likely to be Schenker than the psychologically-based implication-realisation principle of Meyer/Narmour. 'The C-centred area implies E', he writes; 'the rest of the exposition serves to realize that implication.'[42]

The psychological foundations for this are flimsy. Because 4-11 is not given a privileged role over other pitch-class collections on the surface of the music, it would be unlikely that even the expert listener could predict the highly abstract kind of pattern completion proposed by Straus, particularly over large time spans. And in any case the model provided by Ex. 6.1b is hardly explicit in the music. For instance, though it may be true to say that the first theme revolves about C, that C is virtually *never* present in the bass of the music, making the pattern even harder to discern.

All this is to say that, though both Straus and Johnson acknowledge the significance of polarities in the music, the (anti-modern) urge to synthesise remains a strong force in the working out of their ideas (even if its achievement is frustrated) and this undermines what I consider to be the central status of opposition and discontinuity in this music.[43] An analytical rehearing of the Symphony in C clearly needs to take account of the Whittall question: what is modernism and why does music analysis (even of Stravinsky's neoclassical works) need it?

As in the *Symphonies of Wind Instruments*, the ultimate goal of the Symphony in C is a 'chorale', which appears to play a role of both closure and resolution. Gesturally this is certainly so, as its homophonic calm brings the work to rest in a manner in common with the slow coda-like

Ex. 6.2 Stravinsky, Symphony in C, fourth movement (bb. 1–14)

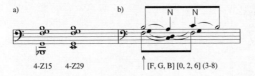

passages to be found at the end of many works from *Les Noces* through the closing 'Alleluia. Laudate Dominum' of the *Symphony of Psalms* and on to the *Requiem Canticles*. For Taruskin, this is an aspect of *uproshcheniye* ('simplification') which progressively became a more marked feature of Stravinsky's neoclassicism. (He discusses the chorale from the *Symphonies*, which was published in advance of the rest of the work: 'Full of *Luftpausen* and, toward the end, full beats and even measures of silence, it comes across as a veritable slap in the face of rhetoric'[44]). In the case of the Symphony, it comes to rest *on* C, recalling the first movement, and implying some sort of resolution. But does it resolve the work's harmonic ambiguities, any more than the *Symphonies*' chorale synthesises that work's oppositions?

With regard to the final movement there *are* senses in which it might be heard as a resolution. The fourteen-bar *largo* with which it begins serves to 'prolong' an important referential sonority: the all-interval tetrachord. An invariant three-note set, F–G–B (3-8), played vertically by trombones and horns, punctuates the horizontal motion of the bassoon lines by combining with it to generate the two different forms of the all-interval tetrachord: E–F–G–B (4-Z29) and F–G–B♭–B (4-Z15); see Ex. 6.2a. The invariant trichord is an insistent feature of these bars, but it also appears to be prolonged by the neighbour-note motions of horn 1 (supported in parallel motion by the other two horns; Ex. 6.2b). The bassoon lines are typical of Stravinsky's circular melodic construction: each line is contained within a fairly narrow intervallic range and keeps revolving round the same limited pitches. In this case, bassoon 2 is contained within a fifth (B♭–C–D–E–F) and bassoon 1 is contained within an octave (D–E–F–G–A–B–D). Taken together they form another instance of Johnson's eight-note diatonic collection, and the pitch classes of the forms of 4-Z29 and 4-Z15 that occur here are also taken from the same collection. The lack of linear direction to the melody, the relative harmonic stability of the verticalities that support it and the unchanging harmonic context of the whole all contribute to the overall static effect of this passage.

Yet there is a strange sense of forward motion to these bars, even if their direction is not strongly expressed. This might be partly the result of the

Ex. 6.3 Stravinsky, Symphony in C, fourth movement

C: ᵛV²₄⁺   ᵀI⁶⁾

Ex. 6.4 Stravinsky, Symphony in C, fourth movement (fig. 138)

4-Z29

listener's expectations (based on classical precedents) of the function of a slow introduction to an *allegro* finale. But the rising upbeat character of the bassoon 1 melody implies a later structural downbeat, and the prominence, as established in the first movement, of the 'leading note' B, even out of the immediate context of anything that might resemble C, also suggests upward resolution on to that C. This sense is compounded by the invariant F–G–B trichord, which might be heard as a final inversion dominant seventh of C suggesting resolution on to a tonic first inversion. In one way, that resolution *is* provided by the final sonority of the entire piece, which is a kind of enriched $^6_3$ chord of C and which, perhaps rather unexpectedly, follows what 'should' have been the final chord rooted on C (Ex. 6.3). In another way, though, that resolution does *not* take place because the leading note both rises and is contained in the final sonority. Stravinsky alludes to aspects of tonal voice leading in order to give the impression of forward motion and continuity, yet this is balanced by a harmony that remains static and discontinuous.

The main body of the movement (fig. 138) begins with the same 4-Z29 sonority, rescored, that ended the *largo*, but otherwise contrasts with it: it is fast, loud and staccato, and it has a new linear idea which seems to have a clearer sense of direction (Ex. 6.4). Nevertheless, though more fragmentary (the line is constantly being broken off), this linear material is similar to the preceding bassoon 1 line in that it consists of diatonic scale segments which nearly always move upwards and which seem to be leading towards a goal. The line gradually ascends through an octave from fig. 138 to fig. 140⁺⁴ (outlined in Ex. 6.5) and then the process is repeated, in altered form, to lead to a varied reprise of the first subject of the first

Ex. 6.5 Stravinsky, Symphony in C, fourth movement (figs. 138–40^{+4})

movement at fig. 143, the local goal of the ascending lines and the first strong downbeat of the movement (until this point, most phrases have begun on weak parts of the bar, confirming the 'upbeat' status of the opening music). Figs. 138–43 thus continue what was begun in the slow introduction: both prolonging an essentially static harmonic configuration and yet, paradoxically, implying through its 'dominant-like' qualities a kind of forward motion.

It is interesting to note how the G is weakly represented here, always occurring off the beat; the leading note, B, and later the leading note of the dominant, F♯, are given far greater melodic and metric prominence. For instance, the arrival at the high G in the scalic passage between figs. 142 and 143 is twice delayed. On three occasions the F♯ appears to be the goal of the upward motion and only after its third appearance does F♯ rise to G but with a *diminuendo*, off-beat and unaccented. Like the B in the opening motif of the first movement, it does 'resolve', but the emphasis is such as to undermine the significance of that resolution.

As an aside, it is amusing at this point to play the model-spotting game. I hazard the suggestion, following Walsh's comparison of the first subjects of the Symphony in C and Beethoven's C major Symphony,[45] that the finale of Beethoven's work also lies behind the opening of the Symphony's finale. Just as Stravinsky's hesitant G-scale figures reach forward to the eventual appearance of the main theme, so the *adagio* introduction to Beethoven's finale consists of an initially fragmentary and gradually expanding G-scale figure which humorously forms an anacrusis to the arrival of the principal theme at the *allegro molto e vivace*. Such 'factitious comparisons to other music' are, as Stravinsky might say, obvious; more importantly, the spirit and function of this passage in Stravinsky's work are quite different. It is no longer funny: fragmentation is now heard as an essential of the musical language rather than a disruption of something more continuous and the arrival of the main theme is not intended to be decisive. As in the first movement, root position C major triads are conspicuous by their absence (note the elaborated $^6_3$ chord again at fig. 143, a temporary resolution, perhaps, of the implied $^4_2$ chord that has been present from the start) and the harmony of the next section, figs. 143–5, is almost as static as that which precedes it. The circular melody and the diatonically saturated harmony lead nowhere: the music simply cuts off at fig. 145 and a new section begins over a relentless 'dominant' pedal.[46]

There are other aspects of this movement which suggest parallels with larger-scale tonal connecting processes, such as the return of the opening *largo* material at fig. 162 to 'reactivate' the all-interval tetrachord and the leading note B; the restatement of the 'dominant' motif from fig. 138 in the 'tonic' at fig. 173; and the long 'dominant' preparation for the final chorale in figs. 174–81 – not to mention the movement's rigorous thematic working. 'Tonics' and 'dominants' exist here insofar as smaller-scale voice leadings suggest motion from one to the other; but even these occur in the context of elements that do not belong in tonal terms (e.g. the 'dominant seventh' in the two bars immediately preceding the chorale contains both F and F♯). As in so much of neoclassical Stravinsky, such connections serve to disguise more fundamental oppositions; the form of the movement is defined not by its voice leading but by the juxtaposition of blocks of clearly differentiated material. Often this material has been 'found' – musical devices from the tonal era in quotation marks, which locally might seem to behave in a functional manner but which operate within the context of a new, non-functional whole.

In this movement, the material has been 'found' in the first movement and is here reworked, reordered and juxtaposed in new ways. These are some of the more obvious inter-movement connections:

1st movement	4th movement
1st subject, fig. 5	theme, fig. 143
bridge theme, fig. 13	fig. 146 (vn1, fl)
2nd subject, fig. 21	fig. 148 (ob)
cadence (tpt), fig. 22	cadence (cl), fig. 150
figs. 39^{+3}–44	figs. 163–9

The most pervasive link is, of course, the three-note B–C–G motif which forms the final chorale melody. Ex. 6.6 shows the counterpoint between the outer voices of the chorale. The closure of the music is signalled when the lower voice comes to rest on the low C and the upper voice halts on the high D without falling back on to the G as it has done in every other phrase. There is a definite sense of movement towards this conclusion even though, as Ex. 6.6 amply illustrates, this is not brought about by conventional tonal voice leading: indeed the graph is almost a parody or inversion of what one should expect, showing 'dissonant' counterpoint and a melodic ascent. Yet this passage almost defines its own contrapuntal rules, whereby the initial sonority, bounded by E and B, is manifestly prolonged until the final lower voice descent and upper voice ascent (Ex. 6.6ii). This

Ex. 6.6 Stravinsky, Symphony in C, fourth movement, final 'chorale'

contrary motion also implies a certain symmetry. Though the reasons for closure are as much gestural as contrapuntal, the voice leading nonetheless helps to define (albeit vaguely) a sense of direction towards an important cadence. However, the fact that this cadence is not quite the end of the piece confirms that such directedness is only one aspect of the music. The harmony, as elsewhere, is much more static (diatonic here) and does not support the movement of the outer voices. Continuity and discontinuity are held in balance. The very last chord is wholly appropriate because it does not attempt to resolve the work's ambiguities but rather suspends the music's principal 'tonal' centres (C major, G major, E minor) in one sonority: though it may be a 'synthesis' (in the sense of a coming together) it is not a resolution, more a bringing to rest. Herein lies the modernity of Stravinsky's apparent antimodernism.

Such a reading coincides with the model offered by Stravinsky in the *Poetics of Music*, where he proposes that the 'function of tonality is completely subordinated to the force of attraction of the pole of sonority'. The 'polar attraction of sound, of an interval, or even of a complex of tones' is certainly evident at the close of the Symphony in C where the poles (not least the 'tonal' and 'non-tonal') are brought together 'without being compelled to conform to the exigencies of tonality'. That this music can be read locally as being 'tonally connected' without denying deeper-level discontinuities is confirmed in Stravinsky's remark: 'I remain for a considerable time within the bounds of the strict order of tonality, even though I may quite consciously break up this order for the purposes of establishing a new one. In that case I am not *a*tonal, but *anti*tonal.'[47]

The first movement of the Symphony in C acts as a model for the fourth not just in terms of thematic material but structurally as well – it is almost as if the finale is a compressed shadow of the opening. Two clear illustrations of this occur at the beginnings and ends of the movements. Like the finale, the first movement begins with an introductory section (twenty-five bars) which has an upbeat character leading towards the

Ex. 6.7 Stravinsky, Symphony in C, first movement (opening)

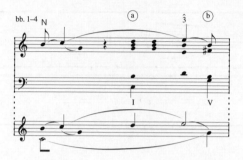

arrival of the apparently more stable first subject. The introduction presents the basic B–C–G cell and, as Cone points out,[48] establishes the
prominence and autonomy of the note B, displaying its reluctance to
behave as the leading note to C as one might expect. Nevertheless, within
the context of 'sort-of-C-major' (see, for example, Ex. 6.7) the B implies
the possibility of voices leading upwards towards the tonic and so, just as
in the finale, imbues the music with a tentative sense of conventional
forward motion. This is supported by the ascending scalic figures
throughout this passage. The harmony, however, tends to contradict the
(implied) voice leading and is much more static. The first instance of this
can be seen in Ex. 6.7. Though the chords marked *a* and *b* are ostensibly
(by virtue of the bass) tonic and dominant, each also contains its own
leading note (indeed, chord *a* seems to contain both tonic and dominant
harmonies); furthermore, the note B remains invariant and is the only
pitch class to be doubled in bars 3 and 4, so undermining the directed
tendencies suggested by Ex. 6.7. Once again we hear the tonal and non-
tonal, the functional and non-functional, held in dynamic tension.

The first theme (fig. 5) is preceded by a bar of 'dominant' just like the
'dominant' bars before the final chorale (see fig. 180[+2]) containing the F of
the dominant seventh, which falls to the E, and the F♯, which rises to the
dominant. The 'definitive' thematic entry in the first movement takes place
not over the expected tonic note in the bass, but over the note E. The first
subject embodies the tension or polarity that Cone identified as lying at
the centre of the movement, namely the 'tendency of B to act as a dominant [of E minor] rather than as a leading-tone'.[49] What is of interest here
is the way in which the oboe melody evinces a certain forward-moving
tendency 'in C' ('progression'), elaborating a C major triad (Ex. 6.8), while
the accompaniment remains static ('succession'), reiterating an E–G dyad.
In fact, the melody is less obviously directed than at first seems to be the
case – the prolonged C does not actually lead anywhere and the melodic

Ex. 6.8 Stravinsky, Symphony in C, first movement, 'first subject'

Ex. 6.9 Stravinsky, Symphony in C, first movement (closing bars)

elaborations are decidedly circular – but there is at least a suggestion of motion, which is entirely lacking from the supporting harmony.

The end of the movement operates in a similar way to the end of the final chorale which, as discussed above, cadences on C before moving away to a different sonority rooted on E. The first movement too appears to cadence definitively on C just before its conclusion (cellos and bassoon 2 move down to the low C at fig. 71^{+2}), but this is subverted both by the insistent presence of the E–G dyad from fig. 68^{+3} and by the marked cadential gestures in the last five bars which reassert the E–G dyad in the bass (despite the attempt by the timpani to impose a cadence in C! – another typically classical gesture in quotation marks, devoid of its original function). Just as the final chord of the entire work freezes the opposed tonic and dominant of the finale into one gesture, so here the final chord contains the two opposed centres of the first movement, C major and E minor. Both cadential chords (Ex. 6.9) contain the note B; the B simultaneously leads to the C and remains unresolved. The movement's polarity of directedness and stasis is expressed in these two chords.

Many commentators on the Symphony in C have attempted to account for its continuity in terms of its motivic unity (White, Vlad) or by looking for substitutes for the tonic–dominant opposition which might articulate its sonata structure (Cone, Straus[50]), perhaps in an effort to discover in what ways the Symphony is symphonic. Others have considered Stravinsky's work as a negation of fundamental symphonic principles:

> Within their own circumscribed terms they [Stravinsky's symphonies] are highly organised, but the motion of symphony is absent. They are exclusively concerned with rhythm and texture rooted in primitive monolithic tonality; when one (or a combination) of these has transiently performed enough of its function, it is replaced, and the total effect, however internally agitated, is as static as a stage upon which dancers are gyrating.[51]

Ex. 6.10 Stravinsky, Symphony in C, first movement (fig. 8)

An examination of the first movement's voice leading inevitably highlights aspects of the music's continuity. However, although voice leading operates locally to generate a sense of directedness, the kinds of large-scale connections made by writers such as Cone and Straus tend to undermine the movement's significant structural discontinuity. Certainly when Cone uses a term like 'bridge passage', we need to question whether the demonstration of such quasi-tonal connectedness is actually pertinent. Take, for instance, the four-bar passage around fig. 8 which connects statements of the first subject 'in' C and 'in' D minor (Ex. 6.10). This does not actually bring about a local modulation. Though the descending lines might smooth over the edges separating the two harmonic areas, the two statements are essentially juxtaposed without any mediation. The rhetoric of the passage is one of transition, but harmonically it is a red herring. The same would appear to be true for the larger context here (figs. 5–11[+3]) which implies a longer-term prolongation of C by outlining a I–II–V–I motion:

    C: I fig. 5
    D: II fig. 8[+2]
    G: V fig. 9[+3]
    C: I fig. 10[+2]

This imitates a tonal procedure, but a closer examination suggests that each of these harmonic areas is discrete and that they are only referentially rather than functionally connected.

    Another 'non-connection' can be heard even more clearly at the end of the so-called bridge passage (fig. 18[+3]) which concludes a long build-up over a D pedal ('dominant of the dominant'). The second theme begins at fig. 19 'in' F. The rupture is extreme, and though the Tchaikovsky-like scalic figure in flute and clarinet forges a surface link, this by no means mitigates the structural opposition between the two blocks. If this is a bridge, it has been built over the wrong part of the river.

    The answer to the question of what kind of C the Symphony in C is in is a complex one. There are undoubtedly aspects of the music which suggest C major and these can be demonstrated, to a limited extent, by the use of voice-leading techniques. There are also many surface gestures and connecting motions that are reminiscent of tonal practice and give the music a sense of directed motion. However, a rehearing of the Symphony invites one to consider whether these conventional aspects of the music are any more significant (despite the provocation of the work's title) than those other non-tonal elements that contradict them. Harmony and voice leading do not necessarily support one another as one would expect in an integrated tonal structure – often they are in direct opposition. The immediate surface of the music suggests a traditional formal, tonal and thematic argument; at a deeper level this traditional structure is constantly confronted so that those elements that are in, or at least on, C are held in a dynamic tension with those elements which are not in or on C. Even in one of Stravinsky's 'purest' neoclassical works – perhaps the closest he ever got to following consistently the strictures of eighteenth- and nineteenth-century models – the structure still invites a modernist interpretation in terms of 'unified fragmentation', of a 'non-synthesising balance'.

Symphony in Three Movements

In *Philosophy of Modern Music*, there are a few works of Stravinsky of which Adorno is not entirely dismissive. One of these is the *Symphony in Three Movements* (1945), Stravinsky's next major work after the Symphony in C. Its very title indicates something less 'symphonic', less integrated than the centricity implied by 'in C'. Robert Simpson has written: 'The more characteristic a work of Stravinsky, the further is it from the symphonic idea . . . The Symphony in Three Movements, a consistent and highly individual work, reveals its virtues most readily if one listens to it as one would approach a ballet score like *Le Sacre du printemps*.'[52] This is supported by the origins of the work, which, Stravinsky tells us, began in 1942 with the composition of the first movement: 'I thought of the work then as a concerto for orchestra.'[53] The second movement began life in 1943 as music for the 'Apparition of the Virgin' scene for Franz Werfel's film, *The Song of Bernadette*, one of a number of examples of what Stravinsky calls his 'aborted film music'.[54] The third movement was composed in 1945 with a 'synthesising' intention – brought about, in the first place, by the simultaneous appearance of both harp and piano (only the piano appears in the first movement, and only the harp in the second). As late as 1963, in a programme note on the work, Stravinsky was still not altogether convinced by its 'symphonic' achievement: 'perhaps Three Symphonic Movements would be a more exact title'.[55] Furthermore, Stravinsky was at pains to point out (albeit retrospectively) the ways in which the *Symphony*, written during the war years, was rooted in the events of the time of its composition, often involving cinematographic thinking: the first movement was inspired by 'a documentary of scorched-earth tactics in China', the third he saw as 'a musical reaction to the news-reels and documentaries that I had seen of goose-stepping soldiers. The square march-beat, the brass-band instrumentation, the grotesque *crescendo* in the tuba – these are all related to those repellent pictures.'

Uncharacteristically, Stravinsky goes so far as to relate specific historical events to precise musical moments, e.g. the turning-point of the third movement (the trombone and piano fugato – itself singled out by Adorno as a fine example of Stravinsky's 'new coloration'[56]) he sees as the turning-point of the events of the war, the movement towards the coda being associated with 'the rise of the Allies' after the victory over the German war machine. His conclusion is intriguing. He denies a programme to the work and reasserts his positivist belief that 'Composers combine notes. That is all.' But, at the last, he does allow for the possibility of a socially/historically conditioned music: 'How and in what form the things of this world are impressed upon their music is not for them to say.'[57] What we do with this information is another matter. Taruskin would have us believe that the conversation books, though attractive and provocative, are unreliable as source material on Stravinsky's pre-serial works.[58] But what Stravinsky's insistence on the 'programmatic' intentions of the *Symphony* reinforces is the fact that it is a fragmented structure, that despite the reference in the title, we should not expect a connected symphonic argument.

I doubt whether this back-tracking by the composer of 'music about music', this half-hearted attempt to justify its 'authenticity', would have cut much ice with Adorno. Nonetheless, it is of interest that he found the *Symphony in Three Movements* 'impressive' on account of the fact that it 'is cleansed of antiquated components, presents contours of cutting sharpness, and applies itself to a lapidary homophony which might well have had Beethoven in mind: he hardly ever before so openly presented the ideal of authenticity'.[59] As Paddison puts it, '"Authentic" art for Adorno always has an echo of the outside world within its material, but sublimated and reconciled by the individual work's law of form.'[60] What is beyond question is the imagination with which Stravinsky is able to build a coherent work by means of the consistent opposition of musical ideas (Adorno identifies the 'static juxtaposition of "blocks"')[61] and in a far less obviously 'constructivist' manner than in the *Symphonies of Wind Instruments*. This, combined with its sparkling orchestration and vibrant rhythmic energy, makes it one of the most widely known (and influential) of his neoclassical works.

The less obvious continuity of the *Symphony in Three Movements* is, then, one aspect of its 'authenticity'. Though some, Vlad among them, have argued a case for Stravinsky's employing a notional sonata form schema here of 'exposition' (beginning–fig. 38), 'development' (figs. 38–88) and 'recapitulation' (fig. 88–end), the working-out of the musical materials does not support this in any meaningful way ('the inner tension . . . is not developed'[62]). But this much Stravinsky himself acknowledged. I would argue that – in a different way from the Symphony in C, but no less effectively – a certain musical continuity *is* achieved in this first movement which does not override but rather complements the obvious discontinuities. As in the Symphony in C, this 'balancing' of the continuous and discontinuous takes place in the context of a coherent body of motivic materials (which has recently prompted van den Toorn to consider the first movement of the *Symphony* in terms of Schoenbergian 'developing variation'[63]), but the working of these motifs is not conventional: 'they do not undertake the dialectical work, which in this case they promised through the very character of the thesis itself.'[64] For Adorno, this is the failure of Stravinsky's symphonic structures, one which he reiterated in 1962: he 'avoided the task of thematic elaboration in his symphonies and quasi-symphonic pieces. This is the origin of the sense of impotence and the illusory in his symphonic work . . . Stravinsky's symphonic structures are forms minus any dialectic with a pure musical content.'[65] Is there really no sense of progress in this work? Is it merely a collage of static fragments? In order to investigate the appropriateness or inappropriateness of Adorno's statement, what follows is a preliminary attempt to account for its (modernist) balancing of discontinuities.

Overall, the first movement might be understood as an inversion of the rhetoric of the sonata model: that is, the 'exposition' is made up of a number of small, opposed blocks of musical ideas only loosely connected (see Fig. 6.1), ideas which return only in part, and then fragmented and varied, in the 'recapitulation', while the 'development' is more obviously continuous. There is an interesting parallel here with Adorno's account of the Berg Piano Sonata, Op. 1. Not for a moment am I suggesting the Berg was a model for Stravinsky, or that Stravinsky's music stands in relation to his sonata form norm (in its detailed working out) in anything like the way Berg's does to his. But Adorno's analysis does show (albeit problematically) how, in the exposition, Berg's motivic material undergoes various processes of transformation, whereas:

> The shaping principle of the development is precisely the opposite: the themes, having been through the discipline of the exposition, can now breathe and allow themselves to sing out . . .[66]

Fig. 6.1 Sectional organisation of 'exposition' and 'recapitulation' of Stravinsky, *Symphony in Three Movements*, first movement

'Exposition'
(147 bars, crotchet = 160)

Figs	Section	Comment
0–5	A	introduces theme (G–A♭ opposition); dynamic character
5–7	B	ostinato; static (transitional) character; introduces (0,4,12) motif; dim. seventh (octatonic) harmony
7–13	C	'jazz-like'; overt seven-note octatonic set; 'walking bass' employs motif from B; static harmonically but rhythmically dynamic
13–16	D	transitional character; form of motif from B in bass
16–19	E (A)	dynamic character of opening; variant of A with rising diatonic scale in bass
19⁺¹–21	F (cf. C)	static (stable) character; continuation of E with falling diatonic scales in bass; alternating wind triads from octatonic subset (cf. C)
21–9	G (B?)	begins statically like B but then begins to 'develop' material; opposes G and D♭ triads (together forming octatonic subset 6-30)
29–34	H	section of closure; mostly over E bass pedal, descending to C in final five bars; continues figuration of G
34–8	D′	transitional character

'Development'
(171 bars, crotchet = 80)

'Recapitulation'
(85 bars, crotchet = 160)

Figs	Section	Comment
88–94	C	transposed up one tone; curtailed
94–5	D′	transposed up one tone; fragment
95–6	C	fragment
96–7	D′	fragment
97–102		material from 'development' (D–B–D motif); crotchet = 80
102–5	cf. B	static (transitional) character; makes use of D–B motif as ostinato; crotchet = 80 (though durations also halved)
105–end	A′	initially transposed up perfect fifth in places, then at original pitch; augmentation; 'C major' close

In the Stravinsky *Symphony*, it is clear that the piano only begins to sing in its own right in the 'development' (beginning at fig. 38, and especially at figs. 45–8). This is enhanced by the role of the (0,3,12/0,4,12) motif from the 'exposition' – 'the incomplete triad so prevalent in Stravinsky's music: an incomplete "minor" or "major" triad with its root doubled and its fifth missing'[67] – which is much more explicitly developed, the kind of motivic working one might reasonably expect of a 'development' section. The flow of ideas certainly seems more seamless than in the 'exposition', though this is perhaps deceptive. Sections built of ostinatos are present – sometimes more overtly than was ever the case in the 'exposition' (e.g. figs. 50–51, 66–7, 70–74, 79–80), sometimes operating in similar ways (e.g. compare figs. 44–5 with figs. 8ff), and on closer examination the flow of ideas is as fragmentary as in the 'exposition'. Like the 'exposition' too, the 'development' seems to end up in quite a different place from where it began. The difference is that in the 'exposition' (and, for that matter, the 'recapitulation') the abrupt oppositions are more obviously foregrounded.

Van den Toorn sums up the *Symphony*'s modernism as follows:

> the first movement of Stravinsky's Symphony would group only very awkwardly with Schoenberg's 'extended', atonal, and twelve-tone repertories, or with the rhythmic and melodic aspects of those repertories; in their progressive and forward-moving impulses, the latter aspects can seem antithetical to the statically maintained blocks and sections characteristic of the Symphony.[68]

The 'exposition' is made up of nine such distinct sections ('blocks'); see Fig. 6.1. Each is individually characterised in terms of harmonic, rhythmic and motivic material, and orchestration (the now-familiar Stravinskian *drobnost'*), with the result that each section also has a different kind of 'energy' on a spectrum between 'dynamic' and 'static'. The way in which Stravinsky here reinterprets the stratification of musical ideas has been of much interest to subsequent composers. To return to just one example: the first 'movement' of Part I of Tippett's Symphony No. 3 alternates musical materials and tempi which the composer characterises as 'Arrest' ('a compression of energy') and 'Movement' ('an explosion of energy'), and which can be understood to correspond to the more 'static' (e.g. section C) and the more 'dynamic' (e.g. section A) sections of Stravinsky's *Symphony*. As discussed in earlier chapters, it is well documented that Stravinsky's work was an important influence on Tippett's Symphony No. 2, but the influence is equally though more subtly apparent in the Third Symphony in various ways, not least because of the Beethoven allusions in both works.[69] Adorno both alludes to the alleged 'Beethoven-like' nature of the

Ex. 6.11 Stravinsky, *Symphony in Three Movements*, first movement (opening, piano reduction)

motifs of Stravinsky's *Symphony* and suggests that it 'applies itself to a lapidary homophony which might well have had Beethoven in mind'.[70] Other allusions to other music shared by these two works include those to 'popular' music: jazz in Stravinsky, the blues in Tippett.

The dynamism of A is immediately apparent – this is Adorno's 'thesis' full of promise, what Arnold Whittall describes as the 'tremendous momentum generated by the opening paragraph'.[71] This is achieved not just in the upward thrust of the theme itself (Ex. 6.11), which dramatises the central conflict between G and A♭ (and also the important neighbour-note motion of G–A♭–G), but also in the way in which rhythmic techniques of augmentation, diminution, compression and shift of metrical stress propel the music to the point where the next section interrupts. It is also worth noting that the basic thematic idea is formed from a four-note octatonic subset (0,1,3,7).[72] This octatonicism is not an overt feature of the music at this stage, but it already suggests the potential for octatonic ('static') working in contradiction to the obvious dynamism of this first section.

Section B (fig. 5) contrasts absolutely with A in its chamber scoring, its soft dynamics and its static character, achieved both by the lack of varied rhythmic activity (repeated quaver ostinato in the clarinets over a C♯ pedal) and its unchanging harmony. It is formed from another four-note octatonic subset (C♯–E–G–B♭), this time a symmetrical formation (0,3,6,9) which further enhances the static character of the section. From this collection the horns and trumpets pick out the other important motif for the work (G–B♭), making a feature of the minor third and its inversion, and the octave. Of course, this set could also be understood as a diminished seventh, though there is no sense in which it functions as such. However, the choice of chord is not, I am convinced, arbitrary. Stravinsky makes use of the chord's associations devoid of any immediate tonal context – in this case, the diminished seventh as a sign of 'expectation', of 'transition', which thus imbues this 'static' section with a tension and a kind of implied direction, even though its directedness is destined to go unresolved (at least, in any conventional tonal sense).

Section C (beginning at fig. 7) is particularly interesting as it appears to combine the dynamic and static aspects of the previous two sections (a procedure, incidentally, which also occurs in the later stages of Tippett's Third Symphony). The section has a jazz-like character which is achieved in a number of ways: an invariant pizzicato 'walking bass' ostinato (A–A–C) in cellos and basses; syncopated, reiterated dyads (E♭–G/G–B♭) in the upper strings; and similarly syncopated 'jazzy' chords in the piano, emphasising its rhythmic aspects, later doubled in the winds (Ex. 6.12a). And, despite the obvious discontinuities, there are also connections with the earlier two sections (which has prompted van den Toorn's motivic reading). The walking bass is clearly a version of the brass motif from section B, as are the upper string formations, which place the thirds and octaves of this motif vertically. The harmony of this section is now explicitly octatonic, thus realising the potential of the preceding sections – the pitch-class material is derived exclusively from the octatonic subset 7-31 (G–A–B♭–C–D♭–E♭–E). Most notable are the jazzy piano chords, the two versions of 4-27 holding G–B♭ invariant. Like the chord employed in section B, these chords – both 'dominant sevenths' – have rich associations, but their functions are ignored; they are 'hypostatised' (hence the parallels with jazz).

Section C, taken out of the context of the rest of the *Symphony*, is a key moment in Stravinsky which resonates backwards and forwards. Backwards as far as the bells of the Coronation Scene of Musorgsky's *Boris Godunov* (original version 1868–9), which similarly alternates chords of the 'dominant seventh', sharing a (different) invariant dyad within an overall octatonic context (Ex. 6.12b). And forwards as far as the minimalism of John Adams's *Grand Pianola Music* and *Fearful Symmetries*, and ubiquitously in Philip Glass. These (and many other) recent examples fetishise the moment ('stasis') brought about by rhythmic repetition, pedal notes and other invariants, and the non-directional alternation of two forms of the same chord by means of neighbour-note voice leading. As seen in Chapter 5, it would seem it is Stravinsky's fate (particularly among minimalists) to have isolated aspects of his music taken and reworked in new contexts. The most immediately attractive moments are plundered and placed under the magnifying glass of repetition. Such an account might at first read like a superficial parody of neoclassicism itself. But the differences revealed by comparing Stravinsky's (modernist) use of materials from the past with the minimalists' (postmodern) appropriation of Stravinsky might help counter some of Adorno's more excessive claims. Stravinsky's moments, when heard in the context of the whole, are never 'impotent' in the way that – like the present-obsessed nature of so much

Ex. 6.12a Stravinsky, *Symphony in Three Movements*, first movement (fig. 7)

Ex. 6.12b Musorgsky, *Boris Godunov*, Coronation Scene

popular music – the most obvious recurrences of minimalism appear to be. It is this music, if any – not Stravinsky's – that wills 'the end of musical Bergsonianism'. In playing off 'le temps espace' against 'le temps durée', the need for memory is eradicated.[73]

As implied above, section C is not just built of static ostinatos, but also inherits something of the dynamism of the first section, achieved rhythmically and melodically. Just as the piano part is made up of only two chords ordered in various ways, so its rhythmic material consists of only two elements: a pair of triplet quavers shared, hocket-like, between right and left hands, and an offbeat *sforzando* chord. This material is also found (appropriately adjusted to suit the instruments) in upper strings and wind. It is the way in which these units are organised, however, which generates a sense of forward momentum. If the triplet quavers suggest continuity (as many as eight of these units are strung together in succession), then the *sf* chords (which, with the exception of the final two beats of the section, only ever occur as single events) disrupt/punctuate the rhythmic flow. The triplet pairs are grouped in progressively longer strings to lead to the first climax (fig. 11, just before the wind enters), and then in smaller groups (pairs or singles) away from this point. This corresponds precisely with an octatonic melody in the top-most voice of the piano in which peak notes are articulated by rhythmic unit b. The increasing frequency of b towards the end of the section serves to disrupt any sense of forward melodic motion, and so the double statement of b calls a halt to the section as a whole. The melody itself is represented in Fig. 6.2. It emerges from the ostinatos below it with a statement of the G–B♭–G motif and then, in typical fashion, builds momentum by cycling through a limited number of pitches (five in this case). Note how the order of the sequence remains fixed and how (with two exceptions marked *) disjunct movement back into the sequence is signalled by rhythmic unit b. This predominantly upward melodic motion further enhances the forward momentum of the passage – a

Fig. 6.2 Stravinsky, *Symphony in Three Movements*, first movement (figs. 7–13); melodic structure (top voice, piano part)

characteristic shared by the walking bass, as well as the bass towards the end of section A (see LH piano, cello and bass, figs. 3–5, dominated by a rising seventh figure). The use of a fixed five-note sequence here, along with the unchanging octatonic harmonic context, and the motivic connections between all the elements of this passage, demonstrate the possibility that Stravinsky already had the propensity for the serial method he was to adopt in the mid-1950s.

I dwell in some detail on section C, not just because it is a familiar Stravinsky 'moment', but also because it demonstrates interesting technical features which have been subsequently exploited in a variety of ways. It is yet another instance of Stravinsky finding ways of balancing distinct materials, which may yet have something in common – of 'unified fragmentation'. Here, circular ideas (most obviously the walking bass) and linear ideas (the piano melody, the rhythmic organisation) are held in balance by the severe limitation of pitch (octatonic) and rhythmic materials, and by their interpretations of the shared (0,4,12) motif. Birtwistle's terms for these distinct but related musical categories are potentially useful here: 'continuum' and 'cantus'. As we saw in the Symphony in C, this music is simultaneously static and dynamic, the two are held in some sort of balance. This, it seems to me, is something far richer than saying, as Adorno does, that these are merely 'apparent progressions'.[74] When this section reappears, to initiate the 'recapitulation', it is, unusually, repeated exactly with the exception that it is transposed up a tone (figs. 88–94) and cut off short of the final four crotchet beats by a varied four-bar fragment of section D (figs. 94–5), similarly transposed up a tone. This is in turn interrupted (figs. 95–6) by a further three bars of section C which present, just once, the five-note octatonic melody (a transposed version of the first full statement from the 'exposition' – bb. 37–9 – but with wind doublings and a 'dislocated' bass), followed by another varied fragment of D (figs. 96–7), before 'development' material returns at fig. 97.

There is little apparent resolution in this 'recapitulation'. Much of the material of the 'exposition' never reappears (the 'return' is substantially shorter), and with the exception of the augmentation in the final section (from fig. 105) the 'recapitulation' seems, if anything, even more fragmentary (cinematic?) than the 'exposition'. The final section feigns tonal closure with a dominant (G) pedal in cellos and basses beginning at fig. 106 (though nothing above it resembles functional dominant harmony) falling to a C chord in the closing bars. Even here, though, the bass clarinet takes over the reiterated Gs almost *too* insistently, undermining the 'finality' of the C in the other bass instruments and drawing our attention to the rogue B in the final thickly scored chord. This could be dismissed as mere 'jazzy' colouration – certainly the case with the unexpected final D♭ chord of the entire piece with its added seconds and sixths ('rather too commercial'[75]). In the first movement, doubling of the B in lower octaves (especially trombone 2) makes such a reading problematical, as it serves to keep B 'in play', a pitch class which has been particularly prominent (in the bass) for much of the 'recapitulation'. Van

Ex. 6.13 Stravinsky, *Symphony in Three Movements*, second movement (bb. 1–2)

den Toorn's solution,[76] predictably, is to interpret the B as 'left "hanging" from the preceding Collection I [octatonic] blocks'; like the conclusion of the *Symphonies of Wind Instruments* before it, this chord, 'with G/B/G positioned over the (CEG) "tonic" triad, equally reflects Collection I's presence'. Though van den Toorn does allow for 'the "feel" of a dominant' from fig. 105 and describes the movement towards the final cadence as a 'tonally incriminating turn of events',[77] the octatonic reading of the final sonority – while undeniably legitimate in the context of the extraordinarily explicit octatonicism of this movement – seems to me to be *too* conveniently synthesising, and to underplay other tensions in the music. The music is undoubtedly 'directed' towards the final cadence by means of the associations of the pedal point and the falling character of the augmented melodic line – implying a partial resolution of the G–A♭ conflict of the opening – and yet it remains 'open' because its harmonic tensions also remain partially unresolved. Like the final chords of the first and fourth movements of the Symphony in C, they are held in balance in a chord that suggests simultaneous resolution and non-resolution. A 'convergence', to use Stravinsky's term, a frozen multivalence, but not a synthesis.

The lyrical second movement, a relatively straightforward ABA song form, anticipates the kind of writing more extensively employed in *The Rake's Progress*. This is 'classic' neoclassicism: 'the Classical setting, typically Classical enunciation of theme and accompaniment'.[78] Allusions to D major are strong, though this is achieved as much by motivic use of the major/minor third/sixth motto from the first movement – indeed, D–F♯ is never heard except in the context of D–F (Ex. 6.13) – as by any strongly functional means. The shift to 'F major' at fig. 118 (described by van den Toorn as a pseudo-modulation: the 'maneuver became a neoclassical habit'[79]) can be understood as a consequence of the D–F in the bass at the opening and can be compared with the shifts found in, say, the opening duet and trio of *The Rake's Progress* ('The woods are green'). Like that trio, too, this movement comes to an end on the weak part of the bar with just an (0,4) formulation – hardly a definitive assertion of the 'tonic' (though, of course, a reassertion of the third/octave which is taken up at the start of the finale). Thus the allusions to tonality here – in such forms as diatonic scales, apparently functional bass progressions and so on – are held in balance by a motivic (i.e. atonal) approach to harmonic organisation. Nonetheless, the general sense of continuity in this movement is occasionally arrested by more explicitly static, punctuating passages, such as at figs. 124–5 and 133–4.

The *con moto* finale restores the propulsive energy of the first movement. If anything, its structure is even more fragmentary than that of the earlier movement, and there is no obvious governing schema – though it could be argued that, like the first movement, it has an initial fragmentary part (figs. 142–70, cf. 'exposition') and a more continuous part (beginning with the fugato at fig. 170, cf. 'development') which progressively takes on the characteristics of the first part once again (from around fig. 182). This is supported by an increase in tempo according to the scheme crotchet = 108–144–(108)–160. Each musical block is again distinctively characterised – the juxtapositions are even sharper here than in the first movement, and each almost seems to be a different Stravinskian 'topic'. For example, fig. 142 is a neoclassical tutti familiar from *Pulcinella* onwards; the woodwind duet at fig. 148 has precedents in the *Symphonies of Wind Instruments* and the *Octet*; the 'rumba' at fig. 152 is like so many of Stravinsky's popular dances, first heard in *The Soldier's Tale*; the ostinatos at fig. 154 look back to *The Rite of Spring*; and the counterpoint at fig. 170 might even look forward to *Agon* (e.g. the 'Bransle double').

The 'rumba block' (figs. 152–4, 161–3, 191–4) is a striking moment and parallels the jazz-like section C from the first movement in its rhythmic momentum, its explicit octatonic formulation and its colourful scoring. Its second appearance is, in van den Toorn's estimation, 'one of the most exhilarating octatonic passages in the literature . . . another triumph of octatonic imagination'.[80] Each layer of the block is clearly distinguished: Db pedal in harp and cello; Db major triads (with Eb passing and Cb neighbouring chords) in woodwind, horns and violins; and alternating G major and E major chords in trumpet, piano and viola (i.e. the same relationship as between the alternating 'dominant seventh' chords in section C of the first movement). What is fascinating is how Stravinsky is able to generate momentum in a static harmonic context, and not just by the general syncopated vitality of these 'rumba' passages. The first appearance (152–4) is, as one might expect, the most stable: the syncopated wind and piano D♭ chords are organised in groups of 4–4–8 crotchet beats. The second (161–3) takes up this metric regularity (4–8 beats), which it then disrupts/compresses (7–4–5 beats) in order to push the music forward. The final appearance (191–4) returns to the regularity of the first (4–4–4–8 beats) and then increases the rate of change (1 bar before fig. 193) while delaying the arrival of the final melodic A♭ until the start of the final block of music (fig. 194[+1]) – in some senses, a highly traditional use of harmonic rhythm to generate motion.

These passages work as effectively as they do because of their positioning in the movement as a whole. Nonetheless, they have been hypostatised by subsequent composers (from Bernstein to Torke), who have been drawn in by their rhythmic energy, their colourful sonorities and their allusions to the immediacy and vitality of popular music. Such moments open a fascinating window on to the origins and reception of Stravinsky's modernism and help account for the strength of his influence – not least the ability of polarised 'foci' to survive into a post-tonal (post-*Agon*) world. Their primitivism ('elemental and vitalizing energy', 'the unaffected and the unstudied, the powerful and the essential'[81]) clearly looks back to Stravinsky's Russian works – especially the rhythmic energy of *The Rite* and *Les Noces* – as well as the persistent use of restricted folk-like melodic formulae. Furthermore, as Watkins tells us, there was in the 1960s and 1970s 'a delayed recognition of the affinities between African rhythm and the processes discovered by Stravinsky between 1912 and 1914'[82] which coincided with the interest being taken by a composer such as Reich in African drumming and may well help to account for the similarities between his music and Stravinsky's. Certainly, the greater self-consciousness in the processing of material in these 'rumba blocks' in comparison with the greater 'spontaneity' of much of *Les Noces* (one would expect allusions to commercial music to be more self-conscious) might suggest a certain 'proto-minimalism' in Stravinsky. When it is written of Michael Torke's music that 'it shares with Stravinsky restless developments of fragmented themes and an irrepressible rhythmic ingenuity',[83] it is surely to moments such as the 'rumba' that reference is being made. The growing awareness in the 1920s of 'the multiple functions of "high" and "low" as musical categories' provides the context for understanding the inevitability of the way in which 'the sounds of jazz . . . were welded to Stravinsky's rhythmic manner previously announced under the Russian Primitivist banner',[84] beginning with *The Soldier's Tale*. Given that processes of globalisation are closely associated with the postmodern condition, the attempts at accommodation in recent music of both 'high' and 'low' culture, and Western and other musical cultures, it should hardly surprise us that moments such as the 'rumba' in the *Symphony in Three Movements* should resonate so loudly with composers of recent decades. Ironically, for Adorno, it was this retrogressive primitivism in Stravinsky that was at the heart of his dispute with the composer.

7   Conclusions: Stravinsky, Adorno and the problem of non-development

The inter-war disputes between the followers of (serial) Schoenberg and the admirers of (neoclassical) Stravinsky found their fullest expression in Adorno's study of 1949, *Philosophie der neuen Musik*.[1] Though its two constituent essays were written some seven years apart,[2] taken together they offer a Hegelian, dialectical view of what Adorno then believed to constitute the 'new music' (he describes the book as 'an extended appendix' to his and Max Horkheimer's *Dialektik der Aufklärung* of 1947).[3] The positive and negative poles of modernism were expressed by Adorno as an opposition of Schoenberg's representation of a progressive, authentic, developmental and free subject and Stravinsky's representation of a regressive, inauthentic, non-developmental and unfree subject; Adorno's dialectical reading was necessarily dependent on a negative view of Stravinsky (the reactionary product of a depersonalised society) standing in antithesis to a positive view of Schoenberg (the progressive product of historical necessity). Adorno was to return to, refine and revise his ideas on Stravinsky on a number of occasions, most notably in 'Stravinsky. Ein dialektisches Bild' in the late collection of essays on modern music, *Quasi una fantasia*.[4]

Appearing at a time when the post-War European avant-garde seemed to be concerned almost exclusively with the Schoenberg–Webern legacy (as we saw in Chapter 1, Boulez was proclaiming that 'since the discoveries of the Viennese School, all non-serial composers are *useless*'[5]), and in the extraordinary light of Stravinsky's own 'conversion' to the serial method (even Adorno expressed his 'pleasure' in 'Stravinsky's departure from the reactionary camp'[6]), Adorno's polemic played a significant role in perpetuating a reading of modernism in which the Schoenberg line remained dominant. Schoenberg's school, according to Adorno, was the only one 'which does justice to the present objective possibilities of the elements of music and stands up to the difficulties involved without compromise'.[7] Even the work of Cage (himself for a brief time a Schoenberg pupil), which was expressing an opposition to rather than a continuity of European traditions, might be understood to occupy a position complementary to that of Schoenberg. (This seems to be borne out by the fact that a fascinating synthesis of these two modernisms was achieved in Europe in the later 1950s: witness the changing perspectives of European music in such 'open form' works as Boulez's Third Piano Sonata and Stockhausen's Piano Piece XI.) Even as early as 1949 (the year of Cage's first visit to Europe), it is possible to see clear parallels between the working of the two 'schools', such that the contemporaneous *Structures Ia* of Boulez and Cage's *Music of Changes* appear as aspects of the same idea. Boulez wrote to Cage in 1951:

> [Your] letter gave me an extraordinary amount of pleasure. Everything you say about the tables of sounds, durations, amplitudes, used in your Music of Changes is, as you will see, along exactly the same lines as I am working at the moment.[8]

This view is reinforced by Adorno's acceptance of Cage. One might naïvely assume that Adorno would have tarred Cage's aesthetic of non-intention with the same critical brush as he did Stravinsky's music, which had rid 'itself of all intentions – that is, of its own subjectivity'.[9] Yet he wrote of being 'deeply moved by a single hearing of Cage's Piano Concerto'[10] and, despite reservations expressed elsewhere, he maintained that one of the strengths of Cage's chance music was 'as a protest against the dogged complicity of music with the domination of nature'.[11] In other words, in accordance with Cage's own views, he identified in his music a freedom comparable in some respects with 'the idea of an unrevised, unrestricted freedom' to be found in the best examples of what he termed '*musique informelle*' (of which he considered *Erwartung* to be the finest instance).

Thus, by 1962, Adorno seemed to be articulating a view of the history of the avant-garde in the first fifteen years after World War 2 in which the apparently competing claims of Paris/Darmstadt and New York, of integral serialism and aleatoricism, were in certain respects both aspects of the same kind of modernist thinking and belonged, in different ways, to the Schoenberg/Webern tradition. Stravinsky's modernism was portrayed as being at odds with all this. The interesting question is why, despite the many fascinating insights he offered into Stravinsky's music, Adorno was not prepared to allow the Stravinsky line to pursue its own separate course through history and to offer a plural view of modernism. Adorno's arguments were certainly not mounted in ignorance of the music: he clearly knew it well. As Subotnik writes, 'Adorno's thorough familiarity with the music he characterizes as well as the aptness and importance of his metaphors are virtually always confirmed by a reconsideration of the music in question.'[12] Andriessen and Schönberger put it more bluntly: Adorno 'detested Stravinsky but . . . sometimes had a clear insight into his music'.[13] But *why* did he so detest Stravinsky? After all, he did not similarly condemn Debussy, whose modernism we saw in Chapter 1 intersects with Stravinsky's in so many ways.

Part of Adorno's 'problem' is that *Philosophy of Modern Music* is very much a text rooted in the history of the time of its writing. Having witnessed first-hand the rise of National Socialism in Germany and, to the extent that he was compelled to flee to America in order to be able to continue to work freely, Adorno, like Schoenberg, was a Nazi victim. Adorno saw prefigured in Stravinsky's music, and preeminently in *The Rite of Spring*, the characteristic features of fascism: the suppression of individual thought, expression and action in favour of a collective identity and collective activity, variously expressed through the idea of the 'Volk' (a timeless concept equated with a 'pure' nature, a primitive nationalism, an idealised past), a belief in the 'destiny' of the race, and the incitement of the collective to the hatred, persecution and ultimate 'liquidation' of particular individual 'others'. Though he does not say so, Stravinsky's on-going admiration for Mussolini must surely have influenced Adorno's attitude. Equally, in the light of Taruskin's revelations about Stravinsky's anti-semitism,[14] one is prompted to speculate whether Adorno might also have been sensitive to this.

At fifty years' distance, it is now possible for us to dissociate Adorno's argument from its historical context. In the same way that, for example, Schenker's analytical methods have been separated (albeit problematically[15]) from the historical, national and political contexts of his theory, so it now becomes possible (though similarly problematically) to reconsider Adorno's insightful analysis of Stravinsky separately from what happened in Germany in the 1930s and 1940s, and from the negative conclusions he inevitably drew. We can understand the historical necessity of pitting Schoenberg – the brave, lone voice, the reluctant revolutionary – who stood for all that was good and genuinely free about new music, against Stravinsky – rooted in a folk culture, reliant apparently on forms and idioms from an idealised past – who represented the evils of the power of the collective. But, in the light of our changed understanding of Stravinsky as a result of what has happened to Stravinsky since his and Adorno's deaths (in 1971 and 1969 respectively) – as charted in Part I of this book – is it not now legitimate to look again at Adorno's argument, removed from its dialectical context? Indeed, we might even speculate that a central part of the 'problem' of Adorno's analysis of Stravinsky lies in the very dialectical method itself – or, more particularly, in the presentation in *Philosophy of Modern Music* of a polarised view of Schoenberg and Stravinsky without any attempt at a synthesis. As Paddison puts it, the

> dialectic of material is brought to a standstill, like Hegel's vision of the 'end of history'. Unlike Hegel, however, there is no ultimate reconciliation of antitheses within the Whole, as Absolute Spirit, but only an absolutizing of

the antitheses themselves in their mutual and total alienation. The extremes, as total integration and total disintegration, become final, and no way forward is offered.[16]

The fundamental antithesis in *Philosophy of Modern Music* is between Schoenberg's (progressive) developmental music and Stravinsky's (reactionary) non-developmental music. For Adorno, the twelve-note method offered 'a textbook model of musical dialectics':

> Its dialectic is one of the architectonic features of music as such. As a developmental structure music is an absolute negation of repetition.... On the other hand, it is only able to develop by virtue of repetition.... A development which leads to something new can only do so thanks to its relationship to the old which is assumed a priori in such a relation and is repeated in however sublimated and unrecognizable a form. There can be no articulated music in the absence of this highly formal constituent of similarity; identity in non-identity is its lifeblood. In serial music this dialectic is taken to extremes. Absolutely nothing may be repeated and, as the derivative of One thing, absolutely everything is repetition.[17]

Central to this dialectic is variation, the 'tool of compositional dynamics'.[18] Through procedures of developing variation, Adorno was concerned to point out Schoenberg's continuity with a figure like Brahms, 'the advocate of universal economy, refuting all coincidental moments of music, and yet developing the most extreme multiplicity – the result from thematic materials the identity of which has been preserved';[19] indeed, Adorno's views on developing variation and twelve-note technique seem to be derived directly (and, arguably, uncritically) from Schoenberg's own views on the matter.[20] Adorno thus both confirms the 'unifying effect' which Schoenberg expressly claimed as the primary province of the twelve-note technique,[21] and asserts the essentially dynamic and developmental nature of serial music. And while, as we have seen, Adorno welcomed Stravinsky's late turn to the serial method, he nonetheless found that little had changed: developing variation was 'no more evident in Stravinsky's serial compositions than in his earlier works. He remained true to himself.'[22] Adorno conveniently forgets to mention Schoenberg's own late (albeit intermittent) turn back to tonality for which, as Paddison points out, Adorno's theory does not account satisfactorily. But what is interesting is that Stravinsky's serialism did at least suggest to Adorno a limited reevaluation of Schoenberg's twelve-note method as presented in *Philosophy of Modern Music*:

> It is not for nothing that in Schoenberg the invention of twelve-note technique goes hand in hand with the use of non-developing dance forms. With

his flair for historical trends the late Stravinsky intuited this convergence with his adversary, took matters to their logical conclusion and thereby implicitly provided a certain critique of twelve-note technique whose static nature contradicted its own origins.[23]

Stravinsky's music is categorically opposed to Schoenberg's. Not that variation is absent from Stravinsky. Far from it: we have seen how, in many respects, it remains central. But for Adorno Stravinsky's variations are not part of a musical dynamics; they do not develop. He presents us with the 'static ideal of Stravinsky's music, its immanent timelessness' in opposition to Schoenberg's 'dynamic, emphatically temporal, intrinsically developing music'. By 1962, Adorno had reconsidered his position and admitted that, in *Philosophy of Modern Music*, he had arbitrarily applied to Stravinsky an 'external norm, a norm which he [Stravinsky] rejected'.[24] Nonetheless, while acknowledging the temporality of Stravinsky's music which (like all music) is 'bound to the fact of succession and is hence as irreversible as time itself', Adorno returned to his argument that, in essence, Stravinsky's music remains stationary 'since it is made up of repetitions'.[25] Mere repetition denies development and so any sense of motion in the music is an illusion – though Adorno does allow that Stravinsky is as hostile to *literal* repetition as the serialists:

> He is beset by the crisis of the timeless products of a time-based art which constantly pose the question of how to repeat something without developing it and yet avoid monotony, or else to incorporate it integrally. The sections he strings together may not be identical and yet may never be anything qualitatively different.[26]

Adorno's ideas here are in part derived from his understanding of Nietzsche's concept of 'eternal recurrence'. It is interesting to see how this notion is given a positive gloss in relation to Schoenberg's twelve-note technique ('Static twelve-tone technique actualizes the sensitivity of musical dynamics in the face of the unconscious recurrence of the same'[27]) whereas a more critical attitude to Nietzsche is used (critically) in relation to Stravinsky:

> Ernst Bloch's comment that Nietzsche's Eternal Recurrence was simply a poor imitation of eternity consisting of endless repetitions applies literally to the inner core of Stravinsky's music. Either his works create the impression of progress, only to disappoint the listener, or – and this may well be a more accurate description of them – they bow to the order of time only to suggest obsessively that time has stopped, that they have abrogated time and achieved a state of pure being.[28]

There is a problem here with Adorno's (and Bloch's) understanding of repetition in Stravinsky. Adorno seems to suggest that Stravinsky's repetitions are absolutely 'primitive' and unchanging, whereas in fact there is nearly always a subtle change of context (which amounts to more than the mere 'impression of progress'). He also seems conveniently to mis-read Nietzsche, where the concept of eternal recurrence was always concerned with the *differences* between repetitions. It nonetheless suits Adorno's dialectic argument to maintain this opposing (and over-simplistic) view of 'progressive' (temporal) repetitions in Schoenberg and 'static' (spatial) repetitions in Stravinsky. Yet we should note that his criticisms were not restricted exclusively to Stravinsky. In Wagner Adorno also found that 'eternal sameness presents itself as the eternally new, the static as the dynamic': the difference between Wagner and Stravinsky is that in Stravinsky 'the concept of progress is repudiated' ('stasis' or 'Being' he describes as the 'ontological ideology of the middle of the twentieth century'), whereas Wagner 'would like to present the regressive element as progress, the static as dynamic'.[29] And, as Paddison tells us, it 'is through Debussy that Stravinsky can be seen to relate to Wagner'. Debussy's music shares with Stravinsky's an objectivity, but Adorno seems more tolerant of Debussy's modernism than of Stravinsky's, as a consequence of his reading of French history (an argument to do with the fact that 'autonomous music in *fin-de-siècle* France was not as alienated from bourgeois society as music in Germany', in which Paddison has identified crucial inconsistencies).[30] 'Stasis' and the 'undynamic' are less of a problem for Adorno in Debussy than they are in Stravinsky; while his reading of Debussy remains contingent, Stravinsky has to be seen to be entirely antithetical to Schoenberg.

In admitting that he had arbitrarily applied to Stravinsky an external norm which Stravinsky himself rejected, Adorno acknowledged that he had violated his 'own most cherished principle of criticism'.[31] This norm, this *a priori* assumption, was that of a dynamic, developmental model which Stravinsky violated. By reconsidering the *a priori* assumption, Adorno might at first appear to be recognising the problem of its ideological status and reversing his earlier position on Stravinsky. But in fact it seems to be more a case of *reculer pour mieux sauter*. As we have seen, Adorno acknowledged that repetition is essential to all music. Nonetheless, his definition of musical temporality is concerned with what he terms its 'transcendence' – the ability of music to become 'something other than what it was . . . [which] *lies in the nature of music and will not be denied*'.[32] Music, he argues, has always stood in opposition to myth, a protest 'against a fate which was always the same'. Therein lies music's freedom, for 'music cannot endure the idea of an avenue from which there is no escape'. This is what, in his view, is 'intrinsically amiss' with Stravinsky's music. Any sense of becoming in his work is a chimera: the 'apparent progressions in every one of Stravinsky's movements are not real, but instead are dammed up to create the illusion of a static timelessness'; they suggest 'that they have abrogated time and achieved a status of pure being'.[33]

Interestingly, this view accords with Schenker's view of Stravinsky, and the Austrian theorist's methods of articulating his case have something in common with those employed by Adorno. In the same way that Adorno attempts to demonstrate that Stravinsky's music was flawed because it continually contradicted the developmental model that Adorno had constructed for it, Schenker's notorious account of Stravinsky's Piano Concerto attempted to demonstrate that Stravinsky's music was not very good because it continually contradicted the background diatonic model that Schenker had constructed for it,[34] that its voice leading was non-directed (undynamic?) – clearly a circular argument. Adorno's assumptions are more explicitly laid out than Schenker's, but in both cases value judgments are made on the basis of the intrinsic 'naturalness' of an underlying ideology – that of organic unity in the case of Schenker, that of a fundamentally dynamic musical temporality in the case of Adorno. Though their political positions were at opposite poles, it is fascinating that both Schenker and Adorno seemed blind to any workable alternative to the Austro-German view of musical structure. We have seen throughout this book how Taruskin has argued for a Russo-centric reevaluation of Stravinsky's achievement. Paddison similarly argues that what, from a Russian perspective, are seen as 'objective' and 'eclectic' in Stravinsky, are, from Adorno's Austro-German perspective, 'irresponsible and dilettantish':

> What were for Schoenberg almost sacred elements of European art music – the need for organic unity achieved from within the material itself, for example – could not, considering his different heritage, have the same significance for Stravinsky.[35]

So how much credence can we now give to an argument that says that a sense of (Austro-German) 'becoming', a musical progress rooted in development, is intrinsic to (all) music, 'and will not be denied'? This statement has, on Carl Dahlhaus for one, 'a singularly irritating effect':

> No-one would deny Adorno's premise that an engagement with time [*la relazione con il tempo*] is essential for Stravinsky's music, as for all music. However, the consequence, that developing variation is the only legitimate way to fulfil the formal law of music as temporal art, is dogmatic.[36]

The corollary of Adorno's proposition – that any music which does not display the developmental characteristic of 'becoming' is dangerous because, like the products of the culture industry, it serves to subjugate the freedom of the individual subject, to bring about the dissolution of individual identity – would now seem, from our present perspective, generally untenable.

Of course, there are examples which might be seen to legitimate Adorno's claim, whether the insistent repetitions of Antheil's *Ballet mécanique* (if ever a work fulfilled Adorno's views on the liquidation of the subject through repetition, this surely is it! – 'Through such shocks the individual becomes conscious of his nothingness in the face of the gigantic machine of the entire system'[37]), or extreme instances of American minimalism (where 'an absolute undifferentiated dynamism . . . lapse[s] once more into the static'[38]). As I proposed in Chapter 5, the origins of minimalism might well be seen to lie partly with Stravinsky, and in particular in what Adorno identifies as a situation where the 'expressive-dynamic model' is replaced by a music in which the spatial dimension becomes 'absolute' (though nothing is so absolute in Stravinsky): minimalism, like postmodernism, 'is the consumption of sheer commodification as a process'.[39] Nonetheless, Stravinsky, while *anticipating* postmodernism in so many ways,[40] is still to be understood in modernist terms: 'still minimally and tendentially the critique of the commodity and the effort to make it transcend itself'.[41] In interpreting Stravinsky's music in the way he does, and in aligning it with the standardised products of industrial mass culture, Adorno appears, in so many words, to be opposing an absolute Schoenbergian modernism with a kind of Stravinskian *post*modernism. (Paddison argues that, in 'Stravinsky: a dialectical portrait', Adorno revised his position to allow for 'a "moment of truth" in the way in which the composer manipulates the debris of a culturally exhausted and disintegrating material'.[42]) It is striking that the features Adorno lists as characterising Stravinsky's objectivity might equally be true of (postmodern) minimalism: mechanical repetitiveness and the fetishisation of rhythm; an identification with folklore (non-Western culture), with the collective ('the expression of the mood of the enchained and the unfree'); a depersonalisation and emphasis on ritual; a regressive primitivism ('refuge in the phantasm of nature', what, in relation to minimalism, Griffiths has described as the 'delight in recovered origins'[43]); and the eradication of 'the subjective experience of time' resulting in the atomisation of musical materials. This is an incomplete picture of Stravinsky. Adorno's dialectical method, while highlighting significant features of Stravinsky's musical identity, has turned Stravinsky into a *postmodernist* by dismissing other key aspects of his *modernism*. In modernism, writes Jameson, there are still to be found certain aspects of the past, of 'nature' or 'being', and culture 'can still do something to that nature and work at transforming the "referent"'; postmodernism, however, is 'what you have when the modernisation process is complete and nature is gone for good'.[44] Such a distinction usefully coincides with Adorno's Schoenberg–Stravinsky dialectic, in which Schoenberg is seen still to 'do something to that nature' (the 'second nature' of the materials of tonality) while, in Stravinsky, 'nature is gone for good', 'referents' can no longer be 'transformed' because their continuity with the past has been severed. Once again, such a view of Stravinsky deserves to be challenged, not for what it usefully tells us about Stravinsky, but for what it fails to say.

Let us, by way of example, take a look at the contrasting attitudes of a Second Viennese composer and Stravinsky to such 'referents', to the directly appropriated music of the past. Berg's appropriation of the Bach chorale 'Es ist genug' for his Violin Concerto has been much discussed. While the emotional impact of the Bach quotation depends entirely on our recognising the difference between it and what surrounds it – its otherness – the melody is nonetheless integrated into the substance of the work, being an aspect of the very row from which the piece is built ('identity in non-identity'). The 'surface' of the music moves from a twelve-note world, to Bach, and back again; at a deeper level, the conflict between the tonal and the twelve-note worlds is attenuated by a commonality, a synthesis of sorts. In the interlude between scenes 1 and 2 of Act III of *Lulu*, as Douglas Jarman has pointed out, the melody of Wedekind's *Lautenlied* undergoes the reverse process by moving from a diatonic original to a twelve-note context – the process of 'absorption' is a *dynamic* one. It is a set of four variations: the first is diatonic C major (with 'jazzy' edges); the second sets a *Nebenstimme* 'in C' canonically off against a *Hauptstimme* 'in G♭'; the third has the melody 'in A' in the bass but accompanied atonally; and the last variation fully integrates the melody (implying a background F♯ major) into the opera's basic serial material.[45] Interestingly, the start of scene 2 returns to a diatonic version of the *Lautenlied*, now in E♭ – the only remaining 'key' of the circle of minor thirds. Thus, the song retains its musical 'otherness' and points indexically, metonymically (as appropriate to the drama) to a decadent, low-life cabaret world, while at the same time belonging entirely to the twelve-note argument of the work as a whole (in this regard, of course, the motion through the symmetrical 'diminished seventh' keys is significant).[46]

Compare this journey backwards and forwards through a 'musical history' in *Lulu* (or, indeed, the fusion of free atonality and serialism in the

Lyric Suite) with Stravinsky's reading of similar historical events in *Agon*. As Taruskin has asserted, the history of the reception of Stravinsky's serial works ever since Milton Babbitt's influential essay[47] has attempted to show a linear *progress* towards the achievement of a fully-formed serial technique, something some writers have alleged occurs within *Agon* itself ('the musical idiom starts with a clear diatonic basis . . . but *progresses* towards chromaticism and serialism, returning to diatonicism at the end'[48]), but which only serves to hide the continuing underlying differences between the contemporary avant-garde and the substance of Stravinsky's work, which was little changed from his earlier music. Evidence, once again, of how a history written in terms of Schoenbergian modernism has for so long influenced our interpretation of Stravinsky's achievements. Watkins discusses differing responses to the question of 'the need for integration in the presentation of systems of potential conflict' but nevertheless asserts that in *Agon* 'tonal and atonal live side by side two decades after Berg's Violin Concerto'.[49] My understanding is, rather, that in Berg there is a clear dialectic between the 'side-by-side' (oppositional) nature of his past and present musical materials and their integration, whereas in Stravinsky the material's 'side-by-sideness' is foregrounded and its 'integration' is achieved in a quite different manner – that is, by means of a 'non-synthesising balance'. Thomas Clifton employs the term 'reconciliation' for *Agon*.[50]

Pulcinella remains one of Stravinsky's most extreme examples of appropriation of music of the past. It began life, at Diaghilev's suggestion, as an orchestration of some eighteenth-century pieces for a ballet. And certainly there are movements which, aside from a few Stravinskian quirks, are little more than transcriptions. Looking back at it many decades later, the *Pulcinella* project took on a much greater importance for Stravinsky. It was his

> discovery of the past, the epiphany through which the whole of my late work became possible. It was a backward look, of course – the first of many love affairs in that direction – but it was a look in the mirror, too. No critic understood this at the time, and I was therefore attacked for being a *pasticheur*, chided for composing 'simple' music, blamed for deserting modernism . . . [51]

Taruskin charts the 'invention' of *Pulcinella* as an original work of Stravinsky's out of its origins as 'Musique de Pergolesi, arrangée et orchestrée par Igor Strawinsky'. He attempts to quash any view that argues it is anything other than an arrangement.[52] And yet his own analysis of the closing bars of the work shows that, at least in places, the source material (here, a Domenico Gallo trio sonata, not Pergolesi) is turned into Stravinsky in ways that conform to the solid Turanian virtues of *drobnost'*, *nepodvizhh-nost'*, and *uproshcheniye*, qualities inimical to the linear, harmony-driven temporality of Western classical music. There is no real accommodation. What attracts the ear to *Pulcinella* is precisely the centrifugal tension arising out of the confrontation of irreconcilable forces.[53]

The music simultaneously suggests a functional relationship between tonic and 'dominant', and a contradiction of that functionality through repetition, ostinato and the substitution for the dominant of, in Taruskin's terms, a chord made up of the notes of an 'anhemitonic C scale' from which the leading note, B, is omitted. These forces may be 'irreconcilable', but they are balanced, they do not cancel each other out. This I examined in greater detail in the Symphony in C, where there is a productive tension between the 'tonal' and the 'nontonal' and their simultaneous resolution and non-resolution. Here, the singular (progressive) subject of the models is fragmented and placed in new contexts, but it does not totally disintegrate.

In this sense, what Stravinsky was doing in *Pulcinella* was an act of criticism, implying a recognition of the *distance* between the model and the new work – and thus, far from a desertion of modernism, was very much in line with Jameson's understanding of modernism, that is, the critique of the commodity and the effort to make it transcend itself. Stravinsky himself described *Pulcinella* and *Le Baiser de la fée* as 'music criticisms'.[54] And Adorno has proposed that a genuinely 'new music constitutes a critique of the old one'.[55] The key question, of course, is whether what Stravinsky did was *mere* critique (simply 'music about music') or whether he was able to make the material 'transcend' itself. I would argue that, even in moments such as the ending of *Pulcinella*, he was: it is neither tonal pastiche, nor the complete destruction of a tonal model, but a balancing act between the meanings implied by the original and by Stravinsky's 'own' procedures. Whittall sums up: Stravinsky 'had rejected traditionally functional harmony, but in doing so he enhanced the distinction between tension and resolution which those functions articulated'.[56]

Berg's many references to the past – whether in the multitudinous use of old forms, or in direct quotation of others as well as himself – make it clear that, while the past remains firmly in the past (the Bach and Wedekind quotations are, in their 'unadulterated' forms, in inverted commas through their alienating scoring for, respectively, four clarinets and barrel organ), its continuity with the present is of equal significance. 'Berg's consciousness of the past was as great as Stravinsky's, but his use of quotation and allusion is scarcely neo-classical in spirit. Rather it is post-romantic – the personal memory, the personal nostalgia breaking through the ordered surface which the new techniques imposed as a necessary basis for coherence.'[57] In other words, Berg maintains not only a meaningful dialectic between past and present but also a musical dialectic between tonal and atonal. In Whittall's statement, much hangs on what is understood by 'neoclassical'. It is the fragmentation and subsequent hypostatisation of material in *Pulcinella* to which Adorno objects, and it is in this context that he lets loose some of his most damning and vituperative judgments. The (bourgeois) listener is implicated in this: 'The work is, of course, lightly colored by speculation upon those listeners who wish their music to be familiar, but at the same time to be labeled modern. This indicates the willingness inherent in this music to be used as fashionable commercial music – similar to the willingness of surrealism to be used for shop-window decoration.'[58] I hope it will be clear by now that, while such an observation may be true of the 'arrangement' sections of *Pulcinella* (Adorno, too, fell into the trap revealed by Taruskin of overplaying the 'original' status of the work), this is in general terms a misrepresentation of Stravinsky.

What Stravinsky suggested in *Pulcinella* and realised in many different ways in his neoclassical works was, to recall Andriessen and Schönberger, a critical attitude towards already existing material. It is possible, with Adorno, to hear *Pulcinella* as Pergolesi-with-wrong-notes, familiar music with just a little diverting modern spice, just as many still choose to hear *The Rake's Progress* as Mozart with wrong notes. Adorno writes of Stravinsky's use of functional components from tonal music 'employed independently of their [original] technical purpose'.[59] This much is mere *Merzbild*. But there is more to Stravinsky than this: as Watkins puts it, a 'personal style was . . . coined not so much through the appropriation of ingredients from a particular historical or cultural model as through their fracture and *purposeful reassemblage*: criticism of received materials becomes the modus operandi for the creative act'.[60] It is the *purposefulness* of this reassemblage which, I would contest, has been one of Stravinsky's most important legacies to the twentieth century: Stravinsky's significance lies not just in his elevation of *drobnost'*, *nepodvizhhnost'* and *uproshcheniye* to primary structural determinants, important though these are, but also in the way fragmented objects are reordered, how new continuities are created – from the abstract balancing of continuity and discontinuity in the *Symphonies of Wind Instruments*, through the dramatic reinterpretation of eighteenth- and nineteenth-century operatic conventions in *The Rake's Progress*, to the late adoption of serial techniques. This is what my analyses (in Chapter 6) of the Symphony in C and the *Symphony in Three Movements* aimed to demonstrate.

One of the principal problems with Adorno's Schoenberg–Stravinsky polemic is that he overvalues those features of Schoenberg's serialism that he finds lacking in Stravinsky. As I have tried to show, just as Adorno fails to say 'everything' about Stravinsky (his reading is selective), so he says 'too much' about serialism (but, once again, a selective reading). In practice, the differences between the kinds of (systematic) repetitions of the 'one thing' (i.e. the row) in Schoenberg's serial music and Stravinsky's constantly shifting (surface) repetitions are surely nowhere near as great as Adorno attempts to make them out to be.

In opposition to Adorno, my project in this book has been to demonstrate the rich possibilities suggested by Stravinsky's modernism. His music, far from allowing merely superficial imitations, has opened up, among other things, new and radical formal, rhythmic and dramatic opportunities. Subsequent composers have worked with this strand of modernism to produce music which, at its best, is not obviously 'Stravinskian' but nonetheless is built on ideas whose origins can, in whole or in part, be identified with Stravinsky. The fragmentation suggested by Stravinsky's music, for instance, has not resulted necessarily in incoherence. The oppositions of the block structures of Birtwistle are held together in new ways: opposition becomes a positive constructive principle (implying a reevaluation of the 'subject'). Carter's music, while clearly owing much to Stravinsky, nonetheless also intersects with Schoenberg's (and others') modernism in fascinating ways, resulting in a music which it is unhelpful to locate exclusively within one strand of musical modernism. While Carter's rhythmic practices and structural concerns are Stravinsky-derived, his atonal harmonic language, it could be argued, owes far more to Schoenberg than to Stravinsky. Thus, despite the attention devoted to Stravinsky in *this* book, it is important to remind ourselves that Stravinsky and modernism are not synonymous – it is, at the very least, inappropriate to view the entire century through Stravinsky-tinted spectacles. The problem with Adorno's interpretation of Stravinsky is that, as a consequence of both his methodology and his prejudices, he tries to evaluate the music in inappropriately Schoenbergian terms, and thu succeeds in proving the truism that Stravinsky's Franco-Russian aesthetic is quite different from Schoenberg's Austro-German aesthetic. To condemn Stravinsky for this is, at best, misguided; at worst, it verges on the authoritarian.

It would seem, then, that the complete dissolution of the subject is not necessarily the only consequence of fragmentation. The 'centre' does not lose hold entirely. Adorno's diagnosis of the mental disorder of schizophrenia – the repressive dissociation and disconnection of ideas – is not the only possible one. The fragmentation of the subject may challenge a single unity, but that does not necessarily mean the end result is incoherent. Rather than implying its liquidation, Stravinsky's music (and that of all those benefiting directly from his legacy) suggests that the nature of the progressive subject needs to be redefined. Paddison quotes Alfred Huber, who similarly asserts that through the 'dogmatically inflexible bearing [of Adorno's philosophical system, he] failed to notice the presence in Stravinsky's work of original, progressive thinking'.[61] The progress of the subject in Stravinsky is still possible, but that progress no longer assumes a linear development, a becoming. An older meaning of progress as a journey would seem to be more appropriate.[62] Though a requirement of Adorno's dialectic, it need not necessarily be the case that Schoenberg and Stravinsky lie at opposite poles (as we saw in Chapter 1, their modernisms intersect in many interesting ways). Stravinsky's subject asserts a different kind of coherence from the 'unity' of Schoenberg's subject. It may not demonstrate the organic connectedness of eighteenth- and nineteenth-century tonal masterworks, but neither is it completely disconnected as in mere collage. As we have seen, the oppositions of materials in Stravinsky's music are held in some sort of balance; discontinuous musical ideas are heard to belong together, offering a new coherence if not a new kind of unity. One wonders whether, were it not for historical circumstance, Adorno, whose understanding of modernism was acutely refined, might have taken a different view of Stravinsky: as Martin Jay reminds us, it is not altogether certain that Adorno was really so 'blind to the genuinely dynamic impulses in our society, as his activist critics always maintain'.[63]

In focusing critically on the central aspects of Stravinsky's aesthetic (stasis, ritual, collectivity, an attitude to the past), Adorno challenges us to listen again to Stravinsky, to reevaluate the ways in which we consider the music to be coherent. Adorno problematises for us the 'timelessness', the 'non-developmental' aspects of Stravinsky's music; we, in turn, need to recognise that these may not, in fact, be problems after all. In 1948, even Adorno admitted to the power of Stravinsky's music as a model for imitation by other composers. But although what he described as the shock impact of works like *The Rite* and *Les Noces* might account for Stravinsky's following by composers during the inter-war years, no one could have predicted the much more elaborate kinds of influence that Stravinsky's non-developmental structures would exert on composers in the latter half of the century. If we follow the logic of Adorno's argument, the history of Stravinsky's modernism remains a mere sub-plot, at an 'angle' (to use Taruskin's word) to the grand narrative of a hegemonic Austro-German modernism. But by the sheer breadth of ways in which Stravinsky's music has impressed itself on composers this century, and increasingly so in the last forty years, it should be clear that Stravinsky's modernism is a central feature of that narrative – the 'very stem', in Taruskin's phrase. To understand this is to begin to make sense of the way in which the multiplicity of the music of our time has emerged. The significance of the Stravinsky legacy should not and cannot be under-estimated.

Notes

1 Introduction: Stravinsky's modernism

1 'Modernisms/Postmodernisms', in Ihab and Sally Hassan, eds., *Innovation/ Renovation: New Perspectives on the Humanities* (Madison: University of Wisconsin Press, 1983), p. 322; quoted at the start of Chapter 1 of Christopher Butler, *Early Modernism: Literature, Music and Painting in Europe 1900–1916* (Oxford: Clarendon, 1994), p. 1.

2 Butler, *Early Modernism*, p. 1.

3 Paul Griffiths, *Modern Music: the Avant Garde Since 1945* (London: Dent, 1981), p. 294.

4 Schoenberg to Rufer, quoted in Malcolm MacDonald, *Schoenberg* (London: Dent, p/b edn 1987), p. 29.

5 'Schoenberg is dead', in *Stocktakings from an Apprenticeship*, tr. Stephen Walsh (Oxford: Clarendon, 1991), p. 214.

6 Anton Webern, *The Path to the New Music*, ed. Willi Reich, tr. Leo Black (London: Universal, 1975), p. 42.

7 'Composition with twelve tones (1)', in *Style and Idea*, ed. Leonard Stein, tr. Leo Black (London: Faber, rev. edn 1984), p. 244.

8 Alastair Williams, '"Répons": phantasmagoria or the articulation of space?', in Anthony Pople, ed., *Theory, Analysis and Meaning in Music* (Cambridge: Cambridge University Press, 1994), p. 196.

9 Peter Nicholls, *Modernisms: a Literary Guide* (Basingstoke: Macmillan, 1995), p. vii.

10 Arnold Whittall, 'Modernist aesthetics, modernist music: some analytical perspectives', in James Baker, David Beach and Jonathan Bernard, eds., *Music Theory in Concept and Practice* (Rochester NY: University of Rochester Press, 1997), p. 157. As an aside, it is of interest to note that Stravinsky asks a similar question in *Poetics of Music*: '. . . what an abortive neologism the word modernism is! Just what does it mean?' (*Poetics of Music in the Form of Six Lessons*, tr. Arthur Knodel and Ingolf Dahl (Cambridge MA: Harvard University Press, 1942; 5th printing 1979), p. 81). A somewhat pointless discussion ensues!

11 Leonard B. Meyer, *Music, the Arts, and Ideas* (Chicago: Chicago University Press, 1967), p. 172.

12 Jean-François Lyotard, *The Postmodern Condition: a Report on Knowledge* (Manchester: Manchester University Press, 1986), p. 3.

13 Paul Griffiths, *Modern Music and After: Directions Since 1945* (Oxford: Oxford University Press, 1995), p. 238.

14 Glenn Watkins, *Pyramids at the Louvre: Music, Culture, and Collage from Stravinsky to the Postmodernists* (Cambridge MA: Belknap, 1994).

15 Frederic Jameson, *Postmodernism, or, the Cultural Logic of Late Capitalism* (London: Verso, 1991), p. 17.

16 Louis Andriessen and Elmer Schönberger, *The Apollonian Clockwork: on Stravinsky*, tr. Jeff Hamburg (Oxford: Oxford University Press, 1989), p. 6.

17 Andriessen in conversation with Michael Oliver, in 'Stravinsky and Influence', BBC Radio 3 interval talk, first broadcast 9 February 1995.

18 Pierre Boulez, *Orientations: Collected Writings,* ed. Jean-Jacques Nattiez, tr. Martin Cooper (London: Faber, 1986), p. 362.

19 Michael Tippett, *Moving into Aquarius* (St Albans: Paladin, 1974), p. 85. Of course, Adorno had spotted early on the link between Stravinsky and Jung: 'The search for musical equivalents of the "collective unconscious" prepares the transition to the installation of a regressive collective as a positive accomplishment.' (Adorno, *Philosophy of Modern Music*, tr. Anne G. Mitchell and Wesley V. Blomster (London: Seabury Press, 1973), p. 162). All references are to the paperback edition (London: Sheed and Ward, 1987).

20 Elliott Carter, in Else and Kurt Stone, eds., *The Writings of Elliott Carter* (Bloomington: Indiana University Press, 1977), p. 301.

21 Harrison Birtwistle in conversation with the author, 'Birtwistle's Secret Theatres' Festival, Royal Festival Hall, London, 2 May 1996.

22 John Tavener, in Paul Griffiths, *New Sounds, New Personalities: British Composers of the 1980s* (London: Faber, 1985), p. 106.

23 Andriessen, 'Stravinsky and influence'.

24 Richard Taruskin, *Stravinsky and the Russian Traditions: a Biography of the Works through* Mavra (Oxford: Oxford University Press, 1996), p. 1599.

25 See, for example: 'Music analysis as human science? *Le Sacre du printemps* in theory and practice', *Music Analysis*, 1/1 (1982), pp. 33–53; 'Musical analysis: descriptions and distinctions', inaugural lecture in the Faculty of Music, King's College London (Dec. 1982); 'Webern and atonality: the path from the old aesthetic', *Musical Times*, 1690 (Dec. 1983), pp. 733–7; 'Tippett and the modernist mainstream', in Geraint Lewis, ed., *Michael Tippett OM: A Celebration* (Tunbridge Wells: Baton, 1985), pp. 109–15; 'The theorist's sense of history: concepts of contemporaneity in composition and analysis', *Journal of the Royal Musical Association*, 112 (1987), pp. 1–20; 'Birtwistle, Maxwell Davies and modernist analysis', *Music Analysis*, 13/2–3 (1994), pp. 139–59; 'Modernist aesthetics, modernist music: some analytical perspectives'.

26 'Birtwistle, Maxwell Davies and modernist analysis', p. 148; 'Tippett and the modernist mainstream', p. 110; 'Modernist aesthetics, modernist music', p. 168.

27 *The Structure of Atonal Music* (New Haven: Yale University Press, 1973), p. ix.

28 Pieter C. van den Toorn, 'Neoclassicism and its definitions', in James Baker, *et al.*, eds., *Music Theory in Concept and Practice*, pp. 154–5.

29 'Stravinsky: a dialectical portrait', in *Quasi una Fantasia*, tr. Rodney Livingstone (London: Verso, 1992), p. 158.

30 Aaron Copland, *Copland on Music* (London: Andre Deutsch, 1961), p. 96.

31 Stone and Stone, eds., *The Writings of Elliott Carter*, p. 305.

32 W. B. Yeats, 'The second coming', from the 1921 collection, 'Michael Robartes and the dancer', in *The Works of W. B. Yeats* (Ware: Wordsworth, 1994).

33 Quoted by Adorno in *Philosophy of Modern Music*, p. 138, n. 2.

34 *Ibid.*, p. 145.

35 Stone and Stone, eds., *The Writings of Elliott Carter*, p. 304.

36 Max Paddison, *Adorno's Aesthetics of Music* (Cambridge: Cambridge University Press, 1993), p. 3.

37 Max Paddison, *Adorno, Modernism and Mass Culture: Essays on Critical Theory and Music* (London: Kahn and Averill, 1996), p. 52.

38 Adorno, *Negative Dialectics*, tr. E. B. Ashton (London: Routledge, 1973), p. 12.

39 See Joseph Kerman, 'How we got into analysis, and how to get out', *Critical Inquiry*, 7 (1980), pp. 311–31; Alan Street, 'Superior myths, dogmatic allegories: the resistance to musical unity', *Music Analysis*, 8/1–2 (1989), pp. 77–123.

40 *Stravinsky and the Russian Traditions*, pp. 16, 18. My emphasis.

41 Paddison, *Adorno, Modernism and Mass Culture*, pp. 116–17.

42 *Stravinsky and the Russian Traditions*, p. 1677.

43 Taruskin gives a fascinating account of Stravinsky's 'French influence' and gives examples from Debussy's *Préludes, Études, Six épigraphes antiques* and *En blanc et noir*, as well as from *Jeux*, to support his argument. See *Stravinsky and the Russian Traditions*, pp. 771–8.

44 *Pyramids at the Louvre*, p. 334.

45 See Richard Langham Smith, 'Debussy and the art of the cinema', *Music & Letters*, 54/1 (1973), pp. 61–70.

46 *Stravinsky and the Russian Traditions*, p. 1678.

47 *Philosophy of Modern Music*, p. 155.

48 Friedrich Nietzsche, 'Of the vision and the riddle', *Thus Spoke Zarathustra*, part 3; in *A Nietzsche Reader*, tr. R. J. Hollingdale (Harmondsworth: Penguin, 1977), p. 251.

49 Arthur C. Wenk, *Claude Debussy and Twentieth-Century Music* (Boston MA: Twayne, 1983).

50 Derrick Puffett, 'Debussy's ostinato machine', *Papers in Musicology*, 4 (Nottingham University, 1996), pp. 32–3.

51 'Debussy', in *Stocktakings from an Apprenticeship*, p. 274.

52 See, for example, Boris Asafyev's *A Book about Stravinsky*, tr. Richard French (Ann Arbor: UMI, 1982); first published in Russian (Leningrad: Triton, 1929) under the pseudonym Igor Glebov.

53 Andriessen and Schönberger, *The Apollonian Clockwork*, p. 100.

54 Adorno, *Philosophy of Modern Music*, p. 208.

55 Brian Trowell, 'The new and the classical in "The Rake's Progress"', in Nicholas John, ed., *Oedipus Rex/The Rake's Progress/Igor Stravinsky*, ENO Guide No. 43 (London: John Calder, 1991), p. 60.

56 Stephen Pruslin's phrases about his libretto for Harrison Birtwistle's opera, *Punch and Judy*, in a note accompanying the recording of the work (London: Decca, 1980), HEAD 24/25.

57 Stephen Walsh, *The Music of Stravinsky* (London: Routledge, 1988), p. 210. For further interesting discussion of these issues in *The Rake*, see in particular Geoffrey Chew, 'Pastoral and neoclassicism: a reinterpretation of Auden's and Stravinsky's *The Rake's Progress*', *Cambridge Opera Journal*, 5 (1993), pp. 239–63; and Chandler Carter, 'Stravinsky's "special sense": the rhetorical use of tonality in *The Rake's Progress*', *Music Theory Spectrum*, 19/1 (1997), pp. 55–80.

58 Taruskin, *Stravinsky and the Russian Traditions*, p. 1675.

59 That of Glenn Watkins in *Pyramids at the Louvre* is by far the most thorough to date.

60 See Taruskin, 'Letter to the editor', and Forte, 'Letter to the editor in reply to Richard Taruskin', *Music Analysis*, 5/2–3 (1986), pp. 313–37.

61 Milan Kundera, 'Improvisation in homage to Stravinsky', in *Testaments Betrayed*, tr. Linda Asher (London: Faber, 1995), pp. 88–9. I am grateful to Craig Ayrey for first bringing this thought-provoking book to my attention.

2 Block forms

1 Drawing (*Nude*) 1910. Charcoal. 48.3 cm × 31.2 cm. Metropolitan Museum of Art, New York, The Alfred Stieglitz Collection, 1949.

2 Georges Boudaille, *The Drawings of Picasso* (London: Hamlyn, 1988), p. 44.

3 John Golding, *Cubism: a History and an Analysis* (London: Faber, 3rd edn 1988), pp. 20–21.

4 Apollinaire, 'Du sujet dans la peinture moderne', in *Les Peintres cubistes* (Paris: 1913), quoted in Golding, *Cubism*, p. 20.

5 'Le Cubisme écartelé', in *Les Peintres cubistes*, quoted in Golding, *Cubism*, p. 21.

6 Virginia Spate, 'Orphism', in Nikos Stangos, ed., *Concepts of Modern Art: from Fauvism to Postmodernism* (London: Thames and Hudson, 3rd edn 1994), p. 90.

7 *Ibid.*, p. 91.

8 Butler, *Early Modernism*, p. 164, quoting from Virginia Spate, *Orphism: the Evolution of Non-Figurative Painting in Paris, 1910–1914* (Oxford, 1979).

9 See *Stravinsky and the Russian Traditions*, pp. 1486–99.

10 Edward T. Cone, 'Stravinsky: the progress of a method', *Perspectives of New Music*, 1/1 (1962), pp. 18–26.

11 All references are to the revised 1947 version of the score.

12 Igor Stravinsky and Robert Craft, *Themes and Conclusions* (London: Faber, 1972), p. 39.

13 Cone, 'Stravinsky: the progress of a method'; Walsh, 'Stravinsky's Symphonies: accident or design?', in Craig Ayrey and Mark Everist, eds., *Analytical Strategies and Musical Interpretation* (Cambridge: Cambridge University Press, 1996), pp. 35–71.

14 See 'The grain of the voice', in Roland Barthes, *Music, Image, Text*, tr. Stephen Heath (London: Fontana, 1997), pp. 179–89.

15 See Peter Brook, *The Empty Space* (London: Pelican, 1972; 1st pub. McGibbon and Kee, 1968).

16 See John Milner, *Mondrian* (London: Phaidon, 1992).

17 *Cubism*, p. 85.

18 See Watkins, '*De Stijl* and the *Mécanique*', in *Pyramids at the Louvre*, pp. 322–38.

19 Milner, *Mondrian*, p. 109.

20 Watkins, *Pyramids at the Louvre*, p. 273.

21 *Ibid.*, p. 264.

22 Ricciotto Canudo, founder in 1913 of the review *Montjoie!* Quoted in Golding, *Cubism*, p. 23.

23 'Ballets russes et français', *La Nouvelle Revue*, 8 (1 July 1913), pp. 116–25, quoted in Watkins, *Pyramids at the Louvre*, p. 232.

24 See Robert Rosenblum, *Cubism* (New York, 2nd edn 1966), p. 40.

25 Igor Stravinsky and Robert Craft, *Expositions and Developments* (London: Faber, 1962), p. 142.

26 Adorno, *Philosophy of Modern Music*, p. 138, n. 2.

27 *Ibid.*, p. 148.

28 *Ibid.*, p. 147. See also Taruskin, 'A myth of the 20th century: *The Rite of Spring*, the tradition of the new, and "the music itself"', *Modernism/Modernity*, 2 (1995), pp. 1–26.

29 Kundera, *Testaments Betrayed*, p. 91.

30 *Ibid.*

31 *Ibid.*, p. 92.

32 *Philosophy of Modern Music*, p. 147.

33 Golding, *Cubism*, p. 36.

34 *Philosophy of Modern Music*, p. 158.

35 *Ibid.*, p. 159.

36 Friedrich Nietzsche, *The Birth of Tragedy*, tr. Walter Kaufmann (New York: Vintage, 1967), p. 60.

37 *Ibid.*, p. 36.

38 *Ibid.*, p. 67.

39 *Philosophy of Modern Music*, p. 167.

40 *Ibid.*

41 Paddison, *Adorno's Aesthetics of Music*, p. 149.

42 Adorno, 'Stravinsky: a dialectical portrait', p. 164.

43 See Christopher Hasty, 'On the problem of succession and continuity in twentieth-century music', *Music Theory Spectrum*, 8 (1986), pp. 58–74; Jonathan Kramer, 'Discontinuity and proportion in the music of Stravinsky', in Jann Pasler, ed., *Confronting Stravinsky: Man, Musician, and Modernist* (Berkeley: University of California Press, 1986), pp. 174–94.

44 'Stravinsky's Symphonies: accident or design?', p. 71.

45 'Vers une musique informelle', in *Quasi una Fantasia*, p. 272.

46 *Adorno's Aesthetics of Music*, p. 182.

47 Paddison, *Adorno, Modernism and Mass Culture*, p. 52.

48 Cone, 'Stravinsky: the progress of a method', pp. 19–20.

49 *Ibid.*, p. 20.

50 *Ibid.*, my emphasis.

51 Pieter C. van den Toorn, *The Music of Igor Stravinsky* (New Haven: Yale University Press, 1983), p. 342.

52 *Ibid.*

53 *Ibid.*, p. 343.

54 *Ibid.*, p. 341.

55 *Stravinsky and the Russian Traditions*, p. 1452.

56 *Ibid.*, p. 1493.

57 Jonathan D. Kramer, *The Time of Music* (New York: Schirmer, 1988).

58 Kramer, 'Discontinuity and proportion in the music of Stravinsky', p. 193.

59 *Ibid.*, p. 194.

60 Whittall, 'Music analysis as human science?', pp. 33–53.

61 'Discontinuity and proportion', p. 177.

62 Adorno, *Philosophy of Modern Music*, p. 192.

63 *Ibid.*, p. 206.

64 I find it equally extraordinary that Watkins fails to mention the *Symphonies* in *Pyramids at the Louvre*.

65 van den Toorn, *The Music of Igor Stravinsky*, p. 26.

66 Jann Pasler, 'Music and spectacle in *Petrushka* and *The Rite of Spring*', in Pasler, ed., *Confronting Stravinsky*, p. 66.

67 *Expositions and Developments*, p. 135.

68 Taruskin, *Stravinsky and the Russian Traditions*, p. 691.

69 *Ibid.*, p. 62.

70 See van den Toorn, *The Music of Igor Stravinsky*, pp. 73–90.

71 Kramer, 'Discontinuity and proportion', pp. 175, 174.

72 *Philosophy of Modern Music*, p. 144: 'Everything characteristic of *Petrushka* is grotesque: the melismata which are misappropriated and restrained to the point of dullness . . . Wherever the subjective element is encountered, it is depraved: it is sickeningly over-sentimentalized or trodden to death. It is evoked as something which is already mechanical, hypostatized, and – to a certain extent – already lifeless.'

73 *Ibid.*, p. 148.

74 *Ibid.*, p. 150 and n. 11.

75 *The Music of Igor Stravinsky*, p. 134.

76 See both *The Music of Igor Stravinsky*, pp. 99–143, and *Stravinsky and The Rite of Spring: The Beginnings of a Musical Language* (Oxford: Oxford University Press, 1987).

77 *The Music of Igor Stravinsky*, p. 127; *Stravinsky and The Rite of Spring*, pp. 174, 178–9.

78 *Stravinsky and the Russian Traditions*, p. 1419.

79 Butler, *Early Modernism*, p. 258.
80 See Jonathan W. Bernard, *The Music of Edgard Varèse* (New Haven: Yale University Press, 1987), esp. Chapter 1.
81 Edgard Varèse, 'The liberation of sound', in Elliott Schwartz and Barney Childs, eds., *Contemporary Composers on Contemporary Music* (New York: Holt, Reinhart and Winston, 1967), p. 197.
82 Taruskin quotes contemporary accounts of the *Symphonies of Wind Instruments* whose language clearly parallels that of Varèse: an arrangement of 'tonal masses . . . sculptured in marble . . . to be regarded objectively by the ear'. Quoted by Deems Taylor in a review of the American premiere under Stokowski in 1924; reproduced by Taruskin in *Stravinsky and the Russian Traditions*, p. 1486.
83 'The liberation of sound', p. 197.
84 van den Toorn, *The Music of Igor Stravinsky*, pp. 470–71, n. 9.
85 'The liberation of sound', p. 203.
86 Zanotti Bianco, 'Edgard Varèse and the geometry of sound', *The Arts* (1924), quoted by Varèse in 'The liberation of sound', p. 205.
87 'I've expressed my admiration for Varèse and people have jumped to the conclusion that I must be a pupil of his, or have been influenced by him. But I wasn't influenced by . . . Varèse. Because you admire something, it doesn't necessarily mean you resemble it. Imitation is an existential mistake.' Xenakis, quoted by Bálint András Varga in *Conversations with Iannis Xenakis* (London: Faber, 1996), p. 212.
88 Igor Stravinsky and Robert Craft, *Memories and Commentaries* (London: Faber, 1960), p. 103.
89 *Ibid.*, pp. 100–101.
90 For a full account of Stravinsky's involvement with the pianola, and a catalogue of his music on piano roll, see Rex Lawson, 'Stravinsky and the pianola', in Pasler, ed., *Confronting Stravinsky*, pp. 284–301.
91 Watkins, *Pyramids at the Louvre*, p. 321.
92 F. T. Marinetti, 'The founding and manifesto of Futurism', in Umbro Apollonio, *Futurist Manifestos* (London: Thames and Hudson, 1973), p. 22.
93 *Philosophy of Modern Music*, p. 145.
94 'Music and new music', in *Quasi una Fantasia*, pp. 265–6.
95 *Ibid.*, p. 267.
96 Walter Benjamin, 'The work of art in the age of mechanical reproduction', in *Illuminations*, tr. Harry Zohn (London: Jonathan Cape, 1970), pp. 219–53.
97 Adorno, 'On the fetish-character in music and the regression of listening', in Andrew Arato and Eike Gebhardt, eds., *The Essential Frankfurt School Reader* (New York: Continuum, 1982), p. 276.
98 Daniel Albright, *Stravinsky: the Music Box and the Nightingale* (New York: Gordon and Breach, 1989), p. 4.
99 Judith Weir, '"Oedipus Rex": a personal view', in John, ed., *Oedipus Rex/The Rake's Progress/Igor Stravinsky*, p. 18.

100 'Discontinuity and proportion', pp. 177–81.

101 *The Music of Igor Stravinsky*, pp. 144–54.

102 *Pyramids at the Louvre*, p. 264.

103 Griffiths, *Modern Music and After*, p. 128.

104 *Memories and Commentaries*, p. 103.

105 Varga, *Conversations*, p. 56.

106 Andriessen and Schönberger, *The Apollonian Clockwork*, p. 100.

107 Olivia Mattis, 'Varèse's "progressive" nationalism: *Amériques* meets *Américanisme*', in Helga de la Motte-Haber, ed., *Edgard Varèse: Die Befreiung des Klangs* (Hofheim: Wolke, 1992), p. 154.

108 Charles Ives, 'Essays before a sonata', in *Three Classics in the Aesthetics of Music*, ed. Howard Boatwright (New York: Dover, 1962), p. 164. Mattis tells us that, on his return to France for five years in 1928, Varèse was responsible for organising concerts and lectures (as director of the Pan-American Association of Composers) which introduced Europe to the music of Ives, Ruggles and Cowell; see Mattis, 'Varèse's "progressive" nationalism', pp. 163–7.

109 See Harold Bloom, *A Map of Misreading* (Oxford: Oxford University Press, 1975). The most sustained application of Bloom's ideas to twentieth-century music is to be found in Joseph Straus, *Remaking the Past: Tradition and Influence in Twentieth-Century Music* (Cambridge MA: Harvard University Press, 1990).

110 Watkins, *Pyramids at the Louvre*, p. 390.

111 Though *Jeux* clearly has a mosaic-like form, the sense of 'progression' within as well as across many of the individual blocks suggests a rather less oppositional structure than that of the *Symphonies of Wind Instruments*. Nonetheless, it was a work which was regarded highly by the post-World War 2 avant-garde. See, for example, Herbert Eimert's analysis ('Debussy's *Jeux*'), in *Die Reihe*, 5 (1959; Eng. edn 1961), pp. 3–20.

112 Cone, 'Stravinsky: the progress of a method', p. 19.

113 Boulez, *Orientations*, p. 407.

114 'Le rythme chez Igor Strawinsky', *Revue musicale*, No. 191 (1939); *Technique de mon langage musical* (1944), translated by John Satterfield as *Technique of my Musical Language* (Paris: Leduc, 1957).

115 Paul Griffiths, *Olivier Messiaen and the Music of Time* (London: Faber, 1985), p. 148.

116 Boulez, *Orientations*, pp. 414–15.

117 For a fuller account of Messiaen's use of colour in *Couleurs de la Cité céleste*, see Griffiths, *Olivier Messiaen*, pp. 202–6.

118 In its persistent use of gongs and tam-tams, among other things, it offers itself as a model for and invites comparison with another static, monumental ritual, Boulez's *Rituel* of 1974, which is also concerned with the 'resurrection of the dead' in that it was written 'in memoriam Bruno Maderna'. See Chapter 5 below for further discussion of this work.

119 Boulez, 'Proposals', in *Stocktakings from an Apprenticeship*, p. 49.

120 Karl H. Wörner, *Stockhausen: Life and Work*, intr., tr. and ed. Bill Hopkins (Berkeley: University of California Press, 1976), p. 252.

121 Robin Maconie, *The Works of Karlheinz Stockhausen* (London: Marion Boyars, 1976), p. 9.

122 See Stravinsky/Craft, *Memories and Commentaries*, pp. 118–21.

123 Griffiths, *Modern Music and After*, p. 119.

124 Arnold Whittall, *Music Since the First World War* (London: Dent, 1977), p. 263.

125 *Ibid.*, p. 261.

126 Wörner, *Stockhausen*, p. 140.

127 See, for example, Tim Nevill, ed., *Towards a Cosmic Music: Texts by Karlheinz Stockhausen* (London: Element, 1989).

128 From a broadcast of *Kontra-Punkte*. See Wörner, *Stockhausen*, p. 30.

129 *Ibid.*, p. 31.

130 Maconie, *The Works of Karlheinz Stockhausen*, p. 58.

131 Stravinsky/Craft, *Memories and Commentaries*, p. 118.

132 In *The Works of Karlheinz Stockhausen*, pp. 146–8.

133 The two numerical series, discovered by the mathematician Leonardo Fibonacci (1170–1240), govern virtually the entire proportions of *Klavierstück IX*. In series 1, each term (an integer) is the sum of the preceding two:

(0) (1) 1 2 3 5 8 13 21 34 55 89 144 etc.

Series 2 is generated by the addition of successive terms in series 1:

0 (+1=) 1 (+2=) 3 (+3=) 6 (+5=) 11 (+8=) 19 (+13=) 32 (+21=) 53 (+34=) 87 (+55=) 142 etc.

134 Originally published as Herbert Henck, 'Karlheinz Stockhausen *Klavierstück IX*/Eine analytische Betrachtung', *Orpheus*, 17 (1976), reproduced in French translation as 'Le *Klavierstück IX* de Karlheinz Stockhausen: considérations analytiques', in *Contrechamps*, 9 (1988), pp. 169–91. All references here are to the French translation.

135 Wörner, *Stockhausen*, p. 36.

136 *Ibid.*, p. 47.

137 *Ibid.*, p. 38.

138 Griffiths, *Modern Music and After*, p. 146.

139 Messiaen's note on *Turangalîla*, tr. Paul Griffiths (Deutsche Grammophon 431 781–2, 1991), p. 14.

140 Wörner, *Stockhausen*, p. 47.

141 *Ibid.*, pp. 52–3.

142 Griffiths, *Modern Music and After*, p. 145.

143 Stockhausen, quoted in Wörner, *Stockhausen*, p. 110.

144 Boulez, 'Sonate, que me veux-tu?', in *Orientations*, p. 143.

145 Jonathan Kramer actually uses the term 'moment' when discussing 'blocks' in Stravinsky. See 'Moment form in twentieth century music', *Musical Quarterly*, 64 (1978), pp. 177–94; also 'Discontinuity and proportion in the music of Stravinsky'.

146 Ian Kemp, *Tippett: the Composer and his Music* (Oxford: Oxford University Press, 1987), p. 323.

147 Tippett (1967) in Meirion Bowen, ed., *Music of the Angels* (London: Eulenburg, 1980), p. 234.

148 Kemp, *Tippett*, p. 327.

149 *Ibid.*, p. 337.

150 Igor Stravinsky and Robert Craft, *Dialogues* (London: Faber and Faber, 1982), p. 27. For a full discussion of this, see Stephen Walsh, *Stravinsky: Oedipus Rex* (Cambridge: Cambridge University Press, 1993).

151 See Chew, 'Pastoral and neoclassicism', and Chandler and Carter, 'Stravinsky's "special sense"'.

152 Ian Kemp, *Tippett*, p. 335.

153 Michael Tippett, *Those Twentieth Century Blues* (London: Hutchinson, 1991), p. 226.

154 Kemp, *Tippett*, p. 370.

155 Kemp calls this a 'monologue' and distinguishes the men's 'monologues' from the women's 'arias'.

156 *Moving into Aquarius*, p. 143.

157 Programme note, quoted in Meirion Bowen, *Michael Tippett* (London: Robson, 1982), p.109.

158 Kemp, *Tippett*, pp. 375–80.

159 Robert F. Jones, 'Tippett's atonal syntax', in Lewis, ed., *Michael Tippett OM*, p. 127.

160 Arnold Whittall, 'Tippett and the modernist mainstream', p. 114.

161 Harrison Birtwistle in public conversation with the author, 'Birtwistle's Secret Theatres' Festival, Royal Festival Hall, London, 2 May 1996.

162 Programme note, quoted in Michael Hall, *Harrison Birtwistle* (London: Robson, 1984), p. 177.

163 Oil drawing (traced) and water-colour on paper. Museum of Modern Art, New York.

164 Hall, *Harrison Birtwistle*, p. 26.

165 See Paul Klee, *Pedagogical Sketchbook*, tr. and intro. Sibyl Moholy-Nagy (London: Faber, 1953), espec. Chapters 2 ('Dimensions') and 3 ('Earth, water and air').

166 See 'Klee and music', in Norbert Lynton, *Klee* (London: Hamlyn, 2nd edn 1975), and Andrew Kagan, *Paul Klee: Art and Music* (Ithaca: Cornell University Press, 1983).

167 Programme note, in Hall, *Harrison Birtwistle*, p. 177.

168 Kramer, 'Discontinuity and proportion in the music of Stravinsky'.

169 See Jonathan Cross, 'Birtwistle's secret theatres', in Ayrey and Everist, *Analytical Strategies*, pp. 207–25, especially Fig. 7.1, p. 211.

170 Sibyl Moholy-Nagy in the 'Introduction' to Klee, *Pedagogical Sketchbook*, p. 10.

171 Cone, 'Stravinsky: the progress of a method', p. 20.

172 Kramer, 'Discontinuity and proportion in the music of Stravinsky', p. 177.

173 'He [Birtwistle] subjected it [*Agon*] to the most detailed analysis he has ever undertaken and echoes of it still reverberate in his music.' Hall, *Harrison Birtwistle*, p. 17.

174 Taruskin, *Stravinsky and the Russian Traditions*, p. 137.

175 But also note Taruskin's argument for the influence of Stravinsky on Debussy; see Chapter 1, n. 43.

176 *Ibid.*, p. 1675.

177 Griffiths, *Modern Music and After*, p. 295.

178 It is also interesting to note that Ferneyhough has declared that '*Octandre* was always extremely important' to him. See Brian Ferneyhough in conversation with James Boros, 'Composing a viable (if transitory) self', *Perspectives of New Music*, 32/1 (1994); repr. in *Brian Ferneyhough: Collected Writings*, ed. James Boros and Richard Toop (Amsterdam: Harwood, 1995), pp. 431–46.

179 See preface to published score (Peters Edition, 1995), and Boros, 'Composing a viable (if transitory) self'.

3 Structural rhythms

1 Taruskin, *Stravinsky and the Russian Traditions*, p. 958.

2 Boulez, 'Stravinsky remains', in *Stocktakings from an Apprenticeship*, p. 110.

3 All references here are taken from 'The phenomenon of music', in Stravinsky's *Poetics of Music*, pp. 21–43.

4 '. . . the voice that speaks to us from the Stravinsky/Craft books . . . was in an indirect but important sense as much the creation of Pierre Souvtchinsky as the voice that had spoken two decades earlier out of the *Poétique musicale*.' Taruskin, *Stravinsky and the Russian Traditions*, p. 4.

5 See Souvtchinsky's essay, 'La Notion du temps et la musique', *Revue musicale* (1939).

6 *Philosophy of Modern Music*, p. 193.

7 *Stravinsky and the Russian Traditions*, p. 958.

8 Richard H. Hoppin, *Medieval Music* (New York: Norton, 1978), pp. 356–7.

9 Umberto Eco, *Travels in Hyperreality* (London: Picador, 1987), discussed by Barry Smart in *Postmodernity* (London: Routledge, 1993), p. 29. It also calls to mind, once again, Jameson's suggestive proposition that Stravinsky 'is the true precursor of postmodern cultural production' (see p. 5 above).

10 *Stravinsky and the Russian Traditions*, p. 713.

11 *The Music of Igor Stravinsky*, p. 214.

12 There are some useful, generalised accounts of Stravinsky's rhythmic practices in monographs. The only authors who go into any substantive detail are, of course, Taruskin, *Stravinsky and the Russian Traditions*, and Pieter C. van den Toorn, *The Music of Igor Stravinsky* (see especially Chapter 8). Among the texts more specifically dedicated to rhythm, the most useful are Boulez, 'Stravinsky remains'; Allen Forte, 'Foreground rhythm in early twentieth-century music', *Music Analysis*, 2/3 (1983), pp. 239–68; Wolfgang Dömling and Theo Hirsbrunner, 'Ordnung in der Zeit: "Rhythmik"', in *Über Strawinsky: Studien zu Ästhetik und Kompositionstechnik* (Laaber: Laaber-Verlag, 1985), pp. 147–71; Kramer, 'Discontinuity and proportion in the music of Stravinsky', pp. 174–94, and *The Time of Music*; Messiaen, 'Le Rythme chez Igor Strawinsky', and *Traité de rythme, de couleur, et d'ornithologie*, vol. 2 (Paris: Leduc/UMP, 1995); and van den Toorn, 'Stravinsky re-barred' and 'Rhythmic structure', in *Stravinsky and 'The Rite of Spring'*.

13 *Stravinsky and the Russian Traditions*, pp. 956–7.

14 *Ibid.*, p. 959.

15 *Ibid.*, p. 961.

16 See *Stravinsky and 'The Rite of Spring'*, pp. 94–6.

17 See 'The Primitive', in Watkins, *Pyramids at the Louvre*, pp. 63–212.

18 Robert Donaldson Darrell in *Phonograph Monthly Review*, 5/4 (January 1931), p. 137; quoted by Watkins in *Pyramids at the Louvre*, p. 194.

19 'Stravinsky remains', p. 64.

20 See Puffett, 'Debussy's ostinato machine', pp. 54–5.

21 John Cage, *A Year from Monday: New Lectures and Writings* (London: Calder and Boyers, 1968), p. 42.

22 Stone and Stone, *The Writings of Elliott Carter*, p. 313.

23 *Ibid.*, p. 48.

24 *The Music of Igor Stravinsky*, pp. 147–9.

25 'Stravinsky remains', p. 103.

26 *Ibid.*, p. 104.

27 *Ibid.*, p. 105.

28 *Ibid.*

29 Harrison Birtwistle, *Pulse Field (Frames, Pulses and Interruptions)* for six dancers and nine instruments (1977).

30 'Stravinsky remains', p. 62.

31 *Ibid.*, p. 64.

32 *Philosophy of Modern Music*, p. 153.

33 *Ibid.*, p. 151.

34 *Ibid.*, pp. 154–5.

35 Allen Forte, *The Harmonic Organization of 'The Rite of Spring'* (New Haven: Yale University Press, 1978).

36 Taruskin, *Stravinsky and the Russian Traditions*, pp. 955, 956.

37 *Ibid.*, p. 954.

38 *Ibid.*, p. 963.

39 Varèse, 'The liberation of sound', p. 197.

40 Whittall, *Music Since the First World War*, p. 201.

41 Kyle Gann, *The Music of Conlon Nancarrow* (Cambridge: Cambridge University Press, 1995).

42 Stone and Stone, *The Writings of Elliott Carter*, pp. 245, 247.

43 *Ibid.*, p. 244.

44 See Carter's own account in *ibid.*, pp. 292–6.

45 See Stravinsky/Craft, *Dialogues*, pp. 99–101.

46 Karlheinz Stockhausen, '. . . how time passes . . .', *Die Reihe*, 3 (1957; English edn 1959), pp. 10–40.

47 Andriessen and Schönberger, *The Apollonian Clockwork*, p. 100.

48 Richard Steinitz, 'Weeping and wailing', *Musical Times*, 1842 (Aug. 1996), p. 20.

49 Messiaen, preface to the score of *Chronochromie* (Paris: Leduc, 1963). My translation. Interversion is the way in which elements from the middle of a given sequence are taken in turn to generate a new sequence, which itself then becomes available for interversion, e.g. the sequence 1 2 3 4 5 6 interverted becomes 4 3 5 2 6 1, which in turn becomes 2 5 6 3 1 4 etc.

50 Griffiths, *Olivier Messiaen and the Music of Time*, p. 193.

51 See Messiaen, 'Le rythme chez Igor Stravinsky', pp. 91–2; also *Traité de rythme, de couleur, et d'ornithologie*, vol. 2.

52 Griffiths, *Olivier Messiaen and the Music of Time*, p. 139.

53 Messiaen himself subjects this movement to an analysis in vol. 2 of the *Traité*.

54 From the composer's note on the work, trans. Paul Griffiths, reproduced to accompany Deutsche Grammophon 431 781–2 (1991), p. 10.

55 Stravinsky, from 'Ce que j'ai voulu exprimer dans "Le sacre du printemps"', *Montjoie!*, 8 (1913), quoted and translated in Taruskin, *Stravinsky and the Russian Traditions*, pp. 877–8. Taruskin gives a full account of the origins and varying accounts of the scenario of *The Rite*.

56 Harold Bloom, *The Anxiety of Influence: a Theory of Poetry* (London: Oxford University Press, 1973), pp. 14, 66–7, quoted in Kevin Korsyn, 'Towards a new poetics of musical influence', *Music Analysis*, 10/1–2 (1991), p. 26.

57 In general terms, Messiaen's 'personnages rythmiques' understood as a consequence of Stravinsky's instrumental role-play is a fascinating concept; in practice, however, Messiaen realises the concept more strictly as three interacting rhythmic characters.

58 Composer's note, p. 10.

59 Birtwistle, quoted in Norman Lebrecht, 'Knights at the opera', *The Independent Magazine* (18 May 1991), p. 58.

60 Nicholas Kenyon, *Observer* (16 March 1986).

61 Andrew Clements, *Guardian* (27 May 1994). It is perhaps interesting to note that another 'layered' work, Ives's *Central Park in the Dark*, was programmed alongside *Earth Dances* at the London Proms performance on 27 August 1994.

62 Michael Kennedy, *Sunday Telegraph* (21 April 1996).

63 Meirion Bowen, *Guardian* (23 March 1987).

64 Edward Greenfield, *Guardian* (16 January 1988).

65 Birtwistle is quoted by Andrew Clements in his note on the work, in 'Endless Parade', programme book to accompany the BBC Birtwistle Festival (London: BBC, 1988), pp. 52–3. The six strata here juxtaposed vertically (simultaneously) perhaps parallel the 'six musical mechanisms' juxtaposed horizontally (successively) in the earlier *Carmen Arcadiae Mechanicae Perpetuum*.

66 See Paul Griffiths, *New Sounds, New Personalities* (London: Faber, 1985), p. 189.

67 Peter Heyworth, *Observer* (17 January 1988).

68 *Ibid.*

69 Arnold Whittall, 'Birtwistle, Maxwell Davies and modernist analysis', p. 153.

70 'Stravinsky remains', pp. 81, 85.

71 'Birtwistle, Maxwell Davies and modernist analysis', p. 150.

72 '... a paradigm of "sonic accumulation." The whole piece is a crescendo brought about by the seriatim addition to the texture of highly individualized separate ostinati, ... each rigidly and immutably maintained from its point of entry to the end.' Taruskin, *Stravinsky and the Russian Traditions*, p. 957.

73 This perhaps, despite the implications of the title, signifies the greater 'symphonic' ambitions of Birtwistle's work (see Whittall's discussion in 'Birtwistle, Maxwell Davies and modernist analysis') in comparison with the 'balletic', 'programmatic' status of *The Rite*.

74 David Epstein, *Shaping Time: Music, the Brain, and Performance* (New York: Schirmer, 1995). Robert Adlington has offered a wide-ranging critique of Epstein's proposals in his review in *Music Analysis*, 16/1 (1997), pp. 155–71.

75 Kramer, 'Discontinuity and proportion in the music of Stravinsky', p. 176.

76 *Ibid.*, p. 181.

77 Stone and Stone, *The Writings of Elliott Carter*, pp. 356, 203–4.

78 Griffiths, *Modern Music and After*, p. 57.

79 Stone and Stone, *The Writings of Elliott Carter*, p. 351.

80 *Tippett: the Composer and his Music*, p. 97.

81 *Ibid.*, pp. 333–4.

82 *Ibid.*, p. 98.

83 I am grateful to Gareth Williams for introducing me to a number of Mathias's orchestral and chamber works.

84 Stone and Stone, *The Writings of Elliott Carter*, p. 204.

85 See Griffiths, *Modern Music and After*, p. 295.

4 Ritual theatres

1 Brook, *The Empty Space*, p. 11.

2 *Ibid.*, p. 44.

3 Stephen Walsh, 'Venice and *The Rake*: the old and the new', essay in Welsh National Opera programme book, ed. Simon Rees (1996), p. 25.

4 Brook, *The Empty Space*, p. 150.

5 Bertolt Brecht, *The Threepenny Opera*, tr. and ed. Ralph Manheim and John Willett (London: Methuen, 1979), Act 1, scene 1.

6 Stravinsky's familiarity with such theatre is well documented by Watkins in *Pyramids at the Louvre*, while the parallels between Stravinsky's theatrical thinking and that of Meyerhold are explored in Walsh, *Stravinsky: Oedipus Rex*; see especially 'Of masks, masses and magic', pp. 11–22.

7 Paddison, *Adorno's Aesthetics of Music*, p. 268. Adorno's views are expressed in his essay, 'On the social situation of music'.

8 *Philosophy of Modern Music*, p. 171, n. 25.

9 *Ibid.*, p. 175.

10 Paddison, *Adorno's Aesthetics of Music*, p. 268.

11 Paddison, *Adorno, Modernism and Mass Culture*, pp. 116–17.

12 Stravinsky/Craft, *Expositions and Developments*, p. 89.

13 Brook, *The Empty Space*, p. 80.

14 Stravinsky/Craft, *Expositions and Developments*, p. 91.

15 *Ibid.*

16 *Ibid.*, p. 92.

17 *Ibid.*, p. 91.

18 Nietzsche, *The Birth of Tragedy*, p. 58.

19 *Ibid.*

20 *Ibid.*, pp. 62, 63.

21 Stravinsky/Craft, *Expositions and Developments*, p. 92.

22 It is worth reminding ourselves here of Stravinsky's own operatic preferences: pro-Verdi, anti-Wagner.

23 Stravinsky/Craft, *Dialogues*, p. 105.

24 Brook, *The Empty Space*, pp. 47–8.

25 Antonin Artaud, *The Theatre and its Double*, tr. Victor Corti (London: Calder, 1993), p. 68.

26 *Ibid.*, p. 42.

27 Brook, *The Empty Space*, p. 63.

28 Adorno, *Philosophy of Modern Music*, p. 169.

29 *Ibid.*, pp. 213, 65.

30 For a full and fascinating discussion of this issue (and the work in general), see Walsh, *Stravinsky: Oedipus Rex*.

31 Quoted in Griffiths, *Modern Music and After*, p. 171.

32 *Ibid.*

33 Pierre Boulez, *Conversations with Célestin Deliège* (London: Eulenburg, 1976), p. 21.

34 Hans Werner Henze, in a note accompanying the recording of the work (DG 2530 212, 1972).

35 Composer's note on the work, in Paul Griffiths, *Peter Maxwell Davies* (London: Robson, 1982), p. 153.

36 *Ibid.*, p. 154.

37 *Ibid.*, p. 153.

38 *Ibid.*, p. 154.

39 Van den Toorn, *The Music of Igor Stravinsky*, p. 201.

40 Messiaen, preface to the score.

41 Dedication to *Rituel*, in Dominique Jameux, *Pierre Boulez*, tr. Susan Bradshaw (London: Faber, 1991), p. 351.

42 Griffiths, *Modern Music and After*, p. 157.

43 See John Kirkpatrick, *A Temporary Mimeographed Catalogue of the Music Manuscripts and Related Materials of Charles Edward Ives, 1874–1954* (New Haven: Library of the Yale University School of Music, 1960; repr. 1973).

44 Stone and Stone, *The Writings of Elliott Carter*, p. 278.

45 Composer's note on the work, quoted in Hall, *Harrison Birtwistle*, p. 173.

46 *Ibid.*, p. 174.

47 Van den Toorn describes them as 'buffers or "spacers" in the delineation of its large four-part framework', but goes on to suggest that 'subsequent appearances of the Prelude (as Interlude) are not altogether convincing (or may appear, with the addition of each miniature [dance], increasingly irrelevant)' (*The Music of Igor Stravinsky*, p. 393). This is, surely, to miss the point. To remove the Chorus from a Greek drama would not unduly affect the plot or the unfolding of the basics of the narrative, but the Chorus's role as both participant and commentator is vital to the formality of a drama concerned primarily with the way in which the tale is told, not the tale itself. (The controversial American opera producer, Peter Sellars, made just this mistake in his production of *The Magic Flute* at Glyndebourne in the early 1990s when he chose to omit all of the spoken dialogue. The dramatic impact of the work was detrimentally affected, and the dialogue was quickly restored for subsequent revivals.) The Prologue/Interludes in *Agon* act like the Chorus – they are both structural markers (objective commentators) and active participants in the musical argument through the process of interlock (albeit to a very limited degree).

48 Boulez, *Conversations with Célestin Deliège*, p. 87.

49 *Ibid.*, p. 88.

50 See Cross, 'Birtwistle's secret theatres'.

51 Whittall, 'The geometry of comedy', *Musical Times*, 1799 (Jan. 1993), p. 17.

5 Minimal developments

1 Andriessen and Schönberger, *The Apollonian Clockwork*, p. 61.

2 *Ibid.*, pp. 100–101.

3 In a radio interview, 'Stravinsky in three movements', a BBC Radio 4 'Kaleidoscope' feature, first broadcast 9 November 1996.

4 Adams, quoted in liner note to recording of *Fearful Symmetries*, 979 218–4 (Elektra Nonesuch, 1989).

5 Quoted by K. Robert Schwarz in his introductory note to the Boosey and Hawkes catalogue of Adams's music (1995), p. 3.

6 Jameson, *Postmodernism*, pp. 15–16.

7 *Ibid.*, pp. 33, 16.

8 *Ibid.*, p. 309.

9 I omit discussion here of another kind of European 'minimalism', the so-called 'holy' minimalism of Arvo Pärt, Henryk Górecki, John Tavener and others, which owes little directly to American minimalism. It is minimal only in the (medieval) simplicity of its materials and means, which are Stravinskian in character: non-functional diatonic harmonies, stasis, metric flexibility, varied repetitions, verse-refrain structures and so on. However, in common with the experimental roots of American minimalism, such simplicity sprang from a dissatisfaction with the 'sterility' of the high-modernist avant-garde, and shares, albeit in very different ways, something of the spiritual intentions of La Monte Young's experiments in its desire to transcend the mundane through repetition.

10 'Life downtown', Andriessen in conversation with Gavin Thomas, *Musical Times*, 1813 (March 1994), p. 141.

11 Liner note to the recording of the work, 7559–79251–2 (Elektra Nonesuch, 1991).

12 Similarly, a younger generation of British composers – most notably Mark-Anthony Turnage and John Woolrich – have rediscovered Stravinsky via Birtwistle.

13 In Greenaway's film this section bears the caption: 'Aural and visual variations on a conundrum of the apotheosis of the spirit of Mozart'.

14 Quoted in note on *De Staat* to accompany CD recording, Elektra Nonesuch (1991).

15 Andriessen and Schönberger, *The Apollonian Clockwork*, p. 100.

16 *Ibid.*, p. 101.

6 A fresh look at Stravinsky analysis

1 Fred Lerdahl, 'Atonal prolongational structures', *Contemporary Music Review*, 4 (1989), p. 65.

2 Forte, *The Structure of Atonal Music*, p. ix. My emphasis.

3 James Baker, 'Schenkerian analysis and post-tonal music', in David Beach, ed., *Aspects of Schenkerian Theory* (New Haven: Yale University Press, 1983), pp. 153–86.

4 Lerdahl, 'Atonal prolongational structures', pp. 68, 82.

5 Paul Griffiths, *Igor Stravinsky: The Rake's Progress*, Cambridge Opera Handbook (Cambridge: Cambridge University Press, 1982).

6 Adele Katz, *Challenge to Musical Tradition: a New Concept of Tonality* (London: Putnam, 1945); Felix Salzer, *Structural Hearing: Tonal Coherence in Music* (New York: Dover, 1962).

7 Martha M. Hyde, 'Neoclassic and anachronistic impulses in twentieth-century music', *Music Theory Spectrum*, 18/2 (1996), pp. 200–35; Marianne Kielian-Gilbert, 'Stravinsky's contrasts: contradiction and discontinuity in his neoclassic music', *Journal of Musicology*, 9 (1991), pp. 448–80; Lynne Rogers, 'Stravinsky's break with contrapuntal tradition: a sketch study', *Journal of Musicology*, 13 (1995), pp. 476–507.

8 *The Music of Igor Stravinsky.*

9 Joseph Straus, 'A principle of voice leading in the music of Stravinsky', *Music Theory Spectrum*, 4 (1982), pp. 106–24.

10 Joseph Straus, 'The problem of prolongation in post-tonal music', *Journal of Music Theory*, 31/1 (1987), p. 17.

11 Derrick Puffett, 'The fugue from Tippett's Second String Quartet', *Music Analysis*, 5/2–3 (1986), p. 258.

12 *Ibid.*, p. 260.

13 Pieter C. van den Toorn, *Music, Politics, and the Academy* (Berkeley: University of California Press, 1995), p. ix.

14 *Ibid.*, pp. 179, 57.

15 Puffett, 'Editorial: in defence of formalism', *Music Analysis*, 13/1 (1994), pp. 3–5.

16 T. J. Samson, review of James Baker, *The Music of Alexander Scriabin*, in *Journal of Music Theory*, 32/2 (1988), p. 354.

17 'Introduction: different trains', in Ayrey and Everist, *Analytical Strategies*, p. 11.

18 See, for instance, Leo Treitler, *Music and the Historical Imagination* (Cambridge MA: Harvard University Press, 1989), p. 17. Dai Griffiths, an acute reviewer with an all-too-rare wit, dubs this Power Analysis™; see *Music Analysis*, 16/1 (1997), p. 147.

19 Baker *et al.*, *Music Theory in Concept and Practice*. It is notable that the two British equivalents to this volume of 1994 and 1996 are already much more open to a reevaluation of the discipline(s) of theory and analysis in the light of interdisciplinary perspectives. They also contain a broader range of anglophone voices than the American collection. See Pople, *Theory, Analysis and Meaning*, and Ayrey and Everist, *Analytical Strategies*. They thus stand closer to such American-originated collections concerned with 'new' musicological issues as, for example, Richard Leppert and Susan McClary, eds., *Music and Society* (Cambridge: Cambridge University Press, 1987); Katherine Bergeron and Philip V. Bohlman, eds., *Disciplining Music: Musicology and its Canons* (Chicago: University of Chicago Press, 1992); Ruth Solie, ed., *Musicology and Difference: Gender and Sexuality in Music Scholarship* (Berkeley: University of California Press, 1993).

20 'Neoclassicism and its definitions', p. 156.

21 Joseph Straus, 'Voice leading in atonal music', in *Music Theory in Concept and Practice*, p. 273.

22 Roger Sessions, 'Thoughts on Stravinsky', *The Score*, 20 (1957), p. 32. My emphasis.

23 Stone and Stone, *The Writings of Elliott Carter*, p. 304.

24 Edward T. Cone, 'The uses of convention: Stravinsky and his models', *Musical Quarterly*, 48/3 (1962), pp. 287–99; Paul Johnson, 'Cross-collectional techniques of structure in Stravinsky's centric music', in Ethan Haimo and Paul Johnson, eds., *Stravinsky Retrospectives* (Lincoln NB: University of Nebraska Press, 1987), pp. 55–75; Joseph Straus, 'Sonata form in Stravinsky', in *Stravinsky Retrospectives*, pp. 141–61, and *Remaking the Past*, pp. 96–103; Walsh, *The Music of Stravinsky*.

25 'Suvchinsky reported that the score of Tchaikovsky's First Symphony was on my piano, and this information, together with the discovery of a similarity of first themes in my Symphony and Tchaikovsky's, was responsible for the rumour that was soon giving model status to the latter. (If Suvchinsky had reported which Haydn and Beethoven scores were on my desk, no one would have paid any attention, of course, yet both of these composers stand behind at least the first two movements of my Symphony far more profoundly than any music by my much-too-lonely compatriot.)' Stravinsky/Craft, *Themes and Conclusions*, p. 49.

26 *Ibid.*

27 Walsh, *The Music of Stravinsky*, p. 176.

28 *Ibid.*, p. 175.

29 Eric Walter White, *Stravinsky: the Composer and his Works* (London: Faber, 2nd edn 1979), pp. 405–8.

30 Roman Vlad, *Stravinsky*, tr. Frederick Fuller (Oxford: Oxford University Press, 3rd edn 1985), p. 142. 'Here he not only adopts the thematic exposition and the technique of development inherent in this [symphonic] form, but he adopts them in a most consequential and rigorous manner, i.e. he accepts the cyclic form based on a single motif or thematic idea which permeates the whole work' (p. 137).

31 Francis Routh, *Stravinsky*, Master Musicians Series (London: Dent, 1975), p. 97.

32 Stravinsky/Craft, *Themes and Conclusions*, p. 50.

33 Ernest Ansermet, taken from his notes to *Les Fondements de la musique dans la conscience humaine*, tr. Eric Walter White, in *Stravinsky: the Composer and his Works*, p. 409.

34 Walsh, *The Music of Stravinsky*, p. 178, citing Robert Simpson, ed., 'Introduction' to *The Symphony*, vol. 2 (Harmondsworth: Penguin, 1967).

35 Straus, *Remaking the Past*, p. 97.

36 *Ibid.*

37 *Ibid.*, p. 103.

38 Johnson, 'Cross-collectional techniques of structure', p. 56.

39 Straus, 'A principle of voice leading'.

40 Straus, *Remaking the Past*, pp. 98–101.

41 *Ibid.*, pp. 98, 102.

42 *Ibid.*, p. 98.

43 This is also true of Kielian-Gilbert's 'interactive equilibriums' (see 'Stravinsky's contrasts: contradiction and discontinuity in his neoclassic music'). Chandler Carter's 'pluralism', however, is more accommodating (see 'Stravinsky's "special sense"', pp. 55–80).

44 *Stravinsky and the Russian Traditions*, p. 1462.

45 Walsh, *The Music of Stravinsky*, p. 177.

46 Another reason why Stravinsky's introduction might seem less bold and humorous than Beethoven's *adagio* has to do with its length. Brevity is the essence of wit: Beethoven's *adagio* is only six bars long; Stravinsky's 'upbeat' lasts thirty-nine bars. Walsh's comments on the first movement are equally pertinent here: 'One other evident quality of this movement which distinguishes it from Beethoven is its lack of conciseness . . . Where Beethoven's music is driven forward by its inherent tensions, Stravinsky's forever turns back on passages which, in themselves, embody harsher tensions than those of classical music but lack a strongly implied resolution.' *Ibid.*, pp. 177–8.

47 Stravinsky, *Poetics of Music*, pp. 35, 37, 38.

48 'The uses of convention'.

49 *Ibid.*, p. 292.

50 'The ambiguity implicit in this three-note motive [B–C–G] evolves into a harmonic polarity powerful enough to generate a sonata form.' Straus, 'Sonata form in Stravinsky', p. 149.

51 Robert Simpson, 'Introduction', in *The Symphony*, p. 11.

52 *Ibid.*

53 Stravinsky/Craft, *Expositions and Developments*, p. 77.

54 *Ibid.*, p. 77 n. 1.

55 Stravinsky/Craft, *Dialogues*, p. 52; see also pp. 50–2.

56 *Philosophy of Modern Music*, p. 211.

57 *Dialogues*, p. 52.

58 *Stravinsky and the Russian Traditions*, pp. 11–12.

59 *Philosophy of Modern Music*, p. 211.

60 Paddison, *Adorno's Aesthetics of Music*, p. 56.

61 *Philosophy of Modern Music*, p. 211.

62 *Ibid.*, p. 212.

63 'Neoclassicism and its definitions', pp. 131–56.

64 *Philosophy of Modern Music*, p. 212.

65 Adorno, 'Stravinsky: a dialectical portrait', p. 166.

66 Adorno, *Alban Berg: Master of the Smallest Link*, tr. with intro. and annotation by Juliane Brand and Christopher Hailey (Cambridge: Cambridge University Press, 1991), p. 45.

67 van den Toorn, *The Music of Igor Stravinsky*, p. 363.

68 'Neoclassicism and its definitions', p. 152.

69 The Ninth Symphony is quoted directly in Tippett's Symphony. 'Someone has even compared the first movement of the *Eroica*, bars 272–5, with the

three chords following Fig. 173 in *Le Sacre*, with Fig. 22 in *Renard*, and with the same musical figure in the first movement of my *Symphony in Three Movements*, bars 69–71.' Stravinsky/Craft, *Memories and Commentaries*, p. 23.

70 *Philosophy of Modern Music*, p. 211.

71 Whittall, *Music Since the First World War*, p. 64.

72 For a detailed account of the movement's octatonic construction, see van den Toorn, *The Music of Igor Stravinsky*, pp. 354–64.

73 See *Philosophy of Modern Music*, p. 193.

74 *Quasi una Fantasia*, p. 153.

75 Stravinsky/Craft, *Dialogues*, p. 51.

76 *The Music of Igor Stravinsky*, pp. 363–4.

77 *Ibid.*, p. 362.

78 *Ibid.*, p. 285.

79 *Ibid.*, p. 287.

80 *Ibid.*, p. 365.

81 Watkins, *Pyramids at the Louvre*, pp. 63, 64.

82 *Ibid.*, pp. 208–9.

83 Mark Swed, Introduction to Boosey and Hawkes catalogue for Michael Torke (1994).

84 Watkins, *Pyramids at the Louvre*, p. 102.

7 Conclusions: Stravinsky, Adorno and the problem of non-development

1 First published in English translation in 1973.

2 The Schoenberg study was written in 1940–41, the Stravinsky essay in 1948.

3 *Philosophy of Modern Music*, p. xvii.

4 First published in 1963 by Suhrkamp Verlag. The English translation was published under the title 'Stravinsky: a dialectical portrait', in *Quasi una Fantasia*.

5 'Schoenberg is dead', p. 214.

6 'Stravinsky: a dialectical portrait', p. 172.

7 *Philosophy of Modern Music*, p. xvi.

8 Jean-Jacques Nattiez, ed., *The Boulez–Cage Correspondence*, tr. Robert Samuels (Cambridge: Cambridge University Press, 1993), p. 112.

9 *Philosophy of Modern Music*, p. 143.

10 'Stravinsky: a dialectical portrait', p. 270.

11 'Vers une musique informelle', p. 315. In *Philosophy of Modern Music*, Adorno had argued that 'Fate and the domination of nature are not to be separated ... Fate is domination reduced to its pure abstraction, and the measure of its destruction is equal to that of its domination; fate is disaster' (p. 67).

12 Rose Rosengard Subotnik, 'Toward a deconstruction of structural listening: a critique of Schoenberg, Adorno, and Stravinsky', in *Deconstructive Variations:*

Music and Reason in Western Society (Minneapolis: University of Minnesota Press, 1996), p. 165.

13 Andriessen and Schönberger, *The Apollonian Clockwork*, p. 119.

14 See, for example, Richard Taruskin, 'The dark side of modern music', *New Republic* (5 September 1988), pp. 28–34, and 'Stravinsky and us', a BBC Proms Lecture, given on 10 August 1996 and first broadcast on BBC Radio 3 the following day.

15 See, for instance, William Rothstein, 'The Americanization of Heinrich Schenker', in Hedi Siegel, ed., *Schenker Studies* (Cambridge: Cambridge University Press, 1990), pp. 193–203; Robert Snarrenberg, 'Competing myths: the American abandonment of Schenker's organicism', in Pople, *Theory, Analysis and Meaning in Music*, pp. 29–56; Snarrenberg, *Schenker's Interpretive Practice* (Cambridge: Cambridge University Press, 1997). Adorno himself wrote astutely that 'notwithstanding insights into structure which have affinities with Schoenberg's practice, he [Schenker] strove to establish for a reactionary aesthetics a solid foundation in musical logic which tallied all too well with his loathsome political views' ('Vers une musique informelle', p. 281).

16 Paddison, *Adorno's Aesthetics of Music*, pp. 265–6.

17 'Vers une musique informelle', p. 284, n. 7.

18 *Philosophy of Modern Music*, p. 61.

19 *Ibid.*, p. 57.

20 See Ethan Haimo, 'Developing variation and Schoenberg's twelve-note music', *Music Analysis*, 16/3 (1997), pp. 349–65.

21 Schoenberg, 'Composition with twelve tones (1)', p. 244.

22 'Stravinsky: a dialectical portrait', p. 171.

23 *Ibid.*

24 *Ibid.*, p. 150.

25 *Ibid.*, pp. 150, 152.

26 *Ibid.*, p. 153.

27 *Philosophy of Modern Music*, p. 64.

28 'Stravinsky: a dialectical portrait', p. 152.

29 Adorno, *In Search of Wagner*, tr. Rodney Livingstone (London: NLB/Verso, 1981), p. 62.

30 Paddison, *Adorno's Aesthetics of Music*, pp. 256, 257.

31 'Stravinsky: a dialectical portrait', p. 150.

32 *Ibid.*, p. 151; my emphasis. Adorno actually writes '[e]ver since music existed'. What music is he thinking of? With the exception of European instrumental compositions since about 1600, very little of the world's music would seem to accord with his definition. The shamanic/ritualistic or functional aspects of the music of most cultures – usually built from simple repetitive patterns – would seem to play conformist rather than oppositional roles within those cultures. Such music does not appear to participate in constructions of the kind of 'otherness' Adorno has in mind.

33 *Ibid.*, pp. 152, 153, 152.

34 See Heinrich Schenker, 'Fortlesung der Urlinie-Betrachtungen', *Das Meisterwerk in der Musik* (Munich: Drei Masken Verlag, 1926), vol. 2, pp. 37–9. This essay is translated by John Rothgeb in the English language *The Masterwork in Music*, ed. William Drabkin (Cambridge: Cambridge University Press, 1996), vol. 2, pp. 1–22 (see pp. 17–18).

35 Paddison, *Adorno, Modernism and Mass Culture*, pp. 117, 116.

36 Carl Dahlhaus, 'La polemica di Adorno contro Stravinskij e il problema della "critica superiore"', in Francesco Degrada, ed., *Stravinskij oggi* (Milan: Edizioni Unicopli, 1982), pp. 47, 48. My translation from the Italian.

37 *Philosophy of Modern Music*, p. 156.

38 'Vers une musique informelle', p. 297. This, *pace* Ivan Hewett: 'Truly radical ideas often hide their possibilities under a plain surface – as minimalism does.' See 'Different strains', *Musical Times*, 1848 (February 1997), pp. 20–23.

39 Jameson, *Postmodernism*, p. x.

40 As Glenn Watkins has so extensively demonstrated in *Pyramids at the Louvre*, the roots of a postmodern aesthetic in much contemporary music can reasonably be shown to lie with Stravinsky.

41 Jameson, *Postmodernism*, p. x.

42 Paddison, *Adorno's Aesthetics of Music*, pp. 269–70.

43 Griffiths, *Modern Music and After*, p. 275.

44 Jameson, *Postmodernism*, p. ix.

45 See Douglas Jarman, *The Music of Alban Berg* (London: Faber, 1979), pp. 144–5, esp. Ex. 180.

46 For an interesting recent discussion, see Raymond Geuss, 'Berg and Adorno', in Anthony Pople, ed., *The Cambridge Companion to Berg* (Cambridge: Cambridge University Press, 1997), pp. 38–50.

47 Milton Babbitt, 'Remarks on the recent Stravinsky', in Benjamin Boretz and Edward T. Cone, eds., *Perspectives on Schoenberg and Stravinsky* (New York: Norton, 1972), pp. 165–85.

48 White, *Stravinsky*, p. 491. My emphasis.

49 Watkins, *Pyramids at the Louvre*, pp. 374, 362.

50 Thomas Clifton, *Music as Heard: a Study in Applied Phenomenology* (New Haven: Yale University Press, 1983), pp. 250–56.

51 Stravinsky/Craft, *Expositions and Developments*, p. 113.

52 *Stravinsky and the Russian Traditions*, p. 1463.

53 *Ibid.*, pp. 1501–2.

54 Stravinsky/Craft, *Expositions and Developments*, p. 109.

55 'Music and new music', p. 260.

56 *Music Since the First World War*, p. 54.

57 *Ibid.*, p. 156.

58 *Philosophy of Modern Music*, p. 203.

59 *Ibid.*, p. 208.

60 *Pyramids at the Louvre*, p. 3.

61 Alfred Huber, 'Adornos Polemik gegen Strawinsky', *Melos*, 38/9 (1971), p. 360
    (tr. Paddison); quoted in *Adorno's Aesthetics of Music*, p. 269.
62 The early uses of the word 'progress' implied 'a physical march, journey or
    procession, then of a developing series of events. There is no necessary ideo-
    logical implication in this sense of a forward movement or developing series.'
    Raymond Williams, *Keywords: a Vocabulary of Culture and Society* (London:
    Fontana, 1976), p. 205.
63 Martin Jay, *Adorno*, Fontana Modern Masters Series (London: Fontana,
    1984), p. 162.

Bibliography

Adorno, Theodor W. *Negative Dialectics*, tr. E. B. Ashton. London: Routledge, 1973

 Philosophy of Modern Music, tr. Anne G. Mitchell and Wesley V. Blomster. London: Seabury Press, 1973

 Introduction to the Sociology of Music, tr. E. B. Ashton. New York: Seabury Press, 1976

 'On the social situation of music', tr. Wesley Blomster. *Telos*, 35 (Spring 1978), pp. 128–64

 In Search of Wagner, tr. Rodney Livingstone. London: NLB/Verso, 1981

 'On the fetish-character in music and the regression of listening'. In *The Essential Frankfurt School Reader*, ed. Andrew Arato and Eike Gebhardt. New York: Continuum, 1982, pp. 270–99

 Prisms, tr. Samuel and Shierry Weber. Cambridge MA: MIT Press, 1983

 Alban Berg: Master of the Smallest Link, tr. with intro. and annotation by Juliane Brand and Christopher Hailey. Cambridge: Cambridge University Press, 1991

 Quasi una Fantasia: Essays on Modern Music, tr. Rodney Livingstone. London: Verso, 1992

Albright, Daniel. *Stravinsky: the Music Box and the Nightingale*. New York: Gordon and Breach, 1989

Andriessen, Louis, in conversation with Gavin Thomas. 'Life downtown'. *Musical Times*, 1813 (March 1994), pp. 138–41

Andriessen, Louis, and Elmer Schönberger. *The Apollonian Clockwork: on Stravinsky*, tr. Jeff Hamburg. Oxford: Oxford University Press, 1989

Apollonio, Umbro. *Futurist Manifestos*. London: Thames and Hudson, 1973

Artaud, Antonin. *The Theatre and its Double*, tr. Victor Corti. London: Calder, 1993

Asaf'yev, Boris. *A Book about Stravinsky*, tr. Richard French. Ann Arbor: UMI, 1982

Ayrey, Craig. 'Introduction: different trains'. In *Analytical Strategies*, ed. Ayrey and Everist, pp. 1–32

Ayrey, Craig and Mark Everist, eds. *Analytical Strategies and Musical Interpretation*. Cambridge: Cambridge University Press, 1996

Babbitt, Milton. 'Remarks on the recent Stravinsky'. In *Perspectives on Schoenberg and Stravinsky*, ed. Benjamin Boretz and Edward T. Cone. New York: Norton, 1972, pp. 165–85

Baker, James. 'Schenkerian analysis and post-tonal music'. In *Aspects of*

Schenkerian Theory, ed. David Beach. New Yaven: Yale University Press, 1983, pp. 153–86

Baker, James, David Beach and Jonathan W. Bernard, eds. *Music Theory in Concept and Practice*. Rochester NY: University of Rochester Press, 1997

Barthes, Roland. 'The grain of the voice'. In *Music, Image, Text*, tr. Stephen Heath. London: Fontana, 1977, pp. 179–89

Benjamin, Walter. 'The work of art in the age of mechanical reproduction'. In *Illuminations*, tr. Harry Zohn. London: Jonathan Cape, 1970, pp. 219–53

Bernard, Jonathan W. *The Music of Edgard Varèse*. New Haven: Yale University Press, 1987

Bloom, Harold. *The Anxiety of Influence: a Theory of Poetry*. London: Oxford University Press, 1973

  A Map of Misreading. Oxford: Oxford University Press, 1975

Boros, James, and Richard Toop, eds. *Brian Ferneyhough: Collected Writings*. Amsterdam: Harwood, 1995

Boudaille, Georges. *The Drawings of Picasso*. London: Hamlyn, 1988

Boulez, Pierre. *Conversations with Célestin Deliège*. London: Eulenburg, 1976

  Orientations: Collected Writings, ed. Jean-Jacques Nattiez, tr. Martin Cooper. London: Faber, 1986

  Stocktakings from an Apprenticeship, tr. Stephen Walsh. Oxford: Clarendon, 1991

Bowen, Meirion. *Michael Tippett*. London: Robson, 1982

Brecht, Bertolt. *The Threepenny Opera*, tr. and ed. Ralph Manheim and John Willett. London: Methuen, 1979

Brook, Peter. *The Empty Space*. London: McGibbon and Kee, 1968

Butler, Christopher. *Early Modernism: Literature, Music and Painting in Europe 1900–1916*. Oxford: Clarendon, 1994

Cage, John. *A Year from Monday: New Lectures and Writings*. London: Calder and Boyers, 1968

  Silence. Middletown CT: Wesleyan University Press, 1978

Carter, Chandler. 'Stravinsky's "special sense": the rhetorical use of tonality in *The Rake's Progress*'. *Music Theory Spectrum*, 19/1 (1997), pp. 55–80

Carter, Elliott. *The Writings of Elliott Carter*, ed. Else and Kurt Stone. Bloomington: Indiana University Press, 1977

Chew, Geoffrey. 'Pastoral and neoclassicism: a reinterpretation of Auden's and Stravinsky's *The Rake's Progress*'. *Cambridge Opera Journal*, 5 (1993), pp. 239–63

Clifton, Thomas. *Music as Heard: a Study in Applied Phenomenology*. New Haven: Yale University Press, 1983

Cone, Edward T. 'Stravinsky: the progress of a method'. *Perspectives of New Music*, 1/1 (1962), pp. 18–26

  'The uses of convention: Stravinsky and his models'. *Musical Quarterly*, 48/3 (1962), pp. 287–99

Copland, Aaron. *Copland on Music*. London: Andre Deutsch, 1961

Cross, Jonathan. 'Birtwistle's secret theatres'. In *Analytical Strategies*, ed. Ayrey and Everist, pp. 207–25

Dahlhaus, Carl. 'La polemica di Adorno contro Stravinskij e il problema della "critica superiore"'. In *Stravinskij oggi*, ed. Francesco Degrada. Milan: Edizioni Unicopli, 1982, pp. 46–59

Dömling, Wolfgang, and Theo Hirsbrunner. 'Ordnung in der Zeit: "Rhythmik"'. In *Über Strawinsky: Studien zu Ästhetik und Kompositionstechnik*. Laaber: Laaber-Verlag, 1985, pp. 147–71

Eco, Umberto. *Travels in Hyperreality*. London: Picador, 1987

Eimert, Herbert. 'Debussy's *Jeux*'. *Die Reihe*, 5 (1959; Eng. edn 1961), pp. 3–20

Epstein, David. *Shaping Time: Music, the Brain, and Performance*. New York: Schirmer, 1995

Forte, Allen. *The Structure of Atonal Music*. New Haven: Yale University Press, 1973

    The Harmonic Organization of 'The Rite of Spring'. New Haven: Yale University Press, 1978

    'Foreground rhythm in early twentieth-century music'. *Music Analysis*, 2/3 (1983), pp. 239–68

Gann, Kyle. *The Music of Conlon Nancarrow*. Cambridge: Cambridge University Press, 1995

Geuss, Raymond. 'Berg and Adorno'. In *The Cambridge Companion to Berg*, ed. Anthony Pople. Cambridge: Cambridge University Press, 1997, pp. 38–50

Golding, John. *Cubism: a History and an Analysis*. London: Faber, 3rd edn 1988

Griffiths, Paul. *Modern Music: the Avant Garde since 1945*. London: Dent, 1981

    Peter Maxwell Davies. London: Robson, 1982

    Igor Stravinsky: The Rake's Progress. Cambridge Opera Handbooks. Cambridge: Cambridge University Press, 1982

    New Sounds, New Personalities: British Composers of the 1980s. London: Faber, 1985

    Olivier Messiaen and the Music of Time. London: Faber, 1985

    Modern Music and After: Directions since 1945. Oxford: Oxford University Press, 1995

Haftmann, Werner. *The Mind and Work of Paul Klee*. London: Faber, 1967

Haimo, Ethan. 'Developing variation and Schoenberg's twelve-note music'. *Music Analysis*, 16/3 (1997), pp. 349–65

Haimo, Ethan, and Paul Johnson, eds. *Stravinsky Retrospectives*. Lincoln NB: University of Nebraska Press, 1987

Hall, Michael. *Harrison Birtwistle*. London: Robson, 1984

Hasty, Christopher. 'On the problem of succession and continuity in twentieth-century music'. *Music Theory Spectrum*, 8 (1986), pp. 58–74

Henck, Herbert. 'Karlheinz Stockhausen *Klavierstück IX*/Eine analytische Betrachtung'. *Orpheus*, 17 (1976). Tr. into French as 'Le *Klavierstück IX* de Karlheinz Stockhausen: considérations analytiques'. *Contrechamps*, 9 (1988), pp. 169–91

Hewett, Ivan. 'Different strains'. *Musical Times*, 1848 (February 1997), pp. 20–23

Hoppin, Richard H. *Medieval Music*. New York: Norton, 1978

Hyde, Martha. 'Neoclassic and anachronistic impulses in twentieth-century music'. *Music Theory Spectrum*, 18/2 (1996), pp. 200–35

Ives, Charles. 'Essays before a sonata'. In *Three Classics in the Aesthetics of Music*, ed. Howard Boatwright. New York: Dover, 1962

Jameson, Fredric. *Postmodernism, or, the Cultural Logic of Late Capitalism*. London: Verso, 1991

Jameux, Dominique. *Pierre Boulez*, tr. Susan Bradshaw. London: Faber, 1991

Jarman, Douglas. *The Music of Alban Berg*. London: Faber, 1979

Jay, Martin. *Adorno*. Fontana Modern Masters. London: Fontana, 1984

John, Nicholas, ed. *Oedipus Rex / The Rake's Progress / Igor Stravinsky*. ENO Opera Guide 43. London: John Calder, 1991

Johnson, Paul. 'Cross-collectional techniques of structure in Stravinsky's centric music'. In *Stravinsky Retrospectives*, ed. Haimo and Johnson, pp. 55–75

Jones, Robert F. 'Tippett's atonal syntax'. In *Michael Tippett OM: a Celebration*, ed. Lewis, pp. 119–42

Kagan, Andrew. *Paul Klee: Art and Music*. Ithaca: Cornell University Press, 1983

Katz, Adele. *Challenge to Musical Tradition: a New Concept of Tonality*. London: Putnam, 1945

Kemp, Ian. *Tippett: the Composer and his Music*. Oxford: Oxford University Press, 1987

Kerman, Joseph. 'How we got into analysis, and how to get out'. *Critical Inquiry*, 7 (1980), pp. 311–31

Kielian-Gilbert, Marianne. 'Stravinsky's contrasts: contradiction and discontinuity in his neoclassic music'. *Journal of Musicology*, 9 (1991), pp. 448–80

Kirkpatrick, John. *A Temporary Mimeographed Catalogue of the Music Manuscripts and Related Materials of Charles Edward Ives, 1874–1954*. New Haven: Library of the Yale University School of Music, 1960; repr. 1973

Klee, Paul. *Pedagogical Sketchbook*, tr. and with intro. by Sibyl Moholy-Nagy. London: Faber, 1953

Korsyn, Kevin. 'Towards a new poetics of musical influence'. *Music Analysis*, 10/1–2 (1991), pp. 3–72

Kramer, Jonathan D. 'Moment form in twentieth century music'. *Musical Quarterly*, 64 (1978), pp. 177–94

  'Discontinuity and proportion in the music of Stravinsky'. In *Confronting Stravinsky*, ed. Pasler, pp. 174–94

  The Time of Music. New York: Schirmer, 1988

Kundera, Milan. *Testaments Betrayed*, tr. Linda Asher. London: Faber, 1996

Lawson, Rex. 'Stravinsky and the pianola'. In *Confronting Stravinsky*, ed. Pasler, pp. 284–301

Lerdahl, Fred. 'Atonal prolongational structures'. *Contemporary Music Review*, 4 (1989), pp. 65–87

Leppert, Richard, and Susan McClary, eds. *Music and Society*. Cambridge: Cambridge University Press, 1987

Lewis, Geraint, ed. *Michael Tippett OM: a Celebration*. Tunbridge Wells: Baton, 1985

Lodge, David. *Working with Structuralism*. London: Routledge, 1981

Lynton, Norbert. *Klee*. London: Hamlyn, 2nd edn 1975

Lyotard, Jean-François. *The Postmodern Condition: a Report on Knowledge*. Manchester: Manchester University Press, 1986

MacDonald, Malcolm. *Schoenberg*. London: Dent, 1987

Maconie, Robin. *The Works of Karlheinz Stockhausen*. London: Marion Boyars, 1976

Mattis, Olivia. 'Varèse's "progressive" nationalism: *Amériques* meets *Américanisme*'. In *Edgard Varèse: Die Befreiung des Klangs*, ed. Helga de la Motte-Haber. Hofheim: Wolke, 1992, pp. 149–78

Messiaen, Olivier. 'Le rythme chez Igor Strawinsky'. *Revue musicale*, 191 (1939) *Technique de mon langage musical* (1944). Tr. by John Satterfield as *Technique of my Musical Language*. Paris: Leduc, 1957 *Traité de rythme, de couleur, et d'ornithologie*, vol. 2. Paris: Leduc/UMP, 1995

Meyer, Leonard B. *Music, the Arts, and Ideas*. Chicago: Chicago University Press, 1967

Milner, John. *Mondrian*. London: Phaidon, 1992

Nattiez, Jean-Jacques, ed. *The Boulez–Cage Correspondence*, tr. Robert Samuels. Cambridge: Cambridge University Press, 1993

Nevill, Tim, ed. *Towards a Cosmic Music: Texts by Karlheinz Stockhausen*. London: Element, 1989

Nicholls, Peter. *Modernisms: a Literary Guide*. Basingstoke: Macmillan, 1995

Nietzsche, Friedrich. *The Birth of Tragedy*, tr. Walter Kaufmann. New York: Vintage, 1967 *A Nietzsche Reader*, tr. R. J. Hollingdale. Harmondsworth: Penguin, 1977

Paddison, Max. *Adorno's Aesthetics of Music*. Cambridge: Cambridge University Press, 1993 *Adorno, Modernism and Mass Culture: Essays on Critical Theory and Music*. London: Kahn and Averill, 1996

Pasler, Jann. 'Music and spectacle in *Petrushka* and *The Rite of Spring*'. In *Confronting Stravinsky*, ed. Pasler, pp. 53–81

Pasler, Jann, ed. *Confronting Stravinsky: Man, Musician, and Modernist*. Berkeley: University of California Press, 1986

Pople, Anthony, ed. *Theory, Analysis and Meaning in Music*. Cambridge: Cambridge University Press, 1994

Puffett, Derrick. 'The fugue from Tippett's Second String Quartet'. *Music Analysis*, 5/2–3 (1986), pp. 233–64 'Editorial: in defence of formalism'. *Music Analysis*, 13/1 (1994), pp. 3–5 'Debussy's ostinato machine'. *Papers in Musicology*, 4. Nottingham University, 1996

Rogers, Lynne. 'Stravinsky's break with contrapuntal tradition: a sketch study'. *Journal of Musicology*, 13 (1995), pp. 476–507

Rosenblum, Robert. *Cubism*. New York: 2nd edn 1966

Rothstein, William. 'The Americanization of Heinrich Schenker'. In *Schenker Studies*, ed. Hedi Siegel. Cambridge: Cambridge University Press, 1990, pp. 193–203

Routh, Francis. *Stravinsky*. Master Musicians. London: Dent, 1975

Salzer, Felix. *Structural Hearing: Tonal Coherence in Music*. New York: Dover, 1962

Schenker, Heinrich. *Das Meisterwerk in der Musik*, 3 vols. Munich: Drei Masken Verlag, 1926. Tr. as *The Masterwork in Music*, ed. William Drabkin. Cambridge: Cambridge University Press, 1994–7

Schoenberg, Arnold. *Style and Idea*, ed. Leonard Stein, tr. Leo Black. London: Faber, rev. 1984

Schwartz, Elliott, and Barney Childs, eds. *Contemporary Composers on Contemporary Music*. New York: Holt, Reinhart and Winston, 1967

Sessions, Roger. 'Thoughts on Stravinsky'. *The Score*, 20 (1957), pp. 32–7

Simpson, Robert. *The Symphony*, vol. 2. Harmondsworth: Penguin, 1967

Smart, Barry. *Postmodernity*. London: Routledge, 1993

Smith, Richard Langham. 'Debussy and the art of the cinema'. *Music and Letters*, 54/1 (1973), pp. 61–70

Snarrenberg, Robert. 'Competing myths: the American abandonment of Schenker's organicism'. In *Theory, Analysis and Meaning*, ed. Pople, pp. 29–56 *Schenker's Interpretive Practice*. Cambridge: Cambridge University Press, 1997

Solie, Ruth, ed. *Musicology and Difference: Gender and Sexuality in Music Scholarship*. Berkeley: University of California Press, 1993

Souvtchinsky, Pierre. 'La notion du temps et la musique'. *Revue musicale*, 1939

Stangos, Nikos, ed. *Concepts of Modern Art: from Fauvism to Postmodernism*. London: Thames and Hudson, 3rd edn 1994

Steinitz, Richard. 'Weeping and wailing'. *Musical Times*, 1842 (August 1996), pp. 17–22

Straus, Joseph N. 'A principle of voice leading in the music of Stravinsky'. *Music Theory Spectrum*, 4 (1982), pp. 106–24

'The problem of prolongation in post-tonal music'. *Journal of Music Theory*, 31/1 (1987), pp. 1–21

'Sonata form in Stravinsky'. In *Stravinsky Retrospectives*, ed. Haimo and Johnson, pp. 141–61

Remaking the Past: Tradition and Influence in Twentieth-Century Music. Cambridge MA: Harvard University Press, 1990

'Voice leading in atonal music'. In *Music Theory in Concept and Practice*, ed. Baker *et al.*, pp. 237–74

Stravinsky, Igor. *Poetics of Music in the Form of Six Lessons*, tr. Arthur Knodel and Ingolf Dahl. Cambridge MA: Harvard University Press, 1942

Stravinsky, Igor, and Robert Craft. *Memories and Commentaries*. London: Faber, 1960

Expositions and Developments. London: Faber, 1962

Themes and Conclusions. London: Faber, 1972

Dialogues. London: Faber, 1982; first pub. as *Dialogues and a Diary*, 1982

Street, Alan. 'Superior myths, dogmatic allegories: the resistance to musical unity'. *Music Analysis*, 8/1–2 (1989), pp. 77–123

Subotnik, Rose Rosengard. *Deconstructive Variations: Music and Reason in Western Society.* Minneapolis: University of Minnesota Press, 1996

Taruskin, Richard. 'The dark side of modern music'. *New Republic*, 5 September 1988, pp. 28–34

'A myth of the 20th century: *The Rite of Spring*, the tradition of the new, and "the music itself"'. *Modernism / Modernity*, 2 (1995), pp. 1–26

Stravinsky and the Russian Traditions: a Biography of the Works Through Mavra. Oxford: Oxford University Press, 1996

Tippett, Michael. *Moving into Aquarius.* St Albans: Paladin, 1974

Music of the Angels, ed. Meirion Bowen. London: Eulenburg, 1980

Those Twentieth Century Blues. London: Hutchinson, 1991

van den Toorn, Pieter C. *The Music of Igor Stravinsky.* New Haven: Yale University Press, 1983

Stravinsky and The Rite of Spring: the Beginnings of a Musical Language. Oxford: Oxford University Press, 1987

Music, Politics, and the Academy. Berkeley: University of California Press, 1995

'Neoclassicism and its definitions'. In *Music Theory in Concept and Practice*, ed. Baker *et al.*, pp. 131–56

Trietler, Leo. *Music and the Historical Imagination.* Cambridge MA: Harvard University Press, 1989

Trowell, Brian. 'The new and the classical in "The Rake's Progress"'. In *Oedipus Rex / The Rake's Progress / Igor Stravinsky*, ed. Nicholas John, pp. 59–69

Varèse, Edgard. 'The liberation of sound'. In *Contemporary Composers on Contemporary Music*, ed. Schwartz and Childs

Varga, Bálint András. *Conversations with Iannis Xenakis.* London: Faber, 1996

Vlad, Roman. *Stravinsky*, tr. Frederick Fuller. Oxford: Oxford University Press, 3rd edn 1985

Walsh, Stephen. *The Music of Stravinsky.* London: Routledge, 1988

Stravinsky: Oedipus Rex. Cambridge: Cambridge University Press, 1993

'Stravinsky's Symphonies: accident or design?' In *Analytical Strategies*, ed. Ayrey and Everist, pp. 35–71

'Venice and *The Rake*: the old and the new'. In *The Rake's Progress*, Welsh National Opera programme book, ed. Simon Rees, 1996

Watkins, Glenn. *Pyramids at the Louvre: Music, Culture, and Collage from Stravinsky to the Postmodernists.* Cambridge MA: Belknap Press, 1994

Webern, Anton. *The Path to the New Music*, ed. Willi Reich, tr. Leo Black. London: Universal, 1975

Weir, Judith. '"Oedipus Rex": a personal view'. In *Oedipus Rex / The Rake's Progress / Igor Stravinsky*, ed. Nicholas John, pp. 17–20

Wenk, Arthur C. *Claude Debussy and Twentieth-Century Music*. Boston MA: Twayne, 1983

White, Eric Walter. *Stravinsky: the Composer and his Works*. London: Faber, 2nd edn 1979

Whittall, Arnold. *Music Since the First World War*. London: Dent, 1977

'Music analysis as human science? *Le Sacre du printemps* in theory and practice'. *Music Analysis*, 1/1 (1982), pp. 33–53

'Webern and atonality: the path from the old aesthetic'. *Musical Times*, 1690 (December 1983), pp. 733–7

'Tippett and the modernist mainstream'. In *Michael Tippett OM: a Celebration*, ed. Lewis, pp. 109–15

'The theorist's sense of history: concepts of contemporaneity in composition and analysis'. *Journal of the Royal Musical Association*, 112 (1987), pp. 1–20

'The geometry of comedy'. *Musical Times*, 1799 (January 1993), pp. 17–19

'Birtwistle, Maxwell Davies and modernist analysis'. *Music Analysis*, 13/2–3 (1994), pp. 139–59

'Modernist aesthetics, modernist music: some analytical perspectives'. In *Music Theory in Concept and Practice*, ed. Baker *et al.*, pp. 157–80

Williams, Alastair. ' "Répons": phantasmagoria or the articulation of space?' In *Theory, Analysis and Meaning in Music*, ed. Pople. Cambridge: Cambridge University Press, 1994, pp. 195–210

Williams, Raymond. *Keywords: a Vocabulary of Culture and Society*. London: Fontana, 1976

Wörner, Karl H. *Stockhausen: Life and Work*, tr. and ed. with an intro. by Bill Hopkins. Berkeley: University of California Press, 1976

Yeats, W. B. *The Works of W. B. Yeats*. Ware: Wordsworth, 1994

Index